Ian Gillan

by

Ian Gillan

with David Cohen

BLAKE

Published by Blake Publishing Ltd,
3 Bramber Court, 2 Bramber Road,
London W14 9PB, England

This edition published in paperback 1998

ISBN 1 85782 3206

British Library Cataloguing-in-Publication Data:
A catalogue record for this book is available
from the British Library.

Typeset by BCP

Printed in Great Britain by Creative Print and Design
(Wales), Ebbw Vale, Gwent

3 5 7 9 10 8 6 4 2

Who to Blame

Bron (B) and Grace Gillan; Janet, Nicola and Lucy Cohen; Matt Aubury (crucial computer advice — many thanks!); Simon (Super-Mec) Clapp; Robert Mazzilli; Fulden Underwood; The Miltons at The Fortescue (Salcombe); Rick and Cheryl at The Creeks End Inn (Kingsbridge); Peter Ehlers at The Thirsty Whale at Altemonte Springs (Florida); The Board of Directors, The Penzance Club Ltd (Paddington Station); Ernie (Goodbye is all she wrote) Birse; Katya Dutton; Richard Hughes and Janet Reeves (Portugal) — very special; Questrn 'P' Kober; Al Dutton; Phil Banfield; Lois James; Adam Parfitt and Charly Helyar at Blake Publishing Limited; Colin Hart; Charlie Lewis; Geoff Aspel; Manjeet Khangura (Electric Echo); BMG Records; Graham (Squiffy) Underwood; Kudos Business Systems (Salcombe); Family G. Doyle — The King of Prussia (Kingsbridge);Al Walls (loan of LP!); Doug McKenzie; Tony Tacon; Gloria Bristow; George Bodnar; Barry Plummer; Chris Hill; Robert Lundgren; Chris Charlsworth; King Print (Kingsbridge); Julian Calverley; Simon Fowler; Simon Robinson (and Ann) for *Darker Than Blue* (Deep Purple Magazine); and RPM Records Limited (Sheffield) — also for discography. Finally, to every single promoter who ever put his neck out for me!

To Rock 'n' Roll!

My Co-Writer

The 'Incredible Bard', David Cohen, thinks this book is straight off the 'do-da'. He says things like that! I called him at home one evening, and his wife, Janet, answered the phone. As I was talking to her, I heard barking in the background.

'Didn't know you had a dog, Janet.'

'It's David,' she said. 'He's barking at a letter from the bank manager.'

My kinda guy!

Married to Janet, and with two daughters, Nicola and Lucy, David has been involved with a number of projects in the creative industries, including with several musicians. He has also worked with Amazon River adventurer, Alan Holman; run a successful writing workshop for HM Prison and co-written a book about street entertainment. He has guested frequently on national and local radio dealing with his work and often controversial interest in inner-city and town centre issues, about which he has been published and which he has lectured on in the UK and overseas. Through his production company (with Al Dutton), The Penzance Club Limited (Penzance Productions), he is involved in several writing projects including for film.

CONTENTS

PROLOGUE

Maybe it's possible to resist the temptation — the beginning was such a long time ago after all; 19 August 1945, to be precise. Two-fifths of a large part of my later life had already been born: just Roger Glover and Ian Paice were yet to arrive. I refer of course to Deep Purple, that enigmatic rock band I have always loved in torment. Jon Lord (keyboards), Roger Glover (bass), and Ian Paice (drums) are essentially moderate people with good hearts and only the normal amount of wickedness. Over the years, they have hovered somewhere near the fulcrum of a musical see-saw, whilst Ritchie Blackmore (guitar) and I (vocals) have danced precariously along the musical extremities.

I use that as an ongoing statement, because although Ritchie left the band after the Helsinki show on 17 November 1993, following an outrage at the Birmingham NEC a few days before, he will never be forgotten — *never!* He is vitally important to the whole spirit of Deep Purple, and it may surprise some readers to know that I have no bad feelings towards Ritchie at all.

I used to room with him in the early days, and over many turbulent years — some exquisite, and some not — I learned to love and admire his supreme musicianship and stage presence. In fact, I do not even dislike him, and admit to having had some great times with him on many occasions.

His perception of me may well be different, because he is on the record as saying that 'one of these days, on the road, I'm going to attack Ian Gillan in a back alley. He's bigger than me and probably a better fighter, so I'm gonna do it with a few friends of mine and we'll beat him up ... but he won't know it's me.'

I'd prefer to think he was just being dramatic, but it was certainly all wrong during the period when I joined the band at The Red Rooster Studio in Munich (1992) for *The Battle Rages On*. Ritchie's own approach to my return was summed up when he told Anders Tengner that he 'wanted to bring somebody else in, but ... was voted down by the other three', and he was no less encouraging when we met.

Just prior to that, I'd spent some time with Roger at a studio in Cookham, Berkshire, working on material I'd be inheriting from the band and the singer, Joe Lynn Turner, who I was to replace, so bringing back together the classic Deep Purple line up. One of the songs was 'Time to Kill', and everybody liked what I'd put down, except the guitar player.

Now I'd not seen Ritchie for a few years, so I thought it would be a great chance in our volatile history to start afresh. He walked into the studio, said 'Hi', and we shook hands. After a couple of minutes of small talk, I said, 'What is it you don't like about "Time to Kill" — is it the lyrics, is it the tune? I can change a bit here and there if you like.

Ritchie said, 'I don't like the words, I don't like the tune and I don't like the title! I mean, the world "*kill*" doesn't exactly fit that chord, does it? To be honest, I'd rather you used the words that Joe wrote.'

I think Ritchie feels the same way about 'Woman from Tokyo'. He claims his favourite artists are Abba and Neil Diamond, so it's not surprising that we have exchanged a few blank looks from time to time.

Consider your position, position your defence
Why don't you let me ask you is it mere coincidence
Feeding speculators on a downhill gravy train
Like vultures ripping out the eyes to reach the dying brain.

My writing of 'Time to Kill' remained unchanged, but the album and tour were a constant struggle, with the band dipping into terminal velocity as we travelled. Ritchie leaving in the manner he chose was critical, and we had to decide whether we could carry on.

We talked about various options and ideas, but it was Mr Udo (a Japanese promoter) who suggested Joe Satriani as a replacement, and so we called him to see if he was interested and available. We all understood it would not be a permanent thing, just a means to save us from drowning. We sent him a tape from the Stuttgart show, and he arrived — a perfect gentleman, perfect professional and a consummate player. We told him we had booked a couple of days for rehearsal, and he walked in, and played immaculately — first time.

We looked through the studio window to see Mr Udo, Colin Hart (our tour manager) and the crew holding up cards. It was like marking an ice skating competition, and the figures were all 9.8, 9.8 and higher! It was a breeze — he was making it so easy for everybody. And then came the moment to play 'Smoke on the Water'. Somebody said, 'Oh, we don't need to do that, do we?'

'I'd kinda like to do it!' he replied.

'OK,' we said.

He smiled and said, 'Gee, I never thought I'd get to play "Smoke on the Water" with Deep Purple!'

After that, he came straight on stage with us.

Joe was very open about the fact he had his band, but he stayed with us and helped us out for quite some time, until the moment came for him to return to his projects. He'd filled a gap which allowed us to continue, regain our confidence, and realise there was life after Ritchie.

It was then that we sat down and decided to find somebody permanent. We had a little poll about who wanted who, and the American musician, Steve Morse, was on everybody's list. We approached him, and after talking him through our situation and ambitions, it was clear he was interested.

When asked if there were any questions he wanted to put to us, there was just one: 'Is there any dress code?' Steve became the permanent guitar player of Deep Purple at the end of 1994.

Chapter 1

I suppose my first real memory is the arrival of my sister, Pauline, on 26 July 1948. She came as a welcome surprise — in fact, a great gift, with much more to offer than the run-of-the-mill-toys I was now trashing as a three-year-old. Sadly, the early excitement of Pauline rapidly diminished and, as a small child, she became something of a disappointment. In fact, she was a complete waste of time!

As we grew older, I tried to encourage her to join me in various games, but she never understood my instructions, seemed to always be crying, and generally turned out to be one of Mum and Dad's worst ideas. When she started to invite her girlfriends round, life degenerated hopelessly, with my space and peace lost to the will of the giggling pack.

For example, I remember Grandad Watkins buying an enormous tent — or so it seemed — and the two of us patiently put it together in the back garden, as my mind ran riot with great adventures in far-off jungles and exotic places. Little did I realise then that my life would allow me just that opportunity, but right at that moment, it was more a case of dealing with Pauline and Co, who now wanted to take over my tent and turn it into a hospital, where they could play doctors and nurses! I believe I refused to be their Doctor Gillan, a decision I'd look back on one day with some regret.

In truth, Pauline and her friends were great. There were moments when things went a bit too far, usually when she was left in the playpen, with Mum out of sight. I'd sneak up to it, give it a good shaking, and roar like a wild animal. In later years, Mum — or Audrey as I call her — would remember these things, and admit that the wrong youngster had been locked up!

Sweet child
In time you'll see the line
The line that's drawn between
Good and bad

All in all, my childhood wasn't bad, so I can't say that mine is a 'rags to riches' story. But it wasn't a cosy life either in Hounslow, and there were many ups and downs to cope with, including time with parents who frequently rowed, and later split up. My father Bill is dead now, but even with all the problems he caused, I cannot think badly of him.

Born in Govan, Glasgow, and one of a large working-class family, he left school at 13 and, with friends of similar backgrounds and attitudes, spent much of his youth in minor skulduggery and enterprise along the banks of the Clyde river.

One of the things they would do to earn a crust was to look for driftwood, which they would painstakingly collect and dry, before selling it to the folk in the tenement buildings. It was a tough area with tough people, and you needed your wits about you to get by.

Childhood memories are often confused, and exaggeration is always a tendency. However, what could not be overstated was Dad's amazing accent. It was 'Govanese', which made Rab C Nesbitt sound like Derek Nimmo. Brought to south-east England, it must have caused problems, because it wasn't until I was about 14 that I even began to understand a word he was saying! Growling and animated gestures, which the inexperienced or uneducated sometimes took as threats, often turned out to be expressions of endearment, and it must have surprised him sometimes to see us all running away, when he was just being nice!

Dad's eccentricities and his contribution to family life were many and varied, ranging from inspirational to downright silly and irresponsible. As for his attitude to me, we got on quite well in the early years, and as time passed by, he'd certainly come to my help when needed.

He was not the central figure in the family, or when he was, it would often be for the wrong reason. There were many causes for friction between my parents, and one was Bill's attitude towards religion, which at best was unorthodox. It didn't help in a house and community where we were supposed to be growing up with Christian values, but his questioning attitude towards God was something I'd come to sympathise with at quite an early age, when I too asked questions about the Almighty and His universe.

I was born into confusion, my mother said to me
When you become a man you'll understand
but it's still a mystery.

I guess I was about 8 years old when I first considered the magnitude and mental challenge of infinity — looking out of windows at the stars, or gazing in daytime at the blue sky, beyond which it is black. The answer to my questions was always given in terms of 'things going on for ever', which seemed crazy. I mean, even I could see that nothing in life went on for ever. Still a child, I saw in every room that there were walls and a door. Standing in the garden there were more walls and a gate, and every street was somehow enclosed as well. But looking towards the sky, there were no walls and no doors. Only space, infinite space, and it just made no sense. But I wanted it to: so in my vivid imagination, I'd dream of ways to enclose all spaces with walls, contain them, and especially the sky! But having achieved this in my dreams, I'd wake up, disturbed by the thought of still more space behind my walls, and so more were built as my torment continued remorselessly, and without answer or satisfaction. Finally, I'd come to terms with the futility of defining space — trying to control it, and *yes*, I know it really does go on for ever!

It did when I was a child, and it would in more mature years, one day to find expression in 'Mr Universe' on the Pye label with Roger Glover in 1967, and later with The Gillan Band, when a different song was released in 1979 on the Virgin label.

Questioning the concept of space, and inevitably asking about God, is no sin in my book, and I still cannot understand how we can justify mass destruction in His name. Right now, I am resigned to live my life on the basis that we are all just a bubble in someone's beer!

I greatly regret not having spent more time trying to appreciate Bill's attitude to life, and what it was that made him reject so much. Unfortunately, many of his opinions (when they were understood in the first place) were considered unhelpful in a virtuous society, so it fell to Audrey to provide the backbone and basic fabric to home life.

It may have helped that her background was nicer than Bill's. Whatever, she was one of four children and, to digress a little, the eldest — 'Aunty Joan' — would later play a helpful role in the early part of my music career. She became Mrs Crewkerne through marriage to an American GI called Charlie, and once back in the States, she would become our first international fan when Episode Six happened. Of course, she wrote to the fan club as 'Joan', which impressed quite a few people.

Back in my childhood, Audrey was ambitious for me, quite religious, hard working, and possessed with considerable determination. Life in those days focused around the West London estates, just inside Heathrow Airport, and the area became quite fertile ground for turning out musicians. Names which come to mind include Screaming Lord Sutch ('Screaming' to his mates), Cliff Bennett of Rebel Rousers fame, Mick

Underwood (whose name crops up often in this story) and, of course, the man he would introduce me to one day: Ritchie Blackmore, who was a 'savage', and whose name will crop up even more often! In fact, our little corner of the 'universe' would make a major contribution to the music scene, beginning in the early days of rock 'n' roll and continuing to this very day.

However, all that is for the future. At home, Pauline and I grew up with increasing confrontation between our parents, poignantly illustrated by a situation which brought them to the brink of separation.

In telling this story, you must accept that the entire family — without exception — loved animals, but some species more than others. For example, Bill wasn't too keen on cats. So, at the height of a particularly bad period between them, Audrey chose to buy one and bring it home, announcing her name to be Sally. Well, the atmosphere became extremely gloomy, and after some dark brooding, Bill stormed out. A few hours later, he returned, and with some degree of triumph introduced us to another pet — a budgie called Puff! He put the bird in a cage he'd also bought, and suspended it on a hoop frame. The frame was then hung on a stand which stood about 5ft high, and the whole thing was placed in the corner of the living room, so the bird could watch the world pass by outside. Although there were two doors to the room, one was blocked off by furniture, leaving space for a settee which faced the fireplace, as well as a table and two single chairs — one of which was Bill's. That one he placed close to the bay window, which meant that nothing could move from the hall without passing him, and which also meant that the luckless cat had the endless frustration of an untouchable lunchbox!

And then came the day when, by some incredible good fortune, Sally and Puff were alone in the room. The cat mounted the arm of the chair, did her calculations on angle and distance, and made the irreversible decision to jump. The leap took her to the cage with sufficient power to set the whole thing into gyroscopic motion, at which point Bill returned. Summing up the situation immediately, he moved with smooth efficiency, grabbed the poor cat in a huge hand, and in the same motion transferred her without parabola to the distant wall, where she stayed for a few seconds, before sliding (without brakes) down the floral wallpaper to the floor. Her life was most certainly saved by the fact that she'd wisely left her claws in the cage, and which Puff idly inspected as they lay spread around the sawdust!

Looking back, never could marriage have joined such an unlikely couple who were simply poles apart. They had different ideas on politics, religion, social and cultural issues. You name it, they didn't share it! Perhaps it was asking too much for the relationship to work, and it all finally came to a head the day Audrey discovered that Bill had an outside interest.

As with so many young men in those days, Bill had stayed in the army, where he'd been promoted to sergeant in the Catering Corps. Although things were poor between them, the situation began to deteriorate rapidly when letters started to arrive on the doorstep, postmarked Liverpool. Eventually, it turned out that Bill had a young girlfriend, and she was expecting his child. Audrey confronted Bill and met his girlfriend at a meeting which must have been devastating for both women. For Audrey, the reason for shock must have been obvious, but so too for the girl, as she now discovered that her lover — and the father of her child — was already married. I believe arrangements were made for the girl to receive 30 shillings a week until the child was born, at which time, matters would be reviewed.

The baby was delivered stillborn, at which point Audrey left Bill, taking us with her. I know it sounds insane, but for all that happened between two sadly incompatible people, and for all I remember of Bill's behaviour, I cannot bring myself to think badly of him, or blame him for the relationship failing. Looking back on the saga, it was doomed from the beginning. How and why it ever began is not my business.

As I leaned forward to kiss my father on his forehead, I noticed his chin. Something strange, what was it?

He badly needed a shave, always so meticulous about his hygiene and appearance. How many mornings had I stood and watched, fascinated as he explained and demonstrated the process, the ritual. First, wash your face with ordinary soap. Then with water as hot as you can bear, apply the brush and shaving cream. Palmolive, the old scent is gone now. Then the blade, leaving his skin even softer, it seemed, than mine. Occasionally, he would reach down, dab some cream on my face and shave me with a bladeless razor. Delicious! 'You're a better man than I am Gunga Din,' he would say.

What was this then? The last time I'd seen him was around 11.00pm the night before as he left my hotel to drive home with a clean chin. He died within the hour at the wheel of his car. Now, here in the morgue, fifty miles away, and twelve hours later, he badly needed a shave.

Yes, that is him, my father William. Yes, Yes!

I stumbled through the formalities of identification. Would you please make sure someone gives him a shave before ... Before! 'Before what?' I thought, turning away to try and hold my composure.

So ... whiskers growing on a dead man's chin sounds like a sea shanty. All of my father's being in me became focused at that time.

Just in case it seems my life was traumatic — or even miserable — in those childhood days, it is not the case. Of course, it was sad to see the parting of parents, and then leaving what had been home to go and stay with grandparents, but there remain many fine and fond memories to look back on.

For example, there was Uncle Alec, the mad inventor, from whom I suppose some of my own inventiveness comes. He was Bill's brother, and as such he seemed definitely *persona non grata* at home. Bill was always very secretive about Alec — in fact, I think he was a little embarrassed by him, which was ironic in many ways!

Alec used to come down from Scotland to see us now and again, and usually arrived with an assortment of cardboard boxes and bizarre paraphernalia. Bill would meet him at King's Cross Station, and steer him and his baggage to the nearest pub, where they would stay until us kids were in bed. Arriving home, Alec would unwrap and show Bill (at very great length) his latest gadget, which he intended taking to the Patents' Office the next day.

On one occasion, I was allowed to see one of Alec's creations, and it was brilliant! It was made up of the most beautifully carved pieces of wood, all of which fitted together perfectly — after a good hour or so. Once assembled, it took the shape of a head and torso, into which fitted a small cupboard. This, when opened, revealed all kinds of mechanical wizardry — there was a left arm that didn't move, but a device in the chest somehow activated the right one, and also caused the head to swivel. A flexible bottle inside the torso was filled with water, and at the press of a button, the right arm would reach out, take a cup from Alec, slosh water into it, and hand it back so my uncle could drink.

His idea was to sell the product to factories on a huge scale, and his enthusiasm was immense. However, as with most of Uncle Alec's ideas, it was useless! That said, my later interest in carpentry (and the occasional useless idea as well) is probably due to his inspiration.

The other memorable thing about Alec was the fact he called my father 'Jock' or 'Willie'. Mr Morgan next door also called him that, but that was about it. Dad hated being called those names, as I found to my cost the night I mimicked my uncle and said, 'Good night, Jock'!

With the parting of parents, all that kind of magic went, which left us to find joy in the older folk, and we found it — especially in Grandad Watkins, who ran the household with a rod of iron, and on very Victorian principles.

For most families at that time (around the early 1950s), life in a good working-class home followed strict codes of behaviour and peer respect. The man of the house — in this case, Grandad — was in charge, and his bidding was law. Sunday lunch (or dinner as we knew it) was, in theory, a moment of 'good feeling'. It meant togetherness on the Lord's day of rest, and a time to be relaxed and happy!

The BBC helped keep spirits high with a good number of great radio comedy programmes — the likes of *Hancock's Half Hour*, *The Navy Lark*, *Round the Horn* and *The Goons* were my favourites. That said, and for sheer neck, Peter Brough's admired and popular ventriloquist act with the legendary doll, Archie Andrews, took some beating. However, his ratings strangely plummeted when he boldly crossed over to television. It was at this point that the importance of facial control dawned on him!

As for the spirit of the day, Sunday lunch was usually beset by a single problem — Grandad forbade laughter while we were at the table. Annoyingly, that rule did not apply to himself, and he was inclined to show no self control whatsoever as the comedy flowed. There were many moments when he lost it completely, usually during the *Billy Cotton Band Show*, which he loved. Also, there was a song which Alan Breeze used to sing: 'Close the door, they're coming through the window … der der der; Close the door, they're coming down the stairs' (or words to that effect). He loved that song, and while he had hysterics, we all looked on — very glumly. He'd have a go at Grandma sometimes, mostly to make some point of superiority, and to impress us, I suppose.

The sort of thing he did included trapping her once in the corner of the living room, and keeping her there while he blew up a huge weather balloon he'd somehow got hold of.

I should mention that Grandma was a very substantial lady indeed; a characteristic which seriously disadvantaged her on the day in question. So while I was trying to do my homework, all I could hear was the sound of huge lungs blowing up this wretched balloon, which increasingly filled the room, threatening to take Grandma from view and, in due course, life itself. The noise was terrible, as Grandad, oblivious to his wife's distress, continued to enjoy himself, until the balloon touched a piece of furniture and exploded!

To his eternal joy, there stood his very large wife, frozen in shock, and covered in a substance similar to bubble gum. Add to that the French chalk that went with it, and, you may imagine, the lady looked a sight!

When Grandad was in a good mood, that sort of thing appealed to him. More seriously — or should I say, differently — Arthur Watkins enjoyed music and song; in fact, the whole of Mum's side of the family did, and Grandad had a fine bass baritone voice. Sadly, any ambitions he may have had for earning a living this way were cut short by a severe bout of diphtheria but, undaunted by this setback, he turned his hand(s) quite successfully to boxing. An obvious move if you think about it!

I suppose it was Audrey who first turned my ear to music; her brave attempts at 'Rondo à la Turque' on the piano always a climactic disappointment at the same bit!

As I said, with all life's ups and downs, my childhood was not too bad as I began to take notice of the world outside, make friends, and show signs of a creative mind.

To give some sort of focus to this, we're still talking early '50s, when Roger Bannister ran the first four-minute mile and Lester

Piggot became the youngest Derby winner at the age of 18. Giving great happiness to the older generation was Johnnie Ray. He cried a lot with his hit, 'Just Walking in the Rain', and made everybody else (including me) cry, too. I always thought him lucky to have such poor hearing!

With all this going on, I thought it time to make my first statement to the world, and it came with the unveiling of one of my many ideas. Now was the moment to introduce my first invention — a low-cost submarine. I built it at the time Cranford Park flooded, and the river Crane rose way over its banks, so the water was in the meadows up to a height of about four feet. There was a little hump-backed bridge leading to Saint Dunstan's Church and Old Cranford House, where Grandad lived as a child, and is now buried. Where the bridge crossed the river, there was a post and rail fence, and beyond that the flooded meadow.

As with most kids, we used to mess around with handmade carts — you know, old pram wheels front and back, with a bit of wood making up the chassis. The whole contraption was steered by legs planted either side of the front axle, and for those short in the leg, a rope pulled left or right worked just as well.

Enter now 'Gillan the Inventor'. Enter also my great mate, Barry Dass. Barry lived next door, and had long before said he'd test the different ideas I had from time to time. When I told him about the submarine, he fairly willingly agreed to keep his promise, although I suspect he wavered a bit when he saw the meadow. Still, I clinched it by saying he would have the title of 'Captain'. In moments of doubt, Barry's ego could usually be relied upon to override his brain. Status aside, however, I can still see him standing with diminishing enthusiasm as I converted the land trolley into a submarine with planks of wood forming a complete enclosure into which he'd finally be entombed. To make sure Barry could share the fullness of the experience while under water, I had cut portholes which were taped over with cellophane. Otherwise, I admit the inside was a bit spartan.

I put Barry's lack of gratitude down to nervous excitement, as I nailed the final plank over him, before towing the vehicle to the top of the bridge. Instructions were concise, so he knew that when the sub had reached the fourth post along the railed fence, he'd have picked up enough speed for him to turn sharp left, under the railing and off under the water. Of course, I'd checked the railing height to be sure it would clear the ship, and had similarly worked out that he'd have enough thrust to carry him the 60 yards or so through the flood, to the other side.

I guess he must have reached about 9mph when we arrived at the fourth post, and he swung left as instructed. To my joy, he disappeared from sight, and I ran to the top of the bridge to get the best view possible of the other bank.

Have you ever had that feeling that something has gone terribly wrong? After quite some time, I noticed that about three feet into the flood, bubbles were surfacing. As I puzzled over this minor distraction — my eyes still concentrating on the far bank — a head suddenly exploded from the submarine right in front of me, with a wooden lid perched on top. Make no mistake, Barry looked huge, with eyes bulging and veins threatening to blow him apart. Frankly, I was shocked, but as soon as he'd returned to normal size, relief turned to anger at his irresponsible incompetence.

At about the same time, and not too far away, story has it that Ritchie Blackmore was also hammering nails into wood. Apparently, he decided to find a load of planks, and one night went down the row of terraced houses where he lived, sealing off the back gates very firmly. His mistake was (I gather) that his house was the only one he left untouched!

With the submarine venture doomed, my thoughts turned to outer space. Johnnie Ray's luck faltered a little with 'Such A Night', which the BBC banned for 'suggestiveness', and rock 'n' roll rumbled into England with the arrival of Bill Haley and his kiss curl. He came into London to perform his hits, 'Rock Around the Clock' and 'Crazy Man Crazy', and caused riots at Heathrow Airport, just down the road. But if I was thinking about anything artistic at this stage, it was in the possibility of films.

However, there needed to be that final juvenile experiment to deal with first, as I told the hapless Barry about the spaceship. He was pleased with the title 'Chief Test Pilot', but less certain about the design, which basically used his parents' kitchen furniture. It was great stuff, American style, so it came with lots of chrome and colour. The stool was the main frame — nice and tall, with an elegant, low back. It was around Bonfire Night, when fireworks were in ready supply, so there was no problem with power. I taped about 30 rockets and crackers to the legs of the stool, carefully avoiding the area where his legs would dangle. The whole thing was linked to a common fuse, made up with bits of newspaper, sticky tape and loose gunpowder, and the structure was then attached by a washing line to the coal bunker, which acted as a restrainer. The reason for this was to limit the height of orbit.

We were all influenced by Dan Dare's adventures in the *Eagle*, and I took it all quite seriously. In fact, such was my concern for Barry, that I insisted on tying him very firmly to the space ship, so he would not come to grief when it turned upside down for re-entry.

I admit to being a bit disappointed at the lack of public interest, but that could not prevent tight schedules, as I lit the fuse and stood well back. Well, we got ignition all right, but then things took a bad turn as the rockets fired randomly, causing the machine to catch fire and fall over. Barry remained safely in place on the doomed ship, but that familiar look of surprise returned to his face, back again to bother me!

Through the ensuing mayhem, I saw my hopelessly inadequate pilot trapped on the ground in a state of shock and panic, as a firework display went off around him. OK, so there were no extinguishers on board, and the nearest tap was some way away, but the fact was that Barry had completely forgotten the training I'd given him, and compounded his problems when he got tangled in the washing line, which, as far as I was concerned, was the only thing keeping him from shooting off through Cranford Park, to the scene of his previous catastrophe.

Although Barry was in deep distress, I couldn't give him the help he needed, because my own attention had been diverted to the nearby block of flats. Unfortunately, a rocket had shot through an open window on the third floor, where an old lady lived, and had set fire to her home. I was now being abused by hysterical noise from two directions — so much so, that I failed to hear Dad arriving. I went to bed thoroughly confused and hurt, but not so much that I could not think about looking for a replacement for Barry. A doodle from that period deals with my wider inventiveness and state of mind:

Remember, remember the Fifth of November
Gunpowder, treason and plot
If Barry can fly
And comes back alive
I'll probably earn quite a lot.

It was another of those moments when I had to feel both admiration and sorrow for my mother, as I heard her apologising and offering to pay for the damage. She seemed to do it with a mixture of embarrassment and pride, as she explained the disaster away through my ability to talk people into sharing an idea with me, whilst also blaming me — and in this case, Barry, too. I believe I heard, through ringing ears, the neighbour telling her not to worry, that she would get the council to pay for the damage, and that she knew it was just 'one of those things'. She also said some quite nice things about me, which I thought most gracious. Pity Barry felt differently!

At the time of all this — I guess I was about 12 — I was a pupil at Hounslow College, where I had been since the age of four. I was neither clever, nor bottom of the class, but I began to show some interest and promise at sport, which I entered into with great enthusiasm, as opposed to skill. Still, it was something I enjoyed, despite the fact the school's facilities were very basic, with poor playgrounds at the school itself, and a long hike to Boston Manor for football, or to Southall for athletics, which I got into quite seriously.

They were good days, but then, to my dismay, I moved up a class, and came across one or two teachers who showed worrying tendencies; let's say their attitude was vigorously disciplinarian. It was unwise to complain and, in my case, life began to take a change for the worse, as I found myself singled out for special attention. The justification was explained to me; that there's nothing like a damn good thrashing to make the boy a man, and for this purpose the preferred weapon was a so-called slipper, even though it was a size ten or twelve plimsoll. I felt that across my backside on a regular basis, and so I came to learn at first hand, one of life's great truisms. That fear is the first principle of movement!

It was a challenge not to cry, and a huge contest of wills between the assailant and victim. Life was not bettered by the fact I was at that age where battles had to be fought on the street as well, and it was my misfortune that I was the only kid in a private school who came from a council estate, and the only kid on a council estate who went to a private school. Audrey, on whose positive characteristics I've already touched, worked herself to the bone to keep me looking nice, and I guess I stood out wherever I went as the guy who was different. I just didn't seem to fit. Wearing a light and dark blue-striped uniform, you may well imagine the misery that an evening walk home could be. For a non-aggressive person, I needed to look after myself, and at 6ft — although as thin as a rake, I managed to cope.

As for the classroom tyranny, there was a piece of business to settle along the way. We had a teacher who used to make the kids crawl the entire length of a classroom, under chairs and desks, pushing a pencil along by the nose. I vowed that the day I was told to perform this humiliation, it would be my last at the school, and so it came to be.

I seem to remember a heavy volume of Chaucer being involved, the teacher concerned holding his head with a detached look about him, and a murmur of approval as I walked away.

Audrey was teaching at the time, and she was able to use her influence to have me transferred to Acton County Grammar School, where I could begin to achieve my best. There, I was able to pick up sport again, and I found a niche in athletics and pole vaulting in particular. In those days, they didn't have the flexible poles we see today, so the whole thing was often quite demanding. You could always tell a vaulter of that period by the nine-inch gap between cuff and hand! With encouragement from the games' master, I was entered into the Southern Schools Championship at the White City, and it was fantastic. I think I came next to last, or maybe even last, but it didn't matter. I felt as if I'd been to the Olympics; I'd performed before an 'audience', and felt my first real sense of achievement.

A sound education also meant most kids went to church as often as necessary, eventually to be confirmed, and then usually to drift away to deal with life as adults. I'd been going quite regularly for some time — to keep Audrey happy at first, I suppose — but there were also some good mates doing the same thing, people like Los Humphries and Barry Higgins who were the main guys I'd hang out with. Both of them would feature at different points in my life over the years.

The place of local worship was The Church of The Good Shepherd, whose minister was a young priest called Father

Stubbs. It was Anglo High Church, and I remember there being an abundance of swinging the incense and all that stuff. However, there were other things going on as well, and the youth club and snooker hall (which formed part of the church) became a focal point where young people could meet. That was great and, as a growing lad, I was becoming aware of girls — 'crumpet', as we called them in those days.

A new world was dawning, as we all began to push school aside, explore our youth and listen, mostly at the youth club or at home, to a new phenomenon — Elvis Presley! 'Heartbreak Hotel', and the whole new dress culture that began to happen in that period, focused my mind (at last) on something I might have a go at doing myself one day.

So I was confirmed at St Paul's Church in Hounslow West, along with Los and Barry, and after that a few of us drifted homeward, past the Odeon Cinema, our futures uncertain, but full of promise!

Now I don't quite remember how it all began, but I do remember seeing these two guys, by which I mean grown men in their late 20s or early 30s, and one had a broken arm in a sling. Both were smoking roll-up fags, and just leaning against a wall, minding their own business. I remember thinking in my reverie just how good life was being to me, and feeling a bit sorry for them, leaning against that wall; the one with his broken arm, and the other with nothing more to look forward to than his next drag.

Anyway, I must have been staring, because one of them shouted, 'What the fucking hell are you looking at?'

Well, God, to whom I'd just promised so much, went out the window. 'What the fucking hell do you think I'm looking at ... c**t? You!'

A slight pause must have alerted my brain to a gross malfunction, which, to be fair, it quickly corrected as it shoved my legs into top gear, giving me a decent head start. So the two guys started chasing me, although it was the one with the broken arm who was the more aggressive. In the race for survival, I remember two things quite clearly. First, and with the exception of Barry, where were my mates? And second, it bothered me just how quickly the geezer was closing me down. Then through the sweat, the puffing and the panting, I wondered how the great movie stars would have behaved in such desperate circumstances and, so inspired, I brought my screaming legs to a real cool walk. The bloke behind had not anticipated the absurd change of pace; it would have been astonishing if he had, and he ploughed into me.

Helped by my recent communion with God, plus, I'm bound to say, perfect timing, it all came together brilliantly. The assailant had no chance, as I moved him effortlessly across my back, dropping him on his head some feet away. Beneath the smiling face of Elvis on Odeon hoardings, I dropped down, and my knee clamped across his throat. With confidence verging on lunacy, I leaned forward and plucked the 'roll up' from his lip — some part of which I'm afraid came away with it. I coolly put the fag in my mouth, before walking away ... just as Robert Mitchum would have done!

From time to time I make apologies to people in my life, so I'll make one now. It's to Father Stubbs, to whom I'm probably a big disappointment!

I used to be a sinner
Used to have my cake and eat it
They warned me of my fate
I was quite prepared to meet it.

I don't know how Father Stubbs would have reacted to the growing sexual awakenings and ambitions of his flock — girls as well as boys — but I guess he might have offered thanks to God over my first sad effort. The girl's name was Heather, and everybody in the street seemed to know her at one time or another. She came well qualified, as I hoped to find out when we found our way to the airfield at Heston. So we began, and it was all fumbling and rolling around on the ground, incredibly frantic, until, eventually, I rolled her over. She had her jeans around her ankles, and started screaming — quietly at first!

I found it all a bit unsettling really, and couldn't work out what was going on. I got the impression she was getting excited, and then I started to feel something I hadn't expected at all, because my crutch started hurting in a strange kind of way. It was very confusing. We had, in fact, rolled into a bed of stinging nettles. That experience put me off sex for quite a while, I can tell you! Funny old days.

Only a little while ago, my wife was reading the paper in our kitchen. She said, 'Hey, Gubbins,' (that's what I'm sometimes called at home) 'it says here that the average man thinks about sex 48 times a day. What do you think of that?'

Well, it puzzled me, but I said, 'I can't understand how the average man can keep losing concentration.' With the paper ringing in my ears, I realised I could have answered the question better!

And so one of the purposes of going to Acton County Grammar — other than to escape the misery I have talked about — was that Audrey wanted me to pass some GCE O-level exams (as they were known in those days). Pauline, I was reminded, was doing extremely well at Twickenham County School, and was not costing Mum a penny for her education. I should mention that Audrey could only afford to have one of us in a fee-paying school and, as the eldest (and a boy at that), I was the privileged one. It seemed to be like that in those days and, to be fair, Pauline didn't seem to mind. I worked quite hard, and did well in the mock exams, taking and passing seven subjects. But as the real tests approached, the crucial exams, I sadly became side-tracked.

To the distress of all who wished me well, I made the momentous decision to be a film star, and became lost in my dreams and ambitions to that end. As with the cat's effort with the budgie before, my own timing could not have been worse and I went through a difficult period as a result. Having almost abandoned my studies at a critical time, I'd be seen in the streets, pretending to be any number of different characters from the movies. On one occasion I'd be a detective hiding in the shadows smoking a cigarette; on another, I'd be seen walking bow-legged down the road, having left my horse tethered to the cinema railing. Perhaps most disturbing of all, I went through a phase of leering at every woman who came out of Hounslow West Station, pretending I was a great lover.

I'd like to think every generation of youngsters goes through fantasies like that, and certainly from my point of view, I thought it quite a healthy pastime. I didn't seem any different to the other guys who went to the movies, it was just that I wanted to be in them. I wanted to be a film star! I did not want to be a film actor — bit parts didn't interest me in the slightest. I wanted to be a film star — a cowboy, a spaceman, a great lover — even a gangster would do! Anything, so long as it was heroic and glamorous.

And so we come to that supreme moment of irony, that moment when something of great significance germinates, rumbles and then explodes into life, taking you in a direction you most definitely did not have in mind.

Chapter 2

As I came out of the cinema, after watching a Presley film, the light dawned, and I realised the easy route to becoming a film star — the way forward. Of course! All I had to do was become a successful rock 'n' roll singer like Elvis Presley.

Now it's in my nature that once an idea is in place, I like to do something about it, so on my way home to where we then lived in Brabazon Road (opposite the Travellers' Friend pub), I stopped this guy, Andy, whom I vaguely recognised and knew to be a young musician. I told him I was forming a band, and asked if he knew any guitar players in the area. He said he'd see what he could do and, true to his word, he found a few 'possibles' whom he brought to the house one Saturday morning. There were five or six of them, all carrying guitars of varying quality — by which I mean in different states of repair.

One of them was Chris Aylmer, who would turn up in later years with Bruce Dickinson of Iron Maiden fame, and another was Paul Sampson of the future band Samson.

At that time, however, the immediate gathering was of more humble stuff, and those with two strings (or less) were bass players, those with between two and five were rhythm, and a full set made you the lead guitar player. As it was my band, I was the singer and drummer, and we went through songs like

'Sheila', written originally in 1960 by the (then) 14-year-old Tommy Roe, 'Hey Baby' and 'Apache' — Shadows version.

Considering this was just a means to an end, I quite enjoyed singing, and the session was momentous, because it was the first time I'd been thrown out of a place, which in this case was my home! Still, it was great while it lasted — the noise, the trampling over furniture and the general wrecking of the place — accidentally, of course.

Having lost that 'venue', I decided to go to Saint Dunstan's Youth Club in Cranford to check out rehearsal room possibilities. It was a fair old hike, but I found the leader, who showed me the back room and said we could use it. When I said we had no money, he replied, 'Well, the fee will be one performance a week, if you're good enough,' and so we got going.

In putting together various bits and pieces of gear, Dad lent me £8 for a drum kit he bought from the Salvation Army. It came with one Gigster drum (with only a couple of strands left on the snare), a stick, a brush, a large bass drum (without pedal or pegs) and a high hat cymbal mechanism with only one cymbal, which went up and down, never finding its partner! We also found a small amplifier, into which one of the guys could plug a semi-acoustic guitar and, finally, we could record our efforts on Dad's Grundig dictaphone, which we sat on the table.

We took the gear to Saint Dunstan's, set up, and quickly discovered several limitations. The biggest was that when I was singing, I had to bend my 6ft frame double, just to get near the microphone, which in turn made drumming impossible. And when I was drumming, singing became impossible! From time to time, the bass drum would set off on a slow rolling journey into the wings, leaving me looking stupid.

It was time to choose between drumming and singing — it was no contest! Our first performance wasn't too bad. Not only that, but I was aware that some girls out there were paying me attention, and that hadn't happened to me before.

Buoyed up with confidence we rehearsed some more and they were pleased enough to let us do another gig the following week. I also did what seemed the cool thing to do at the time, and changed my stage name to Garth Rockett (note the double *t* to distinguish the name from the machine that nearly ruined Barry Dass some years earlier). The group was called The Moonshiners.

Audrey didn't seem to mind about my name — in fact, she took it all in good part, and said she much preferred the noise we made to the days when I used to sit on the stairs banging a biscuit tin!

Our enthusiasm was such that we improved quickly, and played a set which included 'His Latest Flame', 'Good Luck Charm' (both Presley, of course), 'Hit the Road Jack' (Ray Charles), and others by people like Bobby Vee and John Leyton.

There was another group sharing the hall in the early days — Ronnie and The Hi-Tones. In fact, they had got together before The Moonshiners (early 1962), and had built up quite a good local reputation. Their keyboard player, Dave Bone, was brilliant, and could rattle off Jerry Lee Lewis stuff with ease. His problem was that he sometimes decided not to show up, but when they were all together, they were impressive. Although their equipment was basic, it was better than ours, and so we came to share rehearsal space with them, usually on alternate weeks, each coming to watch the other's progress

.The Hi-Tones, enjoyed taking the piss out of us quite a lot, with the most obnoxious of them being their singer, known as Greasy Ron.

The Hi-Tones, however, had a problem within their own set up, and it turned out to be Greasy Ron! Basically, his singing ability did not match his posing, and the buzz was that they had their eye on me to replace him. One Saturday morning, their rhythm guitarist, Tony Tacon, turned up on a borrowed tandem with drummer, Keith Roach. They arrived at the house to be told by Audrey that I was at the sweet shop, which is where they came to find me. Tony asked outright if I would join them, and after a practice session at Dave Bone's house the next day, I agreed.

We changed the name of the band to the Javelins — after the famous Jowett Javelin car — and a further decision was also taken, that the brilliant, but unreliable, Dave Bone should leave.

It was October 1962, and the line up was Tony (Tubby) Whitfield on bass guitar, Gordon Fairminer on lead, Keith Roach on drums, Tony Tacon on rhythm and 'yours truly' singing. With all this change, I changed my name again, this time to Jess Thunder, and had it printed on our calling card.

In terms of the material we rehearsed and played, it covered the spread of our influences: Buddy Holly, Eddie Cochran, Georgie Fame, Howlin' Wolf and, of course, Elvis Presley. We played songs such as 'Oh Boy', 'Rave On', 'Not Fade Away', 'Cut Across Shortie', and one of my favourites, 'High School Confidential'.

There's always a first time when you take a decision that's going to upset people, and this was mine, as I explained my move to The Moonshiners. In fact, the lads took it very well, and we parted amicably. (Garth Rockett and The Moonshiners [different line up] would rise from the ashes many years later, in 1989, for a project.)

With all this activity going on, I became aware of mutterings from Audrey, who was thinking I should be taking my studies more seriously, and considering a responsible career — sooner rather than later! I suspect she was feeling that a bit of fun was setting me up with strange ideas that I might actually want to be a singer for my living, and so I obliged her by walking into a company called Auto Ice Ltd at The National Works in Hounslow. The firm manufactured ice making machines, and I was interviewed by their manager, Bill Brown. Having told him how well I would be doing when the exam results came out, and much else besides, he took me on at the princely salary of £7 a week. I forgot to mention my outside career with the Javelins. In fact, I enjoyed working at the company, and it wasn't long before Mr Brown put me in charge of a department.

I was clearly seen as management material, which may surprise my current manager, Phil Banfield, but at the time I quickly helped build things up, eventually having responsibility for about 110 outlets in Jersey, Scotland and elsewhere. The exam results, which have slipped my mind, were also conveniently forgotten. However, the music was always there, and became the focal point of my life and dreams.

The Javelins were a great bunch of people and musicians to be with. We had a great camaraderie and shared a cruel but brilliant sense of humour, all of which fused the band, and allowed us to progress to regular bookings at Wistow House, The Blue Moon (both in Hayes, Middlesex) and on up to the prestige Crawdaddy Club and The Station Hotel in Richmond, South London. There we took over the spot vacated by the Rolling Stones, who were 'happening' on the back of 'Come On'.

The Javelins were the first band in which I'd be paid, the gig fee being £2 10 shillings. Of course, it all went on travel and booze but nobody cared — we were doing what we wanted to do.

It was also with the Javelins that I had my first brush with heckling, on the night some bright spark shouted out, 'Get yer hair cut.' He did it while I was singing 'King of the Whole Wide World', but I did not falter!

As our business card showed, we were willing (and needed) to play anywhere, so occasionally we'd get private functions such as weddings, barmitzvahs or just a 'do', such as 21st birthdays. The young ladies from good schools seemed to like us, probably because we were everything they and their sort of escorts were not. I guess the idea of mixing with a bit of 'rough' somehow appealed to them, so while the chaps got drunk as lords (some probably were), their naughty rich girlfriends used to show us round the estates, stables, in cupboards, under tables — interesting places like that.

That said, it was always well known amongst musicians that you had a far greater chance of catching a dose from one of these girls, than you had from those who came to normal gigs. So everybody was extremely careful with them. Outwardly elegant, it did seem that the aristocracy took some pride in being quite mucky!

Javelin gigs would usually be performed in two sets of 45 minutes, and we'd play rock 'n' roll and blues. I used to wear a suit, whilst others would be in band-type uniform — leather jerkins being in vogue. My abiding memory of it all is that whatever we chose to wear, it stank to high heaven. Not surprisingly, I suppose, because after a gig, we'd chuck it in the van, and leave it there until the next time. Most usefully, we also had a mattress, which was used quite a lot.

As for the music, we covered material such as Sonny Boy Williamson, Howlin' Wolf, Chuck Berry, Jerry Lee Lewis and Little Richard, but unlike the Stones, Cliff Bennett, Georgie Fame or 'Screaming', we were not writing our own material, although I would soon use one of life's experiences to write my first song, 'Puget Sound'.

That song evolved because there was one occasion when I did let the band down. Audrey was still teaching, and was offered the chance through her work to go to America on a Teachers' Charter. The invitation was extended to allow Pauline and me to go with her, so I first went to see Bill Brown to ask for six weeks' leave. When he said, 'Over my dead body, and your day job,' (I think he must have known about the Javelins) I took that to mean 'Yes'. I then told the lads about it, and they weren't too pleased either, because it meant losing quite a few gigs, just when things seemed to be happening for us. Still, they didn't do an Auto Ice strop, so we flew El Al to New York, where we checked into an hotel.

The next day, we went to the Greyhound Bus Station, where we picked up our $99 touring tickets, which offered three months' travel freedom anywhere we fancied. In four to five days we were on the West coast, and I was in heaven. Somewhere along the road in Pennsylvania, this girl joined the bus — a classic Greyhound — and in the rear smoking section I learned much, including new phrases like, 'Do all English girls do this?' 'Puget Sound' is about that journey across America, to the place of the song title, and it would eventually be recorded on *Mr Universe*.

I remember the bus
Just the Greyhound and us
It was in between St Paul and Fargo
There were two days to go
But we virgins were slow
And my hand hadn't moved since Chicago

We enjoyed the westbound trip so much, that my Ithaca girl did the return journey with me, whilst Audrey and Pauline enjoyed the spectacular scenery.

Back home, I quickly settled in with the Javelins, and managed to get my job back at Auto Ice, this time in the factory, where they were 'short', and where I learned to weld and work on assembly lines. Although, I couldn't conceive of a career in industry at any level, the people at the company were great — particularly Nick, who worked in the office.

There was also a very beautiful, delicious secretary, whose name I choose to forget! Bill Brown was 'top man', too, particularly for giving me a job, when most others would have told me to sod off.

And so life continued at a varied and often hectic pace, with the day job followed by a gig, usually in the West London area. Although we all did our best to find work, Gordon's dad did most of that for us, acting as a sort of booking agent, which I think he quite enjoyed. He ran a sweet shop during the day, from which other things would later emerge. As things progressed, so we improved our image and sound, which brought us at last to the doorstep of a man who would do so much for the music business — Jim Marshall.

Jim would progress to run the most important amp manufacturing company in the world, and it all began for him in July 1960, when he opened up his famous shop, Marshalls, just down the road from us in Hanwell. He entered the entertainment business in 1937, beginning as a dance band singer, before going on to learn drumming under Max Abrams. As Jim would often proudly explain, Max taught Jack Parnell, Eric Delany and contemporary Simon Phillips, with whom I've had the privilege of working (including on the *Naked Thunder* album in 1990). Anyhow, after years of performing and teaching, Jim saw new opportunities through what was happening in popular music, and the rest is history.

By the time we were looking for gear, Marshalls — with Ken Bran — were making and selling their own amps and cabinets, and the word quickly spread about their attitude and workmanship.

As a digression, I believe Jim once played in the same band as Pete Townsend's dad and I, in turn, sat in the same classroom as Pete, in 'our generation'.

Having mentioned Jim, there is a great anecdote to pass on (even though the time is early Deep Purple). The story centres around a piece of music paraphernalia known in the business as 'slaves'. A few of us were hanging out in the pub one day, when our roadie, Mick Angus, turned up to announce the arrival of 'the slaves' we'd ordered. He said they were locked in the van outside. The announcement caused a considerable silence, and much staring at us, as we quickly realised what was going on. Eventually, the girl behind the bar said, 'Excuse me ... but did you say you have slaves in your van?'

'Yes.'

Long pause. 'Don't you realise it's against the law to have slaves these days?'

'It's alright ... nobody knows, and in any case we only use them for our work.'

Persevering, 'But it's illegal; slavery's been abolished!'

'Oh come on, love ... we've only got twelve of them ...'

'Where do you keep them then?'

'I've already told you, in the van.'

Even longer pause. 'How long have you had them?'

'Well, I've just picked this lot up today ... disappointing really ... we wanted white ones, but they are in short supply. So we've settled for black ... we're desperate! And not only that, but they're all called Marshall!'

Back with the Javelins, they were from nice families — comfortably off, I guess, without being wealthy. Perhaps to some extent it was my own personal lack of security, or maybe it was arrogance or impatience, but as the months passed by, I just couldn't see my way to stardom with this band. It was all there, almost, but tantalisingly untouchable. Our photos appeared in local papers, we had fans, and we had loads of work. But something was wrong, and I could not put my finger on it. I could not even fault the musicianship.

There was the Battle of the Bands competition at the Essoldo in Hayes, and it was typical of the things we had to enter in those days. Bands would travel from miles away for just a few minutes on stage, during which they would try to impress five or six judges, one of whom would probably be a DJ. We won the competition that night, beating a band called the Countdowns, who were also very hot in the area. Their singer was Brian Connolly, the bass player was Steve Priest and they had Mick Tucker on drums.

We played 'Sixteen Tons', 'Too Much Monkey Business' and a slow and very unusual version of Conway Twitty's hit 'It's Only Make Believe'. It was risky doing slow numbers in these situations, but I suspect the gamble paid off for us. Well, it didn't really, because for a start, we never got the prize of a working holiday at Butlin's Holiday Camp; then, when I took someone with me to the cinema to use the complimentary tickets, we got chucked out; and finally, the trophy was taken away for engraving, never to be seen again! This was followed by Gordon deciding to audition for the Countdowns, and he got the gig. In some ways, we were not too disheartened, because he seemed to be forever going away — usually to Spain, where perhaps his parents had a house. With the arrival of Gordon in their group, the Countdowns changed their name to The Sweetshop (after his dad's business), and when he was later replaced by Andy Scott, they shortened it to The Sweet. That band would achieve major hits in the '70s, with songs like 'Little Willy' (banned on the Mecca dance-hall circuit), 'Blockbuster' and 'Ballroom Blitz'. They did all this when I was with Deep Purple, and, in fact, they supported us on a number of shows. However, that would be some years ahead.

With the Javelins, things were not going well, and when cards start to tumble, they do so without mercy, as one disaster followed another.

There was the winter night when Tubby (Tony Whitfield) arrived by bus to show off his brand new Framus. It was still in its cardboard case, and we all stood waiting in the snow outside The Travellers' Friend to admire it, as he leapt from the bus. Sadly, Tubby didn't see the kerb, slipped and performed an incredible mid-air manoeuvre, which ended with the guitar breaking his fall, and its neck, so that only the truss and rod kept it as a single item. As Tubby knew we'd not get paid that night if he didn't perform, we strapped and glued the unfortunate instrument back together, and he played it like a bow, tucking it under his arm so the strings didn't pull off the fretboard. The sound was appalling, but we got paid, and his share went as an instalment on the worthless purchase.

After all the excitement, promise and dreaming, 1963/64 was turning out to be demoralising. My work at Auto Ice lost its way, and I left to join another company, which at the time seemed to have as bleak a future as me. That company was Tesco supermarkets!

Musically, I was becoming increasingly frustrated with the Javelins, and we disbanded in March 1964. We would get together in 1994 to make an album of 'reminiscence', which I'll deal with later.

Withdraw from the world, my friend
I said to myself
It's time to heal and mend
And discover yourself

I put together a band called the Hickies to complete outstanding bookings, but we aimed to do no more than that, as I drifted with diminishing enthusiasm into a soul band called Wainrights Gentlemen.

The 'Gentlemen' were originally formed by Brian Connolly and Mick Tucker, and they were a competent six-to eight-piece outfit, well managed and always working. We played the right venues, such as the Rikki Tik in Windsor and the Café des Artistes but, yet again, success was out of reach, and hopes of fame seemed remote. And then, one night, we were playing at Wistow House. I was singing Brook Benton's 'Kidio', when my eyes strayed to a magnificent pair of tits. Life was about to take a turn for the better!

Whilst trying to concentrate on the lyrics, I forced my eyes up towards the face of Gloria Bristow — or Glorious Bristols as she would later be known to me. At that time, Gloria worked for

Helmut Gordon, whose main claim to fame was that he'd discovered the Detours, later to be The Who. Although Helmut would lose that band, before disappearing off the scene himself, it turns out that Susan Seigal at his office had heard of me, and had sent Gloria along to check me out as a possible replacement for Andy Ross of the Hatch End band, Episode Six.

Well, I'd certainly heard about Episode Six, although they came from outside the area. Their line-up was Tony Lander (guitar), Graham Carter (guitar/vocals), his sister Sheila Carter (keyboards/vocals), Harvey Shield (drums) and Roger Glover (bass). They'd all met at Harrow County School, and came together from two bands, The Lightenings and The Madisons. What was attractive to me was that they had turned 'pro' in April 1965, coinciding with Andy's decision to marry and quit the business and, best of all, they seemed to be well managed.

Gloria was very businesslike, which impressed me a lot, and explained that I'd be with people who were 'going places', would make records and tour anywhere and everywhere. Above all, she said we'd become famous. Their stock in trade was harmonies and ballads, and I'd be expected to dress up in various styles of cabaret clothing, and generally do as I was told.

I know Audrey was, well, let's just say ... concerned. After all she had worked for, to help give me a good start in life, suddenly I was 'going on the road', and was now under Gloria's wing. That said, she took it very well.

The Episode Six set up really impressed me the more I got into it. For starters, they had an office at 43 Aylesford Street in Pimlico, London, and they also had a full-time secretary. There was a fan club, and there seemed little doubt that these people seemed to know their way around. They had contacts and Honorary Members such as Ed 'Stewpot' Stewart, Keith (Cardboard Shoes) Skues, Mike Lennox, Colin Nicol and Tony Blackburn — all well-known DJs. Unfortunately, there's always a price to pay for keeping in with these people, and one was that we'd sometimes have to put up with Tony Blackburn joining us on stage to sing. Frankly, it was embarrassing, as he moved around with this silly grin on his face, completely ruining the Ray Charles song, 'What'd I Say', which was a favourite of his, and mine, too, for that matter! He just couldn't keep time with the breaks, and I'm not saying that because he cut me 'stone dead' in one of the Green Rooms at the BBC in my early days with Purple a few years later. It just happens he was a much better DJ!

Tony made his reputation with the first pirate radio station, Radio Caroline, which operated in international waters, offshore, and that whole business caused a great deal of trouble with the establishment. He later joined the BBC, where I suppose he came to see things differently, including my hairstyle, which I understand annoyed him considerably.

To be fair, he wasn't the only one who seemed to want to distance themselves from certain types of progressive rock music and culture when it happened. David Jenson, another great mate, seemed to do it, as did Simon Dee.

Still, all that was for the future; right now, they were happy to be associated with Episode Six, and we were happy to have the chance to appear on radio, most auspiciously on *Radio 1 Club*, the first legal pop programme, which was first broadcast on Monday 21 October 1968, and continued until October 1971. It was a great showcase for many bands, and was recorded either in a club or hall, or from the BBC's Paris Theatre in London. It was a chance to perform live, have your records played and meet other artists from The Tremeloes to Julie Driscoll with The Brian Auger Trinity and even Pink Floyd (who played at the end of 1968).

Between October 1968 and June 1969, we performed eight times for the *Club*, and also gave a couple of interviews. Apparently, that set a record, whilst back at the office, the Fan Club newsletter was also in full swing, and was always colourful and enthusiastic. Here's how it described me:

Ian Gillan

Real Name	Ian Gillan
Stage Name	Ian Gillan
Birthdate/Place	19 August 1945, Hounslow
Personal Points	6' 2", grey eyes, dark brown hair
Brother & Sister	Pauline
Present Home	Hounslow
Where Educated	Acton County School
Age Entered Showbusiness	15
First Professional Appearance	College dance at Twickenham
Biggest Break in Career	None yet
Biggest Disappointment in Career	Too many to list
Biggest Influence on Career	Other groups
Hobbies	Watching Queen's Park Rangers, swimming, water skiing
Favourite Colours	Turquoise
Favourite Food	Anything English
Favourite Drink	Light & bitter, scotch
Favourite Clothes	Suits, American casual
Favourite Singers	Brook Benton, John(ny) Gustafson
Favourite Bands/instrumentalists	None
Favourite Groups	None
Favourite Actress	Elke Sommer
Favourite Actor	Alfred Lynch
Favourite Composers	None
Miscellaneous Likes	Enjoying myself, sunshine

Miscellaneous Dislikes	People with no sense of humour
Best Friend	Barry Higgins
Most Thrilling Experience	Playing at Nottingham Palais to a great audience
Tastes in Music	Anything exciting
Pets	The odd cat here and there!
Ambition	To own a big house in the country
Professional Ambition	To never run out of ambition and to be a good film actor

Against this revealing profile, I suppose the best way to introduce the musicians I'd be with for the next three years or so is to look at the things that interested them; what their ambitions were, and so on. As their own profiles explained, we were all about the same age, and I guess from similar backgrounds, although influences, experiences and interests varied. Graham's favourite colours were red and black, his dress preference was English and Chinese, and so, too, his favourite food. He was a cold coffee drinker, with a taste for cider, vodka and Pepsi or Cinzano, and he had a wide range of musical influences. They included The Beach Boys and the Barron Knights, all of which gives a clue to the type of music we'd play. His best friends were Sheila, a poodle and a budgerigar. He'd already tasted fame on *Ready Steady Go*, and had ambitions to see the world, stand on the moon and never change his profession! When it came to his big break, he had the good grace to admit to meeting Gloria, unlike my own rather ungrateful 'none yet' reply.

Sheila liked the colours blue and purple, steak and Chinese food, the poodle and the budgie. She also went for ice-cold milk and Advocat, but didn't like opening milk cans! Influenced by Cleo Laine, Jimmy Smith, Alan Price, Georgie Fame and the Beatles, her ambitions included owning a chimp and a baby elephant. Her biggest break was also credited to meeting Gloria.

Tony Lander liked purple and blue, Zoot Money, Nina Simone and George Benson. Tony was a sausage and chips freak, with an ambition to live 'happily ever after'! And yes, Tony was also grateful for having met Gloria.

Then there was Harvey, who counted Episode Six amongst his favourite groups, along with The Drifters, the Mamas and Papas, and the Beatles. He also loved himself best, wanted to 'live happily ever after' and admitted to like 'doing nothing'. Harvey Shield's biggest career break was meeting Gloria!

Which brings me to Roger Glover — or the 'stinking hippie', as he was then known. Born in Brecon, South Wales, a month or so after me, Roger liked purple. His favourite food was Chinese, and his musical influences were Tom Jones, Nina Simone, Bob Dylan, The Beach Boys, The Lovin' Spoonful and the Beatles. It would emerge — and continue — throughout a lifelong friendship and collaboration, that Roger's declared dislikes were arguments and violence.

Roger's only nasty streak was his confessed love of driving through puddles in the van but, of course, he was also immensely grateful to Gloria, although Les Reed won his gratitude as well!

Roger came to the business from a background which was pretty helpful in some ways. When he was ten, his family came to London to run The Richmond Arms in the Old Brompton Road. It has since been demolished and is now The Tournament, but while they were there, they had live music, so he had his first taste, mainly through skiffle. He was with The Madisons before Episode Six, and went on to Hornsey College of Art.

With the sudden departure of Helmut from the management (I still owe him £100!), Gloria took full charge of us, and set about making us work very seriously. Under her enthusiastic management we had organisation, a fair degree of discipline, a gig schedule that took us around the UK, to Germany and as far off as Beirut! Above all, and at last, I had a recording contract — I'd cracked it — or so I thought.

Chapter 3

The deal was made with Dick Katz/Harold Davison Ltd, and it took us to Pye Records. Typed up in about 10,000 words, it basically said: 'Dear Episode Six, I'm going to earn you £30,000 this year, and deal with the record company for you.' So we signed a royalty deal with Pye that gave us 75% of 1%, rising to 'of 3%' after 25 years, and on that we were supposed to live and keep our manager happy.

It's easy to be wise with hindsight, but these sort of deals were commonplace, and would continue in a similar vein for many years, until the balance of power shifted more in favour of the artist, helped by a couple of well-publicised court cases.

So, certainly, what was done in those days is not done now, and it's good to know that the artist's status is not as low as it was — that we're now getting our 'fair share of the pie'.

Comparing today with the Episode Six period, it seems to me that the kids have exactly the same that we had, only there's more of it — more problems and more advantages. What we didn't have as an absolute priority was ambition, in the way you see today. At that age, and in that period, we were immortal, and it was very much ideology which drove us to throw everything we had into what we were doing. And the reason we got better was because we wanted to get better.

Apart from competitions like the Essoldo (with the Javelins), you didn't set out to impress people all the time, because you were not really impressing yourself at that point. So in terms of ambition, and looking back on the Pye deal we signed, the kids today are certainly much smarter about what they are letting themselves in for. Most are into the basics of business and contract law alongside their practising and writing, which is an attitude we never had, or even thought about having, for that matter. Our way of getting attention was (for example) to do a spoof advert. It read: EPISODE SIX — APPEARING ON DECCA RECORDS (SOON!) They didn't much like that!

So we went along with Pye, and we went to work with great energy, although it was Gloria who kept the bookings up with weddings, college dates and the odd American bases — but nothing had been forthcoming from our new business and agency associates.

When we decided to take the matter up with them, it was quietly pointed out (before the hysteria began) that what we'd signed meant they would find us £30,000 of work before the year end and, if they didn't, we were free to leave. It was a bitter blow, leaving us to join the chorus of musicians who said success was possible 'despite your agent'. But as I've already suggested, I guess we were willing lambs to the slaughter, and we just put it down to experience, and got on with it.

Our first record for Pye was The Hollies number, 'Put Yourself In My Place', made after a typically brief session in their basement studio at Marble Arch, and done in a very few takes. Tony Reeves produced us, a respected musician, who would later play with a band called Collosseum. Another early studio guy was Glenn Cornick, who went on to play bass with Jethro Tull.

However, things in the studio did not go as we had planned, because instructions came down telling us not to bother to bring our instruments since we'd only be needed for vocals. We arrived to find a group of session players in place, including a drummer, and that seriously upset Harvey. So even though we had the Pye record deal, the attitude was that we were not considered good enough to play on the production, and sadly this compromise continued for most of our early releases.

As for The Hollies song, despite all that happened, we were still glad to get our hands on our first piece of vinyl, and arrangements were made to take us to meet the group to see what they thought of it. We went along, and they totally ignored us! That song, with Roger's composition, 'That's All I Want' on the 'B' side, was released in January 1966, and we followed it up in April with 'I Hear Trumpets Blow', again with a Glover song, 'True Love is Funny' on the other side. Once again, it was a trip to Marble Arch without our instruments, a session in the studio, and an 'OK, boys ... well, off you go now,' from Alan McKenzie.

In the meantime, of course, the Beatles were steaming on with George Martin, and John Lennon was telling Maureen Cleeve of the *Evening Standard* that the Beatles were 'probably bigger than Jesus Christ right now'.

It sometimes needed a sense of humour to be in Episode Six, and we showed that in various ways. Musically, Roger did a spoof on 'Surfin' USA' (The Beach Boys), except our song was called 'Mighty Morris Ten':

Come on, everybody
Grab your automobile
We're going down the Harrow Road
I've got a little old Morris and it's doing fine
Although it's ninety-six years old!

Another way of dealing with the different emotions at the time was to enjoy a drink or two, and there was a gradual increase in quantity — beer and scotch being my favourite. In doing this, I set up a reputation which would cause other people to be concerned from time to time, often needlessly. In fact, it's a drink related story that gave the band a priceless moment to savour, by which I mean it cheered us up, in the days before the 'drink-drive' laws. And just for once, it did not involve me as the guilty party!

Graham was responsible for the group van, which he kept at his home, and he would usually be the driver as well. On this particular occasion, he must have had other things on his mind, as he drove the six-wheel, long-base Ford transit (known as Wagger, from the number plate, WAG), when the lights began to change. Maybe we were arguing, I just don't remember, when this gent, whom we later discovered to be an Irishman, suddenly drifted off the kerb in front of us. Well, Graham thought the way to avoid him was to accelerate, which proved to be a mistake. The next thing we knew, we had a passenger on the windscreen, with a look not 'suggestive of genius'. Frankly, I think Graham panicked, because he slammed on the brakes, and the impromptu hitch-hiker (being only lightly attached) flew off. Graham's foot then slipped off the clutch, the van leapt forward and ran over the unfortunate visitor.

Getting out to examine the extent of the damage to Wagger, Graham stepped on the poor guy's head. To the victim's eternal credit, he got to his feet, and started giving us a hard time! Amid hysterical laughter, we all agreed the moral of the story to be: if you want to run over an Irishman and get away with it, make sure you perform the exercise at least ten times!

We travelled everywhere on wages of £10 a week, and a typical schedule looked like this:

August

Sat 26th	Winter Gardens, Weston-super-Mare, Somerset
Sun 27th	Douglas House, Lancaster Gate, London (not open to the public)

Wed 31st	Surf City Club, Tonbridge, Kent
September	
Fri 1st	Claypidgeon Hotel, Eastcote, Middlesex
Sat 2nd	Lion Hotel, Warrington, Lancashire
Tues 5th	Depart for Germany (Dover/Ostend ferry) 6.30am
Wed 6th	Tele Record; BEAT BEAT BEAT, Frankfurt.
Fri 8th	Arrive Dover (from Ostend) 5.00am
Fri 15th	Depart for Germany (Dover/Ostend ferry) 6.30am
Fri 22nd/30th	Storyville Clubs — Cologne and Frankfurt.
October	
Tues 3rd	Holland; TV film for promotion of 'Morning Dew'
Wed 4th	Return to UK
Fri 6th	Release of 'I Can See Through You' Tiger's Head Catford.

Although this itinerary is fairly late into the development of Episode Six, it is a good example of routine which involved many miles in a van, but with it, many great experiences, including two trips to Germany, which I call 'The Storyville Experience'.

We were put into a B&B under Cologne Cathedral, and were told we'd be doing six or seven shows a night, with a matinée on Saturday and Sunday. And the same went for The Star Club in Hamburg.

Of course, these weren't full-length sets, but we are talking about many hours, and the pay was lousy, with most of it going on accommodation and expenses. Still, nobody complained, and the clubs were great, as were the audiences who 'got off on us'.

Little things please in these conditions, such as the fact that when we bought bockwurst, the rolls came free — and nobody cared how many you had. They were just piled up in baskets. So we always looked forward to our rolls and mustard! The beer was cheap, at least the sort we found was, and at an exchange rate of 4DM to the pound, we found giant bottles of it for 75 pfennigs each, and drank lots of it!

Despite the enormous amount of practice and effort we put in, things often went wrong at the gigs, and I suppose part of the problem was that we were still struggling to find an identity. We were neither The Hollies, nor The Rebel Rousers not for that matter the theatrical Barron Knights, who had found a particular niche. We were Episode Six, a band of mainly copy musicians, working with harmonies and showmanship. We didn't have a lead singer, since Sheila and I shared that role and, at times, I'd play keyboard while she sang. Our set included a medley of various hits: 'A Hazy Shade of Winter' (Paul Simon); 'That's the Way Life Goes' (Jimmy Cliff); 'Light My Fire' (The Doors); 'River Deep, Mountain High'; and 'I'll Be Your Baby Tonight' (Bob Dylan). We had our own material with songs like 'Monsters of Paradise', 'I Am a Cloud', 'I Am the Boss' and the popular 'Mozart v the Rest', and we'd also drop in snatches of 'Running Bear' and 'Rule Britannia' as we went along!

Crucially, we didn't have hit records, and so we continued working our nuts off, coming on stage after all sorts of acts, at all times of night, and in all sorts of places.

It was an eccentric lifestyle, illustrated by the occasion we arrived at one particular club (God knows where), and it was about 1.30am. There were about 15 people there, all hopelessly drunk, and groping one another in the dark recesses, as a comedian closed an hour of wasted talent and time, in which he'd been amusing the walls. Still, he gave the impression he was having a great time, and we were all cracking up on the fire escape, where the gear was stacked ready to bring in. Suddenly, it was all over, and he started hoofing it out, in case somebody woke up to assault him. As he disappeared into the night, his parting words floated back to us: 'Good fucking luck to you!'

Talking of luck, Gloria was somehow able to swing a support spot for us on the Dusty Springfield Tour. It was our first time in theatres, with four minutes to open the first half, and seven to open the second. The discipline was brutal. If we were more than 20 seconds over or under, we would be fined our fee for the night. More than a minute, and we'd be off the tour! The compére was a comedian called Jeff Lenner, and he'd walk on stage and say things like, 'My wife's so thin, she has to run around in the shower to get wet.' *Really!* He used to nip off to the nearest backstage bar between acts and, on his return, he'd hang his raincoat on the doorman's second finger, straighten his tux, and walk into the spotlight, nanosecond perfect!

Impressed by his professional nonchalance, I asked him what he thought of our performance. He tiredly explained that I'd never get anywhere in the business until I could persuade the audience to ignore the band, and focus on me. He said I shouldn't be there when the curtain went up, but should make my 'entrance' whilst the intro was playing. Also, that I should move around within my own scope of comfort, and draw individuals, or small groups in the crowd into a mood of intimacy by means of eye contact. Some things stick in your mind for ever.

There seemed no end to the levels we'd go to try and find our niche in the business — we even did the Bee Gees with false teeth, and they loved that at The Tiger's Head, Catford and The Black Cat, Woolwich, although it didn't go down so well at other venues, where they thought Gene Vincent would be turning up when he was already in his grave!

Manchester was another place where we'd do two or three

clubs a night; 45 minutes at the first, load up the transit (usually in pouring rain), on to the next venue, keeping sweaty and stinking stage gear under macs while we offloaded the gear and waited for our next call. Sometimes, the club would be on the fourth floor of a building, with fire escapes being the only way to get backstage without interfering with an act or the audience. Even so, we tried to keep our dignity in case we were seen, so we tried to look and behave like roadies.

An example of things going wrong for Episode Six was when I moved into the spotlight in my kaftan, red trousers and white shoes, generally looking pretty cool, despite the early hour. Around my neck were about 40 self-made string beads, linked with thin elastic, and we opened our show with something frantic. Well, I'm giving it my best, and generally going berserk, when, for reasons I can't explain, I bent down in this dramatic gesture, and then straightened up. The beads got caught around my knee and the elastic snapped on some of them, shooting them out like bullets, and the rest were launched in rotation round my head. It was definitely a learning time of my life!

In fact, the red trousers mentioned could sometimes cause an uplift of morale, reminding me of the gig we did at Cheltenham Ladies College. The 'pants' were very loud and tight, and showed off the 'three piece suit' to it's very best! In the interval, the headmistress came bustling over, and said words to the effect that she found my organ offensive, and it was upsetting her 'gals'. Well, I had to tell her there was no way we were playing without Sheila's keyboard, and the whole thing ended quite acrimoniously!

One of the newsletters dealt with my dress sense at the time, telling the fans I'd recently spent a lot of money in Carnaby Street: 'And have you seen IAN'S fantasmagorical glitter shirt yet? It's absolutely gorgeous ... and WOW ... speaking of tight trousers, eh, which we were, how about IAN'S new cerise pants?!'

Well, that's how it was in those days! Looking back on these brilliant efforts, the temptation to burst into applause at the end of every Newsletter was overwhelming, but it was a thankless task, and only gratitude and praise is owing to those responsible.

In dealing with many problems during this difficult time, I then added to them by getting married. It was the summer of '65, and I suppose I was vulnerable to any situation which would bring some warmth and hope to my life. I thought I was by now reasonably experienced in life's ways, when I met this girl, Jean, at The Establishment in Greek Street, in London's Soho. It was a famous venue, made popular by the controversial satirists of the time — John Cleese, Peter Cook and David Frost among them. From those beginnings, it went on to become a nightclub, owned by a guy called Raymond Nash. It seemed that Mr Nash (whom I'd never met) owned a number of clubs in the West End. Typical of such places, it employed doormen, bouncers, personal security, call them what you will. It was part of the day-to-day running of such venues, and at the Establishment, there was Dennis Raine.

Well, Jean and I began a spectacular fling, during which she taught me a very great deal! It seemed she also had a great deal of money, certainly more than anybody else I knew, and although she was about ten years older than me, here amid all the insanity of pop and rock, was a person who gave me excitement. So when Los Humphries married Marlene a little while after I'd met Jean, I asked Los if I could bring her along to their reception, and he said, 'Fine.' She turned up (quite late) under her own steam, and seeing her across the room she looked stunning, dressed sensationally under an expensive fur coat, which was OK in those days. With all eyes on her, as she crossed the room towards me, I noticed something very sinister — Jean had been beaten black and blue. With people staring at us, she told me how Dennis Raine had taken exception to her dating a musician at the club, and although he was not entirely sure it was me, he had his suspicions. Anyway, he'd decided to discourage her from continuing the liaison, and her appearance would make the point to whoever was buzzing around her.

Shocked at her injuries, yet somehow flattered by her closeness and vulnerability, I did not handle the situation with great maturity. My suggestion that we went to the police was rejected out of hand on the basis that they had better things to deal with, than become involved in a 'domestic', and all other ideas were similarly dismissed. In the confusion and headiness of the wedding, I decided that the moment was perfect for a gallant gesture, and I asked Jean to marry me.

History is filled with men who have fallen from great heights because they acted on a romantic impulse, and here was another about to join the ranks — and not even from a great height! It's just that the idea of rock singer, Ian Gillan, saving an abused woman from gangland terror by an offer of marriage, had a certain ring to it. A dickhead ring! With my family decidedly unhappy about the whole business, and my buddies the same, our wedding and reception was a modest affair, after which we went to live with friends of Jean's in a one-bed flat over a hairdressers in Copenhagen Street, near King's Cross station.

One thing bothered me a little, as we found our way across London, and it was that between us we only had about £3. To be clear, I had not gone into this relationship because of the money Jean seemed to have (I've never been that interested in it anyway, through good and bad times), but it did surprise me that she had so little on her that day. Still, who wants to talk about such things just after your wedding!

That night, the telephone rang in the hall, and Jean returned with the news that Dennis Raine had committed suicide. Incredibly, she then simply fell apart. Through the babbling hysteria, the truth came out — that she was in love with Dennis, and not me! So much for chivalry, so much for gallantry, for here stood a girl I thought I'd rescued from hell, showing me that I was really an insignificant, penniless twat! So penniless were we, that we did a 'moonlight bunk' when things had settled down a bit, and found even less salubrious accommodation in an attic behind Baron's Court, West London.

It's a funny word 'salubrious', because it's the only word I remember Grandad using to describe the place when I told him about it. But it was one word more than what he thought about my marriage!

A complete decline in morale was saved by Gloria, who kept our careers alive with a diet of touring. I must have been away for a week or so with the band, when either a show had been cancelled, or we drove home through the night. Anyway, I let myself in at home, there to experience the final humiliation for my stupidity. There before me was Jean, and somebody was with her in our bed. Well, it was uncontrolled gibberish, with explanations like, 'He couldn't get home so he …' but I ignored her, and said, 'Well, that's it,' before taking my leave, never to return.

As we toured the country, problems festered within the band, the main one being what I guess was jealousy over the fact that Roger was doing all the song writing. The material he was so often coming up with was consistently good, and certainly as good as the songs we were about to record on the 'A' sides, written by other artists. Unfortunately, the record company wasn't interested in giving Rog a break, but he persevered with his 'B' sides, while everybody else moaned.

I tackled him on the matter one day, saying, 'This is brilliant, I wish I could do that,' to which he replied in a very tough way (most un-Rog like), saying, 'I'm never going to speak to you again until you've written a song!' In fact, he mellowed a little by adding … 'or at least until you've tried!'

Just the possibility that he might be serious, that I might lose a great friend, galvanised me. Of course I can write! I speak English, I can put words together, so I can write lyrics. 'Pudget Sounds' aside, my first effort, inspired at about the time of the 'Yellow Polka Dot Bikini' hit, was called, 'I've Got a Green-Eyed, Curly-Headed Little Pigmy Hanging Round My Neck', but I was unable to have it taken as seriously as it deserved!

Still, Roger and I started working together on lyrics, practising writing poems, dealing with rhythm, looking at the construction of songs written by people we admired, and just getting up, tapping and singing. 'Ticker ... ticker ... ticker ... ticker ... ticker ...ticker ... tick.' Just as I guess the master, Little Richard did! We'd sit up all night doing exercises; one would mention a subject, and the other would have ten seconds to make a poem out of it. It didn't matter if it was a load of rubbish, we were searching for that little piece of magic.

In the meantime, we struggled on, and were in quite regular demand with the BBC, where the pay was pretty reasonable — £75 as I recall. Alan 'Fluff' Freeman was brilliant to us. While other DJs were full of the 'Hello, dear boy, I do like your record,' Alan would play it. *Yes!*

I suppose one of the reasons we were popular with radio, or at events such as Wimbledon Speedway, Brands Hatch or even once at the Hilton Hotel (London) where Sammy Davis Jr was star billing, was because we were safe, clean and fun loving! Unlike those terrible fellows, the Rolling Stones, whose name was mentioned in whispers!

However, it was beginning to dawn on me that being a 'terrible fellow' had its attractions ... let's just say the seeds were sown. For now it was a question of swallowing pride, and watching artists like Tom Jones and The Walker Brothers turning up in limos, miming to their latest hits, signing autographs by the sackful, and going on their way, leaving us to do a live show. Still, our attitude got us on to *Ready Steady Go*, where we met Sandie Shaw, and we also performed on Southern Television for Mike Mansfield.

And so the day came when I met Janie Jones! Janie's early claim to fame was through her singing in various London clubs. In fact, she had a hit called 'Witches Brew', but that was not the reason for her high profile and notoriety, because Janie moved into the 'fixing business'. Known in the '60s as 'fixing storms', Janie was an unofficial playlist compiler, a role I learned more about when I went with a well-known DJ to a party in a very smart London house.

It was quite late when we arrived, and we walked into a very civilised party, where I quickly picked up on 'how the other half lives'. According to my buddy, we'd timed our arrival about right, and on being ushered into the reception lounge, there in the centre stood Janie, a very pretty girl. She was dressed in a cocktail frock, and surrounded by these guys talking business. You didn't need a University degree to realise that three or four of them were big label record producers, whilst there were many other familiar looking media people and one or two politicians. While they were all chatting away, the same records were being played over and over again, and Janie was saying things like, 'Don't you think this deserved to be a hit,' or 'Don't you think that's just fine?' or 'I hope you're going to give this release plenty of plays!'

And all the time she was moving around, offering to top up the drinks — the glasses never seemed to be empty! I remember being particularly impressed because they were beautiful crystal goblets, and mine saw quite a lot of scotch pass through it.

Altogether, it was quite a formal affair until, quite suddenly, Janie drew attention to herself, and pulled her frock up, showing she had nothing on underneath. She then leaned back in a chair, and started playing with herself, before getting to her feet and gyrating across the floor to where I was getting pissed. She looked at me and, after a few moments, asked which of the girls present I thought the most pretty. When I said, 'The one that's dressed like a nun,' she said, 'Well, off you go then!'

With a scotch in one hand, I was led passively by this incredible-looking girl to a room where we began to have lots of fun on a king-sized bed. And then, through the excitement of it all, I became aware of laughter and giggles. Putting two and two together, I leapt from the bed and rushed into the hall to find a gathering of voyeurs and well-wishers looking through the one-way glass!

Well, there are people who get quite upset about being caught out like that, and others, like myself, who try to see the funny side. I remember looking at the gathering and saying, 'I always finish what I start,' before returning to the room to prove my point. Later that night, I was aware of all sorts of goings on in the house, such as a certain gentleman (whom I believe was from the civil service) who had one of the girls kicking and whipping him, whilst I also noticed some 'human parts' of political life the electorate don't usually get to see, as my wanderings took me past open doors and mirrors. I wasn't complaining, though, and thought the whole thing was pretty spectacular — so much so that I was invited back.

Looking back on it all, I held no position of influence, and had nothing really to sell — I wasn't even a famous musician. Still, why question a good thing? It also gave me some clues as to how good life could be if I became successful. It was uplifting at a difficult period of my life.

As for Janie, I believe she got involved in the 1971 Payola Scandal, and went to prison for running a call-girl ring. She was an interesting lady — my kinda gal!

Back in the real world, Episode Six were losing momentum as the Stones, the Beatles, The Kinks and The Small Faces took control of the music and cultural scene that was now ballooning. John Stephen, a Glaswegian, had transformed Carnaby Street from a nondescript alleyway off Regent Street, into an international style centre for the young. *Time* magazine referred to 1966 as the year of 'Swinging London', and it was all about the Pill, pot and freedom.

But we'd missed the boat, and Gloria explained that if we were to survive and stay in the business, we'd have to work abroad. She told us what we really knew — that the gig scene had changed with the arrival of the major acts making albums, and needing the chance to perform them. The days of package tours with Billy Fury, Adam Faith and that generation of headline acts were at an end; we were moving into concerts. Gloria sweetened the pill by saying that our records were selling well in the Lebanon, and 'Morning Dew' was apparently top of the charts in the two shops that had access to copies!

In solemn moments, I wondered if they had been influenced by the Newsletter which described the song as 'a sound that wraps itself around you ... lifts you eight miles high ... dreams you nine miles deep ... moving brilliants ... hues of red and crimson, purple, green ...'

I know Gloria was unhappy about us going to the Middle East, but we were outside the mainstream of activity in Europe, and needed to work and earn money. So there seemed no alternative. I was surprised that after all we had done, we still had to audition for the trip to Lebanon, and that took place at The Marquee in Wardour Street, which Dick Katz had arranged. Charlie Henchis came over from Paris to check us out, and we signed. I was worried about losing our tenuous position, that we might yet be lucky, but we were caught between a rock and a hard place. Of necessity, we took all our gear with us, and it was a considerable amount of hardware to transport. We were a loud band by then, and surprisingly had a lot more equipment than Deep Purple were working with at that time. We had recently taken delivery of a brand-new sound system made by Grampian, and it came with a control panel similar to those used in recording studios. It had loads of effects, such as echo, reverb and the ability to play tapes through speakers which were built into the whole unit. Tony's guitar was a Gretch Country Gentleman which played through twin Vox speakers and a Marshall amp; Graham had a Fender with two Saltma Goliath speakers and a Dynachorde amp; Sheila worked with a WEM organ through two Vox amps; Harvey had a kit which was a mix of Trixon, Ludvic and Avedis, and I had some new clothes!

We took the lot and our wardrobe to Beirut with seriously mixed feelings. Once out there, we continued to gig on the same lines as before, with kaftans, lots of swapping of instruments between us, and all topped off by our unique brand of comedy, which sometimes went down well, and at other times failed miserably! We mixed popular international hits with our own increased record output which was still on the Pye label, and with whom the lifetime commitment felt like a prison sentence. The songs included 'When I Fall in Love', 'Something's Gotten Hold of My Heart', 'Stay with Me, Baby' and 'Light My Fire', to which we added mock stage fire! Then there was 'Jesse James', which Rog performed, and he was funny. Well, we thought he was! For 'Too Much Monkey Business' we used crazy foam and cornflakes, and also played our 'B' sides, including 'Mozart v the Rest', which we'd later record on Les Reed's Chapter One label.

And then at the Casino du Lisbon, I met for the very first time, a name from my past — Mr Raymond Nash. We were well into our set, and I was resplendent in my Mississippi gambler's outfit — black frock coat, bootlace tie, Paisley waistcoat, striped pants and black boots. We were about to begin a number, when this very nice party of diners who'd been buying us drinks all evening were suddenly removed from their table in front of the stage. It was incredible how it happened; there was no fuss, no argument, but quite simply about ten of them were asked to go somewhere else by a group of very large people in ill-fitting suits. As quickly as this had been done, the table was relaid with fresh ashtrays, flowers and so forth and, soon after, a dapper man came and sat down, while four or five cronies formed a semi-circle around him. After watching the show for a few minutes, and eyeing me in particular, a note was passed up which I read while singing. It said, 'Mr Nash wishes you to join him at his table when you take a break.' Mr Nash was, of course, the owner of The Establishment in London, so it was hard to know if I continued to sing the right words, before I did as he asked.

After a long pause, Mr Nash said, 'Tell me, Ian, what really did happen to Dennis?'

After what seemed an eternity, I looked at him and said, 'Mr Nash, I don't know ... I just don't know ...' I remember babbling on about how Jean and I got back to the flat at King's Cross, but he suddenly changed the subject, and was as nice as pie.

Courtesy of his expense account, the band drank themselves silly, and even went back to his fantastic home for more hospitality. I admit to going down feeling extremely unwell, and not being able to join them. In fact, I spent some time thereafter being fairly low-key, and improving my writing skills in the blistering heat.

> *I am a cloud, I am a cloud*
> *Not just any cloud, but a big black thunder cloud*
> *And I am really proud of my capabilities*
> *I have a loud roar and like to frighten poor people*
> *With my flashing fury*
> *They run helter skelter for shelter*
> *Still I am bored and I will retreat and take a back seat*
> *I am a cloud.*

Little things come to mind when looking back on a trip such as the Beirut visit; things you'd never really think of in the normal course of events. For instance, it quickly became evident to us that the showbiz fraternity out there, other than speciality acts or rock bands, were gay. Charlie Henchis explained that to be deliberate policy for contracts other than very short term. Relationships — business and personal were more reliable that way, because pregnancies were avoided, or if they were not, then the contract would have ended before it became a management problem.

As for heterosexuals, it just meant that we could have a lively stay, although I found an English girlfriend for much of the time we were there. It was with her that I experienced one of many strange and troublesome incidents which were typical of that region at the time.

We were stretched out on the beach one day, just quietly enjoying each other's company, in relative isolation. The sand stretched out for ever, with only the odd shack breaking the view — not an ice cream van to be seen for miles! It happened that a recent storm, one of the worst the area had seen for years, had caused incredible damage to the few shanty type buildings around, and one was just a few yards behind us. Suddenly, a load of sand was thrown over me, and when I looked up, there was this guy standing in what was left of a window frame in the derelict structure. The roof had gone, the top floor was mostly missing and the whole situation was bizarre. So I told him (in French) to bugger off, which I think is the same as in English, but he just grinned and did the same again.

I repeated my demand in much more forceful French, but it happened again, only this time he started throwing stones. I picked up a nearby rock and threw it very hard. It caught him smack in the face, and he disappeared from sight. My first thought was, 'Great shot, Gillan!' But then I wondered if perhaps I'd gone a bit over the top, and I went behind the wall to check on him.

What I saw worried me, because his face was badly damaged, and he didn't seem to be breathing. Without thinking about any consequences, I told my girlfriend to find her way back to the accommodation, and left to look for a police station. Some people at a petrol station directed me to a building further down the road, and I arrived, nerves tingling.

I saw the policeman the moment I burst in. He sat at the far end of the room, and appeared to be taking a coffee break. There was nobody else in the room, as I approached him, unsure whether to smile or look sombre. Well, it wouldn't have made any difference, because he sat there on another planet, as I detected some movement under the chintz table cloth. No question about it, the police officer was jerking off, and was clearly somewhere near the 'vinegar strokes'!

Not wanting to spoil his fun, I quietly took my leave and headed for the apartments, where I found some local people with whom we'd become friendly. When I told them the story, they went mad, shouting at me, 'You crazy ... you crazy ... you never go to the police with thing like that!'

I gave it an hour or two for my nerves to settle, and then went back to the scene of the incident where, to my astonishment, there was no body. There was plenty of blood, but no drips to show if he'd struggled away. Maybe he'd just been removed.

Beirut was a brutal place to be in, as we discovered on many occasions. We came across a European once, who looked as if he'd been hit by a truck, as he dragged his broken body along a ditch, which served as the local village sewer. It was horrific — the poor man tried feebly to signal for help but, incredibly, our driver just put his foot down, and refused to get involved. It was explained to us later that if you report an accident, the automatic assumption is that you caused it. We later learned that the man's body was recovered from the stinking hole about three days later.

To get in and out of Beirut on the 'American Highway', you had to pass over the 'Yellow River', which was a euphemism for the open sewer which served the city. Down there in that stinking morass lived a community of Palestinian refugees. Their only source of fresh water was the sprinklers which came on at dusk, and freshened the ornamental shrubs in the central reservation of the highway. From time to time, one of their children would be struck by a vehicle as they crossed the road with little rusty tins, to collect the precious water.

I've often wondered how much dignity can be stripped from human beings, before death becomes more attractive than such an existence, and whether the builders of that road intended it to be such an insult.

On to lighter things, and the night Angel Manchenio tried to kill me in Marmeltain. Angel was a flamboyant dancer of Spanish gypsy decent, and a regular on one of Charlie's bills at the Casino. Manchenio was quite short — about 5ft 6in, I guess — but possessed of great strength. One of the highlights of his show was when he'd climb up to the balcony about 15 feet above stage level, and throw himself off, flying through the air, to land on his knees on stage, then to rise and strut his stuff. It was fantastic, and we spent many a happy time with him and his large, red-haired English girlfriend, or wife as we knew her, and they would come and party with us at the apartments, a feature of which was the plumbing, or lack of it. Basically, we used to go outside and 'water' the rocks, from where there were panoramic views of the village, railway line and Mediterranean.

Often as not, Manchenio would turn up at some stage of the evening, kick bottles off the table, and perform this very dramatic dance routine which involved much clicking of heels, snapping of fingers and macho posing. It could go on for hours, we'd all get drunk, and it was great!

The evening and moment came when I needed to go outside to answer the call of nature, and while 'doing the business', I saw Manchenio creeping round the building until he got to the corner, where I had my ground -floor apartment. It was really strange, because he was tip-toeing along, bent double, and when he arrived at my bedroom window, I became even more puzzled.

What he'd discovered was that his girlfriend was 'having it away' with some fella in my room. Well, I've never seen anybody lift themselves by their own hair, but that was exactly what he did, as he paced around like a crazed animal in total silence. At the time, I didn't, of course, know what was going on in there, so all I could do was watch this ninja-like creature roaming around in the dark. Eventually, I decided to do something about it, and came out of the shadows.

'Hey, Manchenio ... what's up?'

On seeing me, his eyes lit up like torches and, reaching down, he produced this very big knife. Manchenio always wore knee-length boots, and it was only now that I realised he used them to conceal his weapon.

'I keel you. You fucka my wife. I keel you! I thought you my friend ... I keel you!'

So now I was backing up a bit, saying, 'Hang on, Manchenio. What are you talking about?'

But he just repeated, 'I keel you ... you fucka my wife!'

I said, 'Look where I'm standing. I'm taking a piss, you dickhead. How can I "fucka" your wife from here?'

He froze briefly and said, 'My God, Ian ... my God. I'm sorry! I keela myself now ... goodbye!'

I tried to reason with him saying, 'Listen, first you want to kill me, and now you want to kill yourself.'

'No ... no, Ian, I insult you ... there is only one thing a gypsy with honour can do — I take my own life!'

I then said, 'Look Manchenio, there must be some way out of this,' to which he said, 'Well, there eesa one way.'

Funny how some comments cause warning lights to flash, so I said very cautiously, 'Is it dangerous?' When he replied, 'No, eesa no dangerous,' I put my arm around him, as one does in relief.

His solution was that we could get out of this whole mess if we shared blood which, to cut a long story short, we did in the grand tradition of the movies. He took his knife, made a cut in the heel of our hands, took out a filthy neckerchief, and bound our wounds together. We embraced passionately, exchanged words of love and respect and went back into the lounge, where he totally ignored his wife! He simply got back to drinking with us, before dancing again.

My gypsy brother
Tried to take my life
Thought I'd stolen your lover
Faced me with a knife

Life in Beirut wasn't all about problems and stress, and we often experienced generous hospitality. On one occasion, we were invited to a Christmas party by some sailors in the American navy. I guess this would have been in 1968. The fact that we spoke English and were musicians made their day, so they took us on board, where everybody in sight, from top to bottom, was drunk!

We were taken through 'Top Secret' and 'No Admittance' signs to see the missiles and flight deck. We saw the helicopters, which one guy said were radio controlled, meaning that they had no pilot, and far from asking us to leave our cameras behind, they let us take as many pictures as we wanted.

Although we ate a delicious meal in their mess, we couldn't go the whole hog, since we were on stage that night. From all of this, it will be obvious that the music side of our lives was not progressing, and relationships in this hot climate were becoming very strained. The few press cuttings copied from England read well, but disguised many troubles. Harvey and I certainly went through a bad time, so when the fans back home were reading things like 'Sheila turning up late, and so exercising her prerogative as the female in the group,' it must have sounded fine to them, but in reality it was a turn off, and a mask for what was really going on.

Harvey seemed to be suffering the most, and his growing disinterest shone through some performances. In fact, I threatened to throw him over the castle battlements on one occasion if he didn't get his act together. He finally quit the band when he fell for a Greek belly dancer called Natasha, and was replaced by John Kerrison, who was a character and a half!

How else do you describe a drummer, who, when pissed off with our leader, Graham, sets up his kit at the far end of the hall! It was all so eccentric, often depressing, and far away from London, where the music business was so vibrant and full of creative juices. After all our labours, why were we stuck out here, whilst the Moody Blues, The Who and all the rest were riding the waves of success? I found myself asking many questions, particularly whether my writing had progressed or regressed in the Middle East heat.

Decide which way to turn
Or fall, dispirited
Against the wall
Without an aim, a whim or will
And lie there
Where the world is still and comfortable

We returned to England, but unlike the Beatles, only our mums and dads were there to meet us. Bless them! The end was approaching, and Mick Underwood replaced John Kerrison, who later had a horrific accident, and now bravely travels on wheels. Mick came to the band with plenty of experience, having worked with Ritchie Blackmore in The Outlaws. He was also in the early line up of The Herd. Mick's connection with Ritchie would, of course, change my life a year or so later, but in the closing stages of Episode Six, he definitely brought a spark to the dying embers.

Back home, we were still looked after by Gloria, whose ambition and enthusiasm remained undiminished. We joined the MGM label, where we made 'Little One' and 'Wide Smiles' (May 1968), and along the way got involved in another Bristow promotion *par excellence*.

We went along to this club, and there were Gloria and the Honorary Secretary looking like the dead girl in the movie *Goldfinger*. They looked very sexy and the party was fantastic. Later on in the proceedings, we were ushered outside, and there stood a Mini Moke, a tiny 'buggy' car that was very fashionable at the time, very ventilated and very cheap! To our amazement, there sat Sheila, wearing her very short mini-skirt, and sitting with her in the car were two lion cubs, symbolising the MGM corporate image.

A similar stunt was pulled at Bristol Zoo, and that put the band on television. However, MGM and the band parted company — in fact, they told us to leave — and we signed to Les Reed's Chapter One Label, where we put out 'Mozart v the Rest', 'Lucky Sunday' and 'Les Bicyclettes de Belize'. We were earning reasonable money, sometimes £200 a night, and it was then that I met HEC — or should I say, Deep Purple.

Chapter 4

I t was Mick Underwood who unselfishly mentioned me to Ritchie Blackmore, when asked if he knew any good singers to replace Rod Evans in Deep Purple. Looking back, of course, it was all a bit underhand because neither Rod nor Nick Simper, whom Roger would replace, had any idea what was going on. In fact, neither, apparently, did the Purple management of John Coletta and Tony Edwards. While they were beavering away in the office at 25 Newman Street in London, trying to sort out problems and a viable future for the band, Ritchie, Jon and Ian were in America reshaping it for them.

John and Tony's main problems were about the difficulties with the Tetragrammaton label, who owed them a lot of money, so in terms of what the band were up to with me, perhaps they had taken their eye off the ball. As for replacement, Ritchie and Co were looking to find a singer/songwriter who would help them develop into the future. The band had made albums like *Shades of Deep Purple* (1968), *The Book of Taliesyn* and *Deep Purple* (both in 1969), plus the singles, 'Hush' and 'Kentucky Woman' which were quite successful in America. However, they were looking for a harder sound, and against that background, Ritchie and Jon came to see me at the Ivy Lodge Club in Woodford Green, Essex, after which I was asked if I'd meet them to talk things over.

From the first moment, the guys came across very strongly; I mean they looked so 'rich', so confident, so well dressed, with bouffant hair. I dreaded going to meet them, and prepared myself for it by borrowing the best of Roger's clothes to go with some of mine, and then buying 10 cigarettes to help calm my nerves, and also to offer in a gesture of friendship. I set off with just enough money to buy the cigarettes and get me home, and I also had a vile cold and a pocket full of soggy Kleenex tissues.

So we met, and my first impression of these guys was right. I quickly looked to impress by offering fags — 'Anybody want one of these?' — as used and wet tissues tumbled out as well. With snot trickling down my throat and out of my nose, I bent down to pick up the damp mess, as eyes looked on. It was a moment of horrible misery, and I was later quoted as saying, 'I felt smaller than an ant, dirtier than a piece of dog shit, and wishing to be more invisible than the smallest part of the Universe!'

However, they were just great and helped me through the ordeal. We talked rock 'n' roll, and they offered me the job. They then asked if I knew any decent bass players, and I mentioned Roger. So they asked me to see if he'd join as well, which, after a great deal of soul searching — it hurt Rog — he came along. In fact, his 'interview' with them was even more bizarre than mine. First, he'd not really taken to Jon and Ritchie when they came to see us play, and then he went along wearing jeans that had been 'perfect' two years before. He also wore what looked like a tea cosy with arm holes and sandals, and generally looked like he was held together with string. I thought, 'My God, what are they going to do with this?' but to my amazement they all thought he looked very cool. So they offered him the job as well, and he promptly turned it down!

I spent hours with him over the next few days, agonising over the pros and cons, hearing him say that it was bad enough me leaving Episode Six, and so forth, but in the end he agreed, and phoned Jon up to tell him. In fact, he called Jon at about

10.00am, not realising that Jon didn't rise until about 2.00 in the afternoon, and the conversation went something like: 'Jon, it's Roger here,' to which Jon replied, 'Yeah ... so?'

'It's Roger Glover, the bass player!'

Now remembering, Jon told Roger his decision to join was fine, but added that he'd be on trial for three months. He called it probation!

Everything being about settled, we had a clandestine studio session where we recorded 'Hellelujah', quietly moving in full-time while the (still) unsuspecting Rod, Nick and managers completed dates with the band, which saw the end of Mark 1 Deep Purple at the Top Rank, Cardiff on 4 July 1969.

Although there was great upset at Episode Six, and I believe Gloria threatened legal action, from my point of view it was like walking through a revolving door into a brave new world.

As for Deep Purple, well, as most of you know, it was named after the title of a song liked by Ritchie's grandmother, and first recorded by Bing Crosby, but then more popularly by Nino Tempo and April Stevens in 1963. The band had considerable experience, particularly in America and, unlike my own situation, they had recorded quite a lot of material, having also been in the same studios at Marble Arch that we'd been rushed in and out of for Pye during our time with Episode Six.

They were signed to Tetragrammaton in America (EMI in the UK), and seemed to be treated with a lot more style and respect than I was used to. Above all, they were successful, doing well in the American Billboard Hot 100 chart in America. ('Shades of Deep Purple' made number 24; 'Hush', 4; and 'Kentucky Woman', 38.) They had appeared on *The David Frost Show*, and played alongside bands such as The Byrds (London Roundhouse), as well as travelling Europe with the Small Faces, The Koobas, and Dave, Dee, Dozy, Mick and Titch.

It wasn't all plain sailing, however, as became clear when Jack Barrie pulled strings to get them on the bill for the Sunbury

Festival (later the Reading Festival), and was quoted as having said, 'Deep Purple were booked to be the opening act on the Saturday afternoon, and to add salt to my wounds, they died the proverbial death. My only defence at the bar later was a simple, just wait and see ... they are a little before their time.'

In fact, the band were booed off stage, but these things have happened to most of us at one time or another, and it didn't stop them being looked after like stars, with limos to a party at The Playboy Club in the States, where they met Bill Cosby, and Paicey behaved badly trying to organise something with Jackie De Shannon. They supported Cream on their Farewell Tour, but were thrown out after San Diego. They partied with Jimi Hendrix, and played with their heroes Vanilla Fudge at Edmonton. In a nutshell, their lifestyle was a world apart from what I'd become used to.

As to how they came across, well, they were very different to the rather well behaved group I'd just left. Ritchie had already set his image for the future by dressing in black, and wearing the Puritan hat which became a trademark for some years. He was also developing his ability to be dramatic, and play quite high stakes at brinkmanship, as shown when he decided not to arrive at a David Frost television show until just half-an-hour before it went on air. Roadie Mick Angus was already psyched up to fill the slot somehow, when the guitarist arrived to announce that unlike the rest of the band, he wasn't going to waste time hanging around for nothing.

Ritchie had also started to play long solos, into which he would drop bits of 'God Save The Queen' or 'White Christmas' and, of course, that became part of the Deep Purple tradition, which remains to this very day. This guitar player was brilliant, and as a founder member of Deep Purple, he came to the band with a background of working with The Outlaws, 'Screaming' and generally learning his trade as a backing musician to artists like Gene Vincent. As for Paicey, he had started in Oxford, worked through various bands, including M15, where he met Rod Evans in Slough, and then as the Maze they recorded for Parlaphone and travelled to Hamburg, where they met Ritchie at The Star Club.

That left 'Gentleman Jon', whose wisdom I came to see when I visited his flat. It was covered wall to wall with his score for what would eventually become The Concerto for Group and Orchestra. Although trained at The Royal College of Music and The Royal Academy of Dramatic Arts (RADA), from where he developed his fine stage presence and proud voice, Jon had struggled for years, with help from his mum, on £1 a week, I'm told. He joined the Art Woods, and they were with the Decca label. Influenced by Jimmy Smith, Graham Bond and Bobby Timmins, Jon would bring to Deep Purple a unique stage presence and fine command of the Hammond organ. Just watch it rock!

Together, these musicians behaved and played loudly, and as America moved into the love and peace age, audiences were sometimes confused by what was going on. At a UCLA graduation party, Ritchie smashed the mirrored false ceiling above the stage, while Paicey played with his tongue sticking out. He still does sometimes!

So these were the guys I fronted on that tiny stage at The Speakeasy in Margaret Street, London on the night of 10 July 1969. There I stood before my peers — pros, other musicians, people in the music business and girls. As soon as we started, the place just went wild. It was awesome, and I just coasted through, the feeling of power indescribable. There was 'Mandrake Root' and whatever else, and I played congas for want of something to do during an instrumental. And I cried — oh, I cried! That night I reflected on all the bands I'd travelled with, the turmoil of the transition from Episode Six to Purple, and all the people who'd been hurt along the way; on all the ruthlessness it seemed I'd been part of by dumping one band after another in order to tread my way along the line to this moment.

On that tiny stage, all those emotions touched me so deeply. I'd enjoyed each and every band, but now it seemed that all these friends, musicians and relatives had been lined up along the path to this very moment, for THIS WAS IT! And I salute and love them all.

Earlier on, I'd made reference to the Stones as 'terrible fellows', and now with Deep Purple there was scope to join them, as we quickly developed into a lethal cocktail of creativity and energy. Whatever the circumstances, when we were together, things would happen, and this would be the case for many years to come — on stage and off!

A good way to find out about new mates is to spend time relaxing with them, and the River Thames proved an ideal playground for that. Ian Paice's interest in fishing and Ritchie's enthusiasm for causing chaos in fast boats introduced me to their personalities quite well.

It's difficult to select examples, but an early one started at Bushnell's Boatyard, where we hired The Gay Joker. It was an old wooden boat and, tethered to the dock, it audibly groaned at the sight of two long-haired musicians approaching, accompanied by Bert Bushnell himself.

Once aboard, the first job was to load the various bits and pieces, which in my case took a few minutes. However, Paicey needed at least six journeys to and from the car and, while he sorted himself out, I did the inventory with Mr Bushnell. It was impressed upon me that all damaged or missing items would have to be paid for, and I willingly signed a contract to that effect. It was not much more difficult to do than so many other pieces of paper I'd put my mark on, and the proprietor then took us through the rudiments of river cruising ... or should I say he took me through them, since Paicey was still organising his wordly possessions. I heard about the dos and don'ts of river etiquette, and 'this is the steering wheel, and this thing makes you go forwards or backwards,' at which point he took us to Boulters Lock. Satisfied with our confident approach to the adventure, he then leapt lightly ashore, to leave me in control. Or was it 'command'?

Paice let go of the ropes and, as the lock gates opened, I selected forward gear, and we moved towards a gap that didn't look quite wide enough. As captain of the moment, I made my first major decision: if we can't make it forward, let's try sideways! The next thing I did was opt for a 'time to think position', as an increasing number of well-wishers looked on. And then after a zero contribution so far, my first mate made his final connection to the massive stereo system he'd brought along, and with 'Shotgun' raging out of the speakers, several things seemed to happen at once. The engine immediately found a surge of enthusiasm, which, assisted by crashing gears, put us into full thrust. A holidaying Commodore fell overboard (nobody heard the splash), and J G Ballard ignored us — but then he was busy trying to land his light aircraft! As we planed towards open water, I looked over my shoulder to see a tableau of frozen faces and, somewhere down river, Bert Bushnell was trudging back to his yard, head bowed and shaking, contract in hand! 'Got the stereo going then, Paicey,' I said, as we crabbed and rammed our way into a bright future, and towards the first pub, to check our position.

Ritchie had rented a different boat, which was a modern fibreglass type. It only had a couple or so berths, as opposed to the six or seven we had in our more sedate craft. His vessel turned out to be quite quick, as he demonstrated when the two boats arrived unannounced during the Henley Regatta. As I recall, there were all sorts of signs on the river saying, 'Don't do this' and 'Don't do that', as well as quite a few well 'blazered' people who were shouting, pointing and waving at us. We were fairly accommodating in the larger and slower boat, but

Ritchie very quickly got bored with the whole affair, and decided to show the many onlookers that his craft could reverse, just as quickly as it could go forwards. He also showed its ability to manoeuvre, by scribing circles around The Gay Joker so fast that it mattered not if you were on the river or on the shore. Wherever you stood, you got soaked, as 'You Keep Me Hanging On' helpfully entertained the audience. I've never seen so many pissed off Hooray Henrys and Carolines in all my life, and there were a lot of Carolines — mostly with their tits out. Anyway, we all waved back at them!

As the impoverished newcomer to Deep Purple, there were many things I'd come to terms with quite quickly. For example, having seen Paicey offload serious material wealth, I'd then find myself in his 'wake' as we'd leave the boat moored up somewhere, so we could top up in a riverside pub. Off he'd go, in hipster jeans with a wide belt, loaded with bank notes which he had folded in the belt so that half the money would be hanging out for all to see. He'd strut around just willing people to wonder who this guy was! However, approaching the bar, he'd usually allow others to get there first.

An early problem was also his total disinterest in personal hygiene on board and, apart from having smelly feet, he showed a resolute reluctance to clean out the toilet, which was basically a bucket. After a while, I decided not to do it for him anymore, and we used the pubs instead. It didn't seem to bother him too much, even though his bunk was next door to the cubicle, but unfortunately we moored up badly on one occasion, and the boat tilted sideways. To be fair, he rolled up his sleeves to help sort that problem out.

Back on the river, Ritchie and his German-born wife, Babs, would meet up with us from time to time, as I began to learn more about this eccentric and moody musician. On one occasion he decided to explore an island, and got the engine tangled up with the roots of trees. Unperturbed, he hopped ashore, leaving Babs (whose figure would have proudly adorned the prow of the finest galleon) to amuse herself with their dog, Strokie. It happens that Strokie was a clever animal who would entertain anyone for hours with his backward somersaults and other party pieces. Left alone and stranded with Babs, he started his routine.

After a while, Babs, resplendent in her bikini, began to get lonely and a little agitated, so I stripped down to a pair of jeans, and gallantly dived under the hull to cut the boat free with my knife. Coming to the surface, I realised to my horror that the vessel was rapidly disappearing downstream on the current, at which point Ritchie returned. With Strokie picking up on the excitement of the occasion, and performing his routine to the point of collapse, there stood Babs screaming, 'Ach, Ritchie ... vot I do!'

The guitarist shouted back, without much enthusiasm, 'Turn the wheel, you soppy cow!' and promptly went back to his wanderings on the island, as Babs disappeared into the distance.

There were a few relaxing moments on the river, although nothing was ever normal. Paice, for all his expensive fishing gear, never seemed to catch anything, and I often suggested that he turn down Vanilla Fudge, or try playing Nat King Cole. Well, he'd have none of that, but the point was probably rammed home the day this kid was fishing the bank, using just a bamboo pole, a length of line, a bent pin and some bread. Over a few hours, he filled his bag with trout, and towards the end of the day, Ian, who'd not had a single nibble, went over to him to see if he'd like the treat of fishing from our boat. They swapped places and, as Paicey threw out his line and cranked up the stereo, the kid continued pulling the fish in from the comfort of the boat.

Later, in the pub, the drummer started making up bait for the next day. He used a biscuit tin full of maggots, which he put on the wall while I went (again) for the beer. From the bar, I heard all this shouting and screaming, and looked out to see that the tin had fallen off the wall in the wind and his vile maggots were crawling in the sandwiches, hair and private parts of other punters. They were evil smelling things, and it hurt him a lot to remove notes from his belt, to replace food and drink.

Meanwhile, while we were taking things easy, Ritchie was somewhere up river with his airgun (or maybe it was a catapault), popping off at the river banks. He finally went too far at Windsor, where the river police caught up with him, and he was brought before the magistrates. That's one of the few incidents the press didn't hear about, and was my first awareness of the management skills of Messrs Tony Edwards and John Coletta, who got him off somehow!

On joining Deep Purple, my salary doubled to £20 a week. I knew of their financial troubles with the record company, and that they were owed a considerable sum because of that company's (apparent) bad investment in other entertainment projects, but it was not my affair. Eventually, the whole thing would be sorted out when Warner Brothers came to the rescue. As far as I was concerned, I now had two managers, two roadies in Mick Angus and Ian Hansford, and was with a band that was going places.

I quickly learned about my managers, who were very different characters, and worked out how to approach John for one thing, and touch Tony for another. For example, an early mistake was when Roger and I approached John to ask him for a sub, so we could buy decent clothes to wear on stage. His reply was not exactly positive, to say the least! It was a salutary lesson, and an introduction to big-time management. Still, in those days, they were a united front, with good and bad ideas, but generally fine to be with.

Then there was our full-time accountant and my future mentor, Bill Reid. Bill was a jovial James Robertson Justice lookalike, with offices in Wallington, Surrey, and he would become a key player in the development of the Deep Purple business. In the early days, my introduction to the set-up involved completing 'Hellelujah' (I'm not on the B-side!) released on the EMI label (Harvest) in July, and later in America. In fact, it's not a performance I'm terribly proud of — they weren't my lyrics, and showed me more as I'd been with Episode Six. Still, it got me my first press release with the band, when Tony Barrow International Ltd printed that my 'voice sings powerfully on revivalist lyrics and tells us that it's time for smiles and Deep Purple'.

In fact, it wasn't all smiles really, because when the managers told us we'd be doing the song on *The David Frost Show* (not *Top of the Pops* or *Ready, Steady, Go)*, Ritchie refused. It was the beginning of things to come, but at that time, nobody could foretell the future, even if they had wanted to.

Song writing with Roger also began in earnest, and we were ready for it. Until then, I'd been going through what I see as my formative years, but they had been years where there was restraint, holding back. We were nice people! Now we didn't have to be nice people any more; we could just stick two fingers in the air and go for it, and I think this is what Purple had been looking for.

You could feel it in the music, the way the band played, and it's why songs like 'Speed King' took off. Now my entire music background — Little Richard, Elvis Presley and Chuck Berry — had meaning and focus. I could put into practice what I had learned.

Good Golly, said little Miss Molly when she was rockin'
in the house of blue light
Tutti Frutti was oh so rooty when she was rockin' to the
east and west
Lucille was oh so real when she didn't do her daddy's will
come on, baby, drive me crazy, do it, do it

The early months of Purple were something of a blur, partly

because of the energy and work, but also because I had come to the band a good drinker, and the band weren't exactly teetotallers, either. Because of our whole way of going about things, people thought we were on drugs, because that's what everybody was doing, but the simple fact then was that we were a drinking outfit, into which I slotted quite easily. As the momentum and excitement increased, I'd go (almost daily) to buy a bottle of sweet Martini and a very sweet Vermouth, which I'd use to set me up, poured into a tumbler loaded with ice. A bit later, I'd move on to gin and sweet Martini, and although it wasn't very macho, it did at least hit the soft spot quite quickly. Then I'd get into the day properly, and by nightfall I'd be having a sociable time in some bar or other, finally to find my way home perfectly well, with about ten pints of beer inside me.

It made no difference if it was a working day or not, so come the day we went to Germany, I began very early at the airport, drinking gin and Vermouth before the noon departure. During the flight, I must have had three or four miniatures of gin and tonic, chased by a similar number of beers to see me through the short trip. I then found myself in a restaurant somewhere doing an interview, and quaffing German beer — many large Steins — before going on to do a TV show, and then having an evening meal, where the wine flowed. The session then transferred to a club where I'd get back to scotch and beer to dilute the taste of wine (which is not my favourite beverage) before eventually crashing out in bed.

Come the morning, I'd feel great and ready to carry on! However, the abuse would one day catch up with me, but as with so many of us in that situation, there was nobody to put me straight, and the indulgence therefore went on without comment, and possibly unnoticed. It certainly didn't affect my performance on stage during the many months the band toured relentlessly, and produced some of its greatest music.

The monks of vine who crush the wine
And get it on their smocks
It dribbles down their legs
To their intoxicated socks
They roll about in ecstacy
And frolic on the lawn
Until they hear the bells that signal
Matins.......after dawn!

With two new members to ease into the band, we rehearsed a lot, while John and Tony mapped out a huge touring schedule and personal appearances (PAs). There was the need to balance early gigs with material written before my arrival, and new songs. So we'd perform 'Hush', 'Kentucky Woman' and 'This Bird Has Flown', plus instrumentals, all from *Shades of Deep Purple* and *The Book of Taliesyn*. And then we'd do stuff like 'Speed King', 'Child in Time' and 'Into the Fire', none of which had yet been recorded. We were now in the early stages of putting together our first album, *Deep Purple in Rock,* on which they would feature, at which time Jon's Concerto started to emerge from the walls of his flat, and become a project.

It was something we all found very difficult to cope with, Ritchie in particular, and words were spoken to the effect that we were a rock band making a major album, and so on. The discontent rumbled on, as we rehearsed and wrote at the Hanwell Community Centre, and it was there, in that great echoey space, that Jon first started to play those few notes ...

We'd recently heard an album by a new band called It's a Beautiful Day, on which there was a track called 'Bombay Calling'. It was mainly an instrumental, and was quite fast, but Jon had become fascinated by it and was musing around with it on the keyboard. And then I started to sing, 'Sweet child in time...' and rock history was made! It was totally spontaneous, and conceived without a storyline, as would happen later with

'Smoke on the Water', and through it — with the help of tight trousers — I discovered 'the scream'.

That song, 'Child in Time', remains elusive for me to sing to this very day. The timing and weighting of delivery can be a nightmare if I'm not in the right frame of mind, and for a number that was written without a narrative style, it would shock me to learn — as far away as the '90s, that it was adopted as an anthem by some resistance groups operating underground in eastern European countries. That's one of the scary parts about being a singer/songwriter.

Other songs would be developed in their own surroundings, starting usually with working titles. 'Speed King' began in a smaller room at Hanwell, and was called 'Kneel and Pray' for some time. It was performed at early shows, including one for the BBC. 'Flight of the Rat' began as a joke, when 'Flight of the Bumble Bee' was mentioned, and once again Jon started doing variations around it. The 'rat' was, of course, a drug habit, and we'd often play with words that way. 'Into the Fire' was similarly drug associated and anti the habit — but with a collection of material like this, in addition to 'Bloodsucker', everybody presumed we did drugs. When we said we didn't, the stock answer was, 'Well, you would say that, wouldn't you!' So we gave up arguing about it. We did dabble with substances — at least I did — but that would be later.

Other songs — 'Highway Star', for instance — found their inspiration elsewhere and, in this particular case, it came from a journey on a bus to Portsmouth. We'd hired it with some journalists, and one asked Ritchie how our songs were written. Caught in a helpful mood, Ritchie picked up his guitar, and said, 'Like this.' So he started a rhythm, and I came in with, 'We're on the highway; we're on the road; we're a rock 'n' roll band.'

We were in the mood, and by the end of the night the seeds had been sown for what would become our standard opening song for many years — 'Highway Star'. It has been moments like that which have made me realise why Deep Purple became the band I'd later admit being 'willing to die for', and looking back to the camaraderie (most of the time), and the willingness to be experimental and innovative, I realise so powerfully that my lapses of disillusionment in later years were based on sound logic. Then, as now, we were unafraid and wonderfully creative and, against that kind of backdrop, our rapid emergence as one of the foremost progressive hard rock bands, makes total sense.

As mentioned, my first appearance with Deep Purple was at the Speakeasy and, although a small venue, it nevertheless became the main watering hole in London for musicians, whilst the roadies seemed to hang out at The Marquee. So you could walk into the Speak at any time, and find yourself in the company of people like Keith Moon, The Kinks, or perhaps one of the Yardbirds, and so on. At last, I was mixing with the heavyweights of music on equal terms and, although the best was yet to come, it felt great!

My hair was halfway down my back, and I was comfortable in flared jeans, vest and buckled boots. With this new-found confidence (which some took to be arrogance), I happily fell into the rock lifestyle, which existed in a microcosm at the club. It became truly famous — or should I say infamous — and you could eat in their funky little restaurant, or just sit at the bar talking to some guy whose show you'd just seen a while back.

There was always the nonchalant blow job (BJ), whilst ordering another pint, but, of course, it didn't interfere with the conversation. We always used to say that the ideal groupie stood four feet tall, with a flat head — so you had somewhere to put your beer!

Groupies came to feature greatly in the culture of rock 'n' roll, and willingly helped create the basis for a lifestyle no self-respecting parent would wish their daughter to associate with! Come to think of it, there were not many self-respecting parents who were keen on their sons becoming musicians either, but over the years, there would be many wonderful occasions when the girls would enhance our lives, and that of the roadies and crew.

Their own rules and logic would sometimes defy belief, as I would discover later when I owned the De Lane Lea studio in Holborn. In fact, it was during The Gillan Band days — making *Clear Air Turbulence* — when an enthusiastic German girl managed to work her way into the studio, and was gradually working her way through my band and the crew! An old mate of mine, Jonathan Crisp, turned up, and as befitted a young and highly successful entrepreneur, he was extremely well dressed and elegant in the way businessmen can be. He must have found the scene he walked into a bit of a culture shock so, just to wind him up (he looked frightened to death), I shouted through the studio to the Fraülein, that she should look after my friend. Her reply was vintage, and extremely indignant. 'I most certainly vill not ... he iss vearing a suit!' Now that's what I call a groupie — what style!

Incredible as it may seem, BJs are the ultimate sign of affection in rock 'n' roll; far less emotional, you don't end up getting married and the whole thing is far less stressful. Sadly, for all concerned, the situation was stamped on by the women's movement who chose to represent the whole of their sex (including the groupies) on such matters. As I recall, it was usually the larger-bodied females who made all the fuss, and I also remember getting a bit shirty about it at the time. It all seemed so unfair that just when the time was right for me, people were putting a downer on a bit of consenting fun.

I accept the fact that rock 'n' roll (and what sometimes goes on in it) horrifies some people, or might even put parents off letting their kids go to a show, but to reassure them, it doesn't happen to entire audiences. Well, not every night! So I had finally made it into rock 'n' roll, and from day one had come to grips with its culture.

Even when I'm crazy
On fire — naked
Just as nature intended
With no style that's easily blended

You'll always know where I'll be found
I'm hanging somewhere near the ground
Help me up or help me down
Don't want to lose those days
When everything is just a haze

Sometimes things went a bit wrong. One of many concepts I have learned to test is the 'Concept of Throwing Up', and where better to try it out than in the restaurant of the Speakeasy, where I found myself at the table with my girlfriend, Zoe. After probably 15 or 20 minutes of sound sleep, with my face buried in the spaghetti Luigi had so wonderfully prepared for me, somebody bumped into the lamp over our table, and it woke me. I looked up, spaghetti dripping from my face, and stared at Zoe, who was now in a moving light.

Well, I felt nauseous — not because of her, but because of the moving light and the copious flagons of alcohol I had quaffed. And so, in my state of nausea, it was time to get up from the table (as so many had before me) and try to reach the toilet, where I could vomit.

Now, it is one of the absolute quests of civilised man to throw up and still to keep your dignity. Unfortunately, my legs could not keep up with my stomach, and I ended up spoiling a good fight!

All of this is very well, but we had managers who were on a mission, and it was clearly explained to me that the money I was spending was an advance against future earnings, so there was a serious side to the business, and we all threw ourselves into it, with *Deep Purple in Rock* and, alongside it, Jon's Concerto which he continued with, to the increasing fury of the guitar player, and, to some extent, the rest of us. We also began extensive touring, and doing high-profile appearances. August 1969, for example, saw us undertaking a schedule along the following lines:

August

2nd	Radio Brighton
11th	BBC Radio
13th	The Revolution Club, London.
15th	Mayfair Ballroom, Newcastle
16th	Rebecca's Club, Birmingham
24th	Bilzen, Amsterdam
26th	Klooks Kleek, Windsor
28th	Lyceum, Leicester Square, London
29th	BBC Radio, *Noise at Nine*
30th	Gravesend

It was the beginning of heady days, and I guess I may not have been handling things that well sometimes, as I was reminded the time I went back to my old drinking haunt The Traveller's Friend. I went there to repay mates like Barry, Mick, Dave, Los and all those guys who had 'subbed' me when they were better off than I was a while back. But now I was on £20 a week — big bucks!

So I went into the pub, and said, 'I'm the singer with Deep Purple, drinks are on me!' There was a lot of back-slapping as I ordered a round, and then, before the glasses were empty, I put in for another. 'Same again, please, landlord,' and then I did it a third time.

At this point, little Dave King, whom we called the Professor, came up and said, 'I think that's enough, don't you, Ian?'

I replied, 'Hey man, what do you mean?'

'We enjoy you buying us drinks, and we're enjoying

tonight,' he said, 'we're really pleased you got the job! But don't rub our noses in it! Buying three rounds on the trot's enough, so don't be an arsehole — stick your money in your pocket, and behave yourself!'

A sobering moment. In any case, I was only spending my advance and, thinking about it, I could see John (Coletta), and it steadied me. Over a drink or several, John could be great value, and at cards — at which he gambled furiously — we enjoyed taking *his* money off him, which for the most part he took in good humour. However, when his dander was up, it could be a problem if you pushed your luck at his expense, and then I'd certainly not catch his eye. It wasn't fear, just that when he lost control, his protruding teeth couldn't keep in the spluttering that went with the outburst, and in full rage it was impossible for me to keep a straight face. In moments of doubt, I'd remember that John was not above 'landing one on you', and I'd been warned he'd been a champion boxer in the RAF.

I know we began to cost the management quite a lot of money as we settled into being successful at 'rock 'n' roll in the early seventies. In the beginning, it was limited to chucking a few bits of furniture out of our hotel rooms — just to test the reaction! Then when the complaints started, the management would do their bit and say, 'Very sorry,' before handing over the notes, by which I mean our 'advance'. But we were not out to offend others by our behaviour, it's just that we'd be 'having a go at one another'.

Sadly, it wasn't often seen that way, such as the time we crossed the Forth Bridge, to get to The George Hotel, Edinburgh, after a gig in Dunfermline. This happened in the days before flight cases, so our gear was only protected by plastic and canvas covers. On this occasion, we were driving back in the band limo — a Jaguar 420G — and as we lined up for the toll queue, we all attacked Rog, putting an amp cover over his head and pulling it down, before tying it firmly to his waist with string. So now he was trussed up like the proverbial chicken and, having crossed the bridge, we stopped the car, and chucked him out — right in the middle of this busy multi-lane highway. The sight was incredible, as cars screeched and swerved to avoid the writhing creature on the tarmac. We thought some drivers were needlessly abusive, as we reversed and put our Rog back in the car.

Dear Rog, whose Episode Six profile said he didn't like arguments, was livid, and when Rog *does* fume, steam literally comes out of his ears. So we all said, 'Oh please, Roger, forgive us ... we're so sorry ... let us buy you a drink, Roger ...' and all that bollocks, at which moment we pulled up at our very elegant hotel. Now, Roger, being the forgiving sort of person he is, said, 'Oh, alright then,' at which moment we jumped him again, and stripped him stark naked! Reduced to his birthday suit, he made mutterings along the lines of 'Fuck you lot,' and stormed through reception, up the stairs, pausing only to ask for the key to his room. We strolled in a few moments later to a sea of waxwork faces, frozen over gin and tonics! Gloria Bristow would not have approved!

Whatever misgivings we had about Jon's Concerto, Tony Edwards got behind it after one of those meetings I'd become familiar with, when he or John (Coletta) would say something like, 'Well, boys, what shall we do next?' And there was 'Lordie' with this opus he'd started back in The Art Woods days giving him the big sell. The next thing we knew was that Tony had booked the Royal Albert Hall, and then, when Jon had completed the score (in Purple time), it went to the publisher, Ben Nesbitt, who took it to the conductor of the Royal Philharmonic Orchestra, Malcolm Arnold. He was, in fact, 'Doctor' Arnold, but I'd later tell him that with his standing in the business, 'Sir' had a much better ring.

Anyway, Malcolm said he'd do the show with the Royal Philharmonic Orchestra and, with the die cast, we 'sort of' got behind it. Time was not on our side — I think we only had about a week or so to work with the orchestra, who seemed even less keen than we were. In fact, some of them positively hated it, and it was only Malcolm's enthusiasm and energy that kept the whole thing on track. It was most certainly different, being performed in a cavernous building with 110 musicians, including a 60-piece string section and assorted percussionists. But despite this scale, it was brilliant to see that Ritchie could blast the whole lot of them away, if he chose. The first session with orchestra and band ended with different emotions running high. On the one hand, there were John and Tony sitting in the auditorium, heads deep in hands, looking quite intellectual, while on the other hand a female cellist stood up and shouted something about not playing with second-rate Beatles. Malcolm told her not to be so silly. Then there was another lucklustre performance by the RPO, which prompted our conductor to stop all the nonsense in a manner which quite shocked us.

Their attitude so angered him that he raised his hands up, and said something like, 'I don't know what you think you are doing. You are supposed to be the finest orchestra in Britain and you are playing like a bunch of c**ts! Quite frankly, with the way it's going, you're not fit to be on stage with these people. So pick yourselves up, and let's hear some bollocks!'

He was less aggressive during the rehearsal for the National Anthem, which the orchestra also hated, but warmed them to the thought that 'We're going to make history tonight, so we might as well make music while we are doing it!'

Our attitude in the build up must have upset Jon quite a lot, but as we saw it, it cut two ways. There we were, trying to make *Deep Purple in Rock*, and Jon was increasingly unavailable to rehearse, while on the other side of the coin, we were being asked to support a high-profile, non-rock project of his own. I admit that my own contribution — writing lyrics — was made very late in the day, and it was only during the afternoon performance, just prior to the concert that night, that Jon approached me to ask when I would be 'doing my bit'. I did it over a couple of bottles of Chianti in a nearby Italian restaurant, and contributed to a great night for Jon.

Ritchie played brilliantly, Ian Paice was stunning — as was Roger — and we drove along with the orchestra in great style. I was proud of the band, and we generally got a good reception — in fact, a 15 minute ovation!

Sir William Walton came to see us afterwards and said he'd enjoyed it immensely, although there were some who confessed to being uncertain how to deal with the whole thing. Tom Hibbert is reported to have seen a violinist stifle boredom with a coughing fit during Ritchie's five minute 'speed solo', but if that's the case, there's no way it would have been heard. Finally, the audience didn't really know whether to applaud, dance or just sit tight. What is certain is that it was a stunning success for Jon, and did Deep Purple no harm at all, once a few follow-up difficulties had been resolved. Jon's first child, the lovely Sara, was born that night just to add to his triumph. (We would also perform the Gemini Suite for Jon at the Royal Festival Hall in September 1970, at the invitation of the BBC, with the Orchestra of the Light Music Society. However, I remember little about that, on account of the fact that I was drunk for much of the time. That said, I'm told my performance was acclaimed!)

The Concerto was recorded live, and also filmed by British Lion. From the footage, a programme went out to several countries, whilst BBC *Omnibus* also showed it on 4 April 1970. As for the recording, it went out on the EMI label in the UK, where it reached number 26, and so became this rock band's debut in the charts! It also went out on the Warner Bros' label in America, and made number 149.

One of the side benefits of the project was that it 'blooded' co-engineer Martin (The Wasp) Birch. Martin started his career as a musician, but then moved into production at the De Lane Lea

Studio. The Concerto, however, took him into a totally new role, where he not only had to cope with the complex desks, each with eight tracks, but he also had to deal with audience noise, the orchestra and, loudest of all, Deep Purple. Martin would soon cross over to becoming the sixth member of the band, staying with us for many years on tours and recording work. Further down the line, he'd join Iron Maiden, where he became Martin (The Juggler) Birch.

As hinted at, there were one or two problems to sort out after the Concerto, the biggest being that, as we toured, some promoters and music lovers weren't quite sure what to expect. Or more accurately, they were sure what to expect, and didn't get it! It happened a few times. One occasion was in Folkestone, where we pulled into town to see posters saying, 'Deep Purple in Concert with The So and So Silver band'! Ritchie took one look at that and went berserk, ranting on about the Concerto having become a millstone around our necks. It was extremely embarrassing because this promoter (like others) had obviously heard about the Albert Hall concert, and presumed that's how we liked to do things. If we could play with an orchestra, we could obviously play with a silver band. It was a sad mistake for him, and a wasted journey for us.

So we needed to straighten people out about who we were, and did this through a period of heavy touring, rock 'n' roll behaviour and the release of our album *Deep Purple in Rock* in June 1970. As we became more famous, so our pay went up and we progressed through 1970 either headlining, or at least taking second billing to bands like Canned Heat.

A typical itinerary around this time showed us being in Paris on 5 January; doing *Magic Roundabout* for BBC radio the next day; playing Reading University on the 10th; and then doing two shows in Amsterdam on the 15th and 16th. Then it was back to the Civic Hall, Dunstable, and on to a plane to play The Big Apple in Munich, while shows in the UK at the close of

January included a return to the Royal Albert Hall, which we did very differently to the first!

Looking back on it all, it's clear that we began to go through all sorts of attitude changes; for example, it was suddenly 'uncool' for anyone in Deep Purple to smile, in case people thought (a) we were having a good time, (b) we were being paid good money for it, and (c) that we were not taking things seriously. So we were definitely 'cool', and that showed in publicity shots, album sleeves and so forth.

On stage, Ritchie had begun to take things a little further by refusing encores, and when challenged he'd just say the audience hadn't deserved it. So there we'd be with the audience refusing to leave (as they did in the early days), having paid good money to see us, and we'd leave them begging for our return, only to do so without the great guitar player. There were a lot of arguments and soul searching about all that as we came to terms with fame, and developed a free-flowing set which took us in all sorts of directions.

It has always been said that no two Purple shows are the same, which is why bootlegging out music became such a good business for certain entrepreneurs. Still, good luck to them, that's what I say.

As Ritchie and I developed a close stage relationship, swapping guitar licks with matching vocals, our bond made for a great chemistry, with Jon sharing the same spirit of adventure. Ritchie then took us into riffs of 'The Teddy Bears' Picnic' or 'An English Country Garden', and as his solos became longer, I could otherwise amuse myself, depending on the opportunities available.

One came at a gig we did where there was a Steinway piano on stage. It was covered with a green canvas sheeting which trailed to the floor, and they refused to let the roadies push it aside, neither would they let them build any stacks on it. However, given the lack of space left for us, a compromise was reached. Cardboard protection was added to safeguard the beautifully polished surface.

During a guitar solo, this girl got on stage — sadly, we were never properly introduced — and as Ritchie played on, we fell to the ground and rolled under the piano, where we became fully acquainted. With a brilliant 20-minute solo needing to end, getting the pants back on was a problem, but God bless the long guitar solo, that's what I say!

Nobbing was the order of the day, and you have to be glad that AIDS wasn't the concern it is today. The popular 'dose', beloved of sailors, was well within the curing capabilities of competent doctors, and I caught it a couple of times. Still, in the balance of things, it was worthwhile, and we enjoyed a life of unlimited debauchery.

There was no end to the surprises in store, such as Dirty Doreen, called that because the girl was game for anything — and simply very rude. The way she used her orifices to amuse herself, and anybody who was interested, never ceased to amaze, and there was the extraordinary example of the time we played the Queen Elizabeth Hall, supported by Wishbone Ash. Just before going on stage, one of their band came rushing into the dressing room, saying he'd lost his hairbrush, and could he borrow one. It happened that Doreen had mine tucked between her legs so, lifting her frock, I removed it, and passed it, handle first, to the musician, who drifted out with a very puzzled look on his face. These things were just commonplace in my business.

I guess we must have been affected by our lifestyle, but I won't excuse anything because of it. We just did things spontaneously, and it snowballed. Sometimes we'd be the cause, and on other occasions it would start elsewhere. So if I started getting grief from a hotel switchboard, such that I couldn't get what I wanted *immediately*, I'd rip the phone out of the wall and put it in a lift with a note saying, 'This phone doesn't appear to be working. Will you send another up, please.' I did that quite often, because I did get the distinct impression sometimes that we were not as welcome as other guests, and yet we were certainly better for business.

A barman would occasionally give me a hard time, which I'd find unacceptable. If you have to scowl, or be indifferent to a customer who's drinking the bar dry, there has to be some kind of price to pay. So when it was time to leave, people like that would see me roll a large banknote — of whatever currency we were dealing with at the time — before lighting it, putting it into the ashtray and saying, 'Your tip ... goodnight!' It sounds nasty, but we are all entitled to deal with our dignity as we feel appropriate.

In terms of the really serious money, our ability to release *Deep Purple in Rock* was delayed because John and Tony were still trying to sort out the relationship with the bankrupt Tetragrammaton. Fortunately, Warner Bros bought the company, which allied us to a ready-made label in America, as well as bringing a $400,000 advance. Joe Smith, Warner's President, basically bought Deep Purple as a small asset among bigger contracts, and the irony was that they didn't really know what to do with us. Still, we quickly solved that dilemma for them with delivery of the album, and they were delighted. *Deep Purple in Rock* went to number 4 in the UK charts, and made 143 in the States, followed soon after by 'Black Night', which went to number 2 in the UK (behind 'Band of Gold' by Freda Payne). The band I'd joined just about a year ago were helping me achieve my wildest dreams!

I'm told we played about 50 gigs during the first part of 1970, as well as 15 or so on the Continent. Our fees rose to around £350 a night, and radio and TV work kept flooding in. There was the BBC's *Making a Musical* on 8 February; the BBC's *Sound of the Seventies* in April, May and June; Granada TV's *Doing Their Thing*; plus LWT's *South Bank Summer*. And finally we went into July knowing the problems with Tetragrammaton had at last been settled, that we were now with a great label, that we had a major album in the charts, and that we'd be touring the States in August.

Ahead of that, and at the National Jazz and Blues Festival at Plympton (9 August), Ritchie decided to add another dimension to our act. As our version of the Stones hit 'Paint it Black' drew to a close with a blistering solo from Ian Paice, Ritchie told our roadie, Ian Hansford, to douse his speaker with petrol and set fire to it. Ian was extremely reluctant, but went along with the order, finally torching the gear with a long broom handle. Well, the whole damn lot went up and someone got burnt trying to put the fire out. Ritchie explained it was all because the band Yes had deliberately failed to turn up on time, and so we had been manipulated into being the support act. It didn't work out like that though, because we very effectively closed the show for ourselves — and for them. The incident caused a lot of bad feeling all around, but Ritchie didn't give a toss, and we all felt pretty much the same. Ritchie went on to make quite a habit of trashing guitars on stage, and cheap Japanese models would eventually be bought for the purpose of sending the crowd home happy. Well that's how he saw it anyway, and it worked. (He was doing it right up to the moment of his departure in 1994!)

It was in Dundee that I heard the album had gone into the charts. We were having lunch when Tony Edwards announced it and, after so many years of struggle and disappointment, I just burst into tears. Within one year everything had changed, and now it all seemed, for once, so very simple. I mean, look how we made it with 'Black Night', which we only did because the managers told us we needed a single. So we went to the studio in the afternoon, tried to find a riff, failed, and went to The Newton Arms, where we got pissed. Then Roger and Ritchie went back to try again and, after a few hours, the backing tracks were down. We borrowed the title from the words of an old

Arthur Alexander song, and Roger and I then worked out the lyrics which was quite tricky, given the condition we were in!

As *Disc and Music Echo* reported in September 1970: 'Deep Purple's Roger Glover admitted he's no idea what the words of "Black Night" are all about. Never mind, he only part wrote it!' So we delivered it to the managers, and it succeeded. Why had it all been so difficult before?

Other things started to fall into place for us, beginning with another hike in wages to £100 a week, plus a PR team and increasing publicity to increase our profile even more.

Sadly these days, a bomb scare is no laughing matter, but nearly thirty years ago, it wasn't such a nasty issue.

It was in Offenbach, Germany, that a scare emptied the hall during a concert, as the *Melody Maker* more fully described what we seemed to be doing, and what others did also:

'Talking of riots, Deep Purple caused one during their highly incident-prone European tour. After their skirmish with East German border guards and a bomb scare at Offenbach, which prevented them from finishing a set, they even found trouble in neutral Switzerland. 2,500 people were crammed into a none-too-big venue at Basle, so the people who couldn't get in rioted outside.'

With all this going on, I received a call from out of the blue — it was Tim Rice. He'd heard me sing 'Child in Time', and thought the way I did it would be ideal for a project he was working on with Andrew Lloyd Webber (now, or course, Sir Andrew). I went round to Andrew's flat, where the two of them took me through the concept of their musical *Jesus Christ Superstar*. Tim was fantastic — effusive, enthusiastic, driving, a warm, gentle giant of a man. He introduced me to Andrew, who sat at the piano wearing his 'inside-out look', and said, 'It goes like this,' at which point Andrew started playing.

Every so often, he'd look over his shoulder for appreciation, but I found it difficult to show enthusiasm as I worked with the lyrics. The choruses were great, well worked out and crafted, but we seemed not to communicate too well.

In fact, it was only because of Tim that I really bothered to stay, and we had one of those 'It goes like this, and now change to that' sessions. Tim kept encouraging me with, 'Go on ... go on' and 'Hey, that's great,' until I began to see where the whole thing was going.

Then he said, 'OK, let's take it to the studio,' where I did my whole contribution to the part of Jesus in a few hours.

It's not a project I got close to at all, although I was very pleased with it in the end and, as for the two writers, well the rest is history!

There were two high points, the first being 'In the Garden of Gethsemane', which is an important piece, and there I have to admit having to do two or three takes of the scene at the Cross, which closes the show. That moved me significantly — in fact, it almost brought me to tears. Tony Edwards earned his commission on that venture, because he negotiated a royalty payment of one penny, instead of the flat fee on offer of (I believe) £100. Yvonne Elliman had a similar arrangement, and from my point of view, it was financially very successful, since the original album went on to sell about 8 million copies. It was released in November 1970, and went to number 6 in the UK charts and number 1 in America.

A little while later, I received a call from Tony, saying that Tim was hassling him to get me to play the lead in the movie. I had the voice, the figure — tall and slim — and, of course, long hair. I suppose it's been proven that that's how Jesus looked — I mean, he might have been short and fat, mightn't he?

Well, for many reasons — mainly because Deep Purple was my life — I'd already turned down the stage part, so the film didn't really seem any different. However, Tony said I should at least go and find out more about it, so I went to Pinewood Studios to meet the producer, Norman Jewison. The idea was to chat and screen test and, on balance, my mood was very positive, as I remembered the ambitions of youth. I mean, not even Elvis Presley had the credentials for a part like this, so perhaps everything was going to work out as originally planned all those years ago.

In the back of my mind was the absolute love and loyalty I felt towards the band and, of course, there had been the Concerto project a few months earlier, when I participated in giving Jon such a hard time for being less than 100% committed. All of that was in my mind as I arrived magnificently at the studios in my new Rolls Royce Silver Cloud III complete with 'L' plates, and went to find Mr Jewison's suite, where coffee was served. And then, with his secretary in constant attendance, Mr Jewison looked me up and down and said, 'Well, Tim is keen for you to play the part, and I'm sure everything's going to be just fine. What's your schedule?'

As it happened, I was able to tell him that things were a bit quiet for a month or so, to which he said they'd be going to Israel in a few weeks, and we'd be on location for about ten. There was lots of 'I'm interested', 'let me talk to the band', 'fine ... see if something can be wangled' and 'yes, you look great,' as I stood up to leave. And then I made a mistake. If only I'd had the experience to know when to speak, and when to shut up, because if I'd kept my mouth closed, and let Tony follow things up, I'd probably be a movie star by now. But it wasn't to be. At the door, I said, 'Hang on a second,' to which Mr Jewison replied, 'Yes?'

'What's the deal?'

In fact, my motives were perfectly well intended, because I went on to explain that if I was going to be out of circulation for three months, I'd have to ask what the band would have to say about it. This wasn't about financial gain, it was about the guys being covered for loss of earnings, gig cancellations and so forth. So I repeated the question.

'What's the deal?'

Well, he said it was $1,000 a week, which I took to mean 'expenses'. So I said something to that effect, which he misunderstood, because he said, 'Correct — but you have to pay your own bar bill.' 'That's great,' I said, relieved. 'Now how much do I get paid?'

'Well, I've just told you, $1,000 week.'

After a pause, I said, 'Do you mean I'm being offered about $10,000 "all in" to star in this film, whilst my mates sit around for weeks on end, twiddling their thumbs?'

Puzzled, he said, 'What are you talking about?'

So I laid it on the line. 'Mr Jewison, this band I'm with can take $20,000 a night, that's what I'm talking about!'

The man was absolutely shocked, and it all started going downhill from there. Gestures and recovery noises were made, so when it came to the crunch and he asked how much I wanted, I told him I wouldn't get out of bed for less than $250,000, and was soon on my way to the car and pub, to reflect on the fact I'd nearly become a film star. I told Tony about the meeting, and he said he'd see if he could pick up the pieces but, of course, that never happened, and Ted Neeley got the gig. As a result of that, I discovered I now had two managers who saw me as a trouble maker. With the management now finding me difficult, the first trip by Deep Purple to America that August was relatively uneventful — in fact, a total anti-climax really. We went with great reluctance, because Warner Bros wanted us to perform the Concerto at The Hollywood Bowl, and even Jon was unenthusiastic about that. However, the label were also looking to give us loads of publicity for *Deep Purple in Rock*, so we did an abbreviated version of Jon's work, and followed it with pure Purple which went down brilliantly to the packed venue, although we were then glad to close the door on the Concerto part of our lives. Roger was particularly glad, because he'd played the show having just had a jab to deal with something nasty that he'd picked up along the way!

We played Albuquerque, Salt Lake City and Pasadena, and earned just over £7,500, which was a lot less than the cost of the trip. It also failed to generate the record sales we were hoping for, and ended as a tour beset by niggling problems. Expected bookings failed to appear, keeping us on one occasion hotel-bound in Los Angeles. We borrowed gear in Arizona after the tour bus broke down in the desert, and it was all symptomatic of not quite realising what kind of project Deep Purple was, while back home, 'Black Night' was doing the business, and we were in huge demand.

So, too, was Sandersons wallpaper, the story of which illustrates how we sometimes struggled with the management over concept of style and direction. I'm not entirely sure when the Sandersons incident occurred, but we went to one of those interminable meetings at number 25, where John would order the drinks and then run ideas past us. These were generally 'Let's sort things out, boys' moments — a chance to bounce ideas around. One such idea was to do a deal with Sandersons, who would make Deep Purple (coloured) wallpaper! It was the sort of brainwave that had everybody looking at the table fiddling with pencils or taking a deep swig of drink, at which moment the two of them would swing into a tried and tested strategy. John would take two of the band to lunch, Tony would take the other two, and I'd be left to make my own arrangements. So I'd take myself off to the pub, and eventually we'd all reconvene to hear the outcome of collective deliberations.

The script would follow a predictable pattern, along the lines of 'Well, Jon, what do you think?' and he'd say that he thought 'whatever' a pretty good idea. And then 'Well, Ritchie, what do you think?' and Ritchie wouldn't be bothered at all. And then Roger would be asked, and would say he'd go along with the majority; and finally Paicey, who'd just want to know how much money we were going to get. So with a rub of hands, the management would then say, 'Good, so we're going to do it then lads. Right?' And as they all nodded, I'd go, 'You fucking prats, I don't believe this!' But sadly, that's how so many things seemed to be handled from time to time. It's called democracy.

The deal we had with our managers didn't really bother me in those days. I was young and doing what I'd always wanted to do. I hadn't a care in the world, and the detail of money was a very low priority indeed. In fact, it's a matter I've never really taken that seriously and, if I was a millionaire in the halcyon days of Purple, I was the only one not to realise. People kept telling me how rich I was, but they obviously had better access to my life than I did. Of course, I exhibited wealth by owning a lifetime's ambition — the Roller — for which I paid £3,750, and then I went on to buy my first house — Hyde House in Pangbourne. That cost £12,500, but it was only a neo-Georgian thing on a small private estate, and efforts to make it more palatial by building a small swimming pool in the garden were unsuccessful. So I was basically happy to leave my earnings in the hands of John, Tony and Bill Reid, as Deep Purple became 'bankable'.

Similarly, it never really bothered me how much the management and other professionals were earning, although I did question the percentages when it was decided to drop the agency we used, and handle the matter 'in house'. The figure of 27% comes to mind, but maybe the internal costs and staffing had increased. Still, if I wasn't interested enough to ask properly then, why should I now.? On the other hand, why shouldn't I?

I've already touched on Bill, and he became a major part of our lives. His own introduction is the stuff of folklore, and deserves a mention. As I recall (or, in fact, am reminded), it was decided that we needed a top firm of accountants to give substance to our image and standing in the music business, so a few of us went to this big city firm, where we marched into reception and asked to see one of the senior partners. We said we were Deep Purple, which was enough to attract a fairly serious-looking chap, in a pin-stripe suite, and alongside him was an older, rather wise-looking gentleman who was introduced as a manager. There was clearly a misunderstanding as to what the partner thought Deep Purple was, so the meeting went no further than the reception lobby, and was very brief!

However, someone got the vibe that the old geezer seemed amused and interested, so we lowered our sights and telephoned him, asking to speak to Mr Reid. It takes several factors to come together for a moment of good fortune and, in the case of Bill, it was that he had probably reached the pinnacle of opportunity at this firm, that his kids were approaching independence and, above all else, that he was probably very bored. So he handed in his notice, and bravely took the plunge with us, just before 'Black Night' was released.

A few weeks later and Bill was travelling ahead of us, setting up deals and contracts on a worldwide basis — and deservedly having the time of his life! His modest offices in Wallington became a financial centre for a major part of the music business, and he also represented many stars in sport. Old enough to be our father (he took on that kind of role), Bill became an anchor — at least in my life. He'd sit in his panelled offices overlooking the high street, gold discs on the wall, scratching his balls and dressed in multi-coloured shirts, Bermuda shorts and sandals, enthusing himself, and us — it was great!

It was often said we'd play our best shows when Bill was backstage — or out front — but when it came to after show parties, he'd hover, resplendent with a huge Havana cigar. After a glass of wine or two, he'd take himself off to bed, leaving us to abuse the expense account. I'd love to know how he'd explain away receipts like the 'Chicken Wey' in Frankfurt, which was not a restaurant! But equally, a lot of our leisure activities and expenses were looked after by the promoters, who quite enjoyed themselves as well. So maybe it wasn't that big a problem, while other things about the man deserve my discretion. Bill told us what we could afford, and he paid the accounts — all of them! He was the one who dished out the weekly money and, if I ran short, I'd call him to say, 'Bill, can I afford this?' or 'May I do that?' and he would make it possible. It seemed that we were a bottomless pit of money, but everything was channelled through him, and we respected that.

On the domestic scene, Ritchie was married for the second time; Jon was with Judith (and child); Paicey was engaged to his money and Roger and I were in love!

In fact, I was in this full time relationship with Zoe, whom I'd first met back at Pye Records, and later started up with during my Episode Six days. I'd always had a spark for this mysterious girl, which is what attracted me to her in the first place. I then met her at a gig, which she turned up to with a friend in her Austin A30. I was sitting in the back of a limo, and just got out, jumped into her car, and we drove down to her home in Salisbury, after which things drifted on for ten or twelve years.

It's hard to know what to say about the relationship, and because Zoe has felt unwilling to disclose much here, I'll deal lightly and politely with a part of my life which saw me at my youthful prime, but in which any personal regrets are best kept that way. To have stayed with Zoe Dean for so many years, when I had so many other opportunities, speaks for itself.

As our touring intensified, I suspect the close-bonded relationship within the group began to crack when I brought Zoe along with me, and we started to live in separate quarters and hotels to the band, and even took to having our own limo. In fact, I played the 'star' part to the limit and, I guess, I was a pain quite often. But this wasn't the real world — or, at least, if it was, it was a fantasy to be enjoyed while it lasted. Eventually, all the women in our lives joined the circuit, and began to compete, bitch, and generally screw things up, mostly when we were doing that well enough between us, without their help!

Otherwise, little seemed to be a real problem. Perhaps the most difficult situation for me was when I had my ego severely dented when I failed my driving test in April 1971. Having decided not to be flash by using the Roller, I used the test school's 1100, and apparently indicated left before taking a confident right! Still, it was worth it just to see the instructor's face, when I climbed into the Rolls (L-plates still on) and drove away. Perhaps I should have had my hair cut, but I'd been failed, and remained a learner for many years thereafter!

Chapter 5

With album and single success, plus a huge following in the UK, the management clearly realised that they were sitting on a goldmine, and upped the pressure and routine. I can't say we complained because we were so hyped up, and it just didn't matter. We pushed our notoriety ever further, with a four-day visit to Scotland in October 1970, where we took the place by storm.

29th	Edinburgh Odeon
21st	Dundee Caird Hall
22nd	Dunfermline Electric Ballroom
23rd	Aberdeen Music Hall
24th	Glasgow Electric Ballroom (changed to Tiffany's)
25th	Hamilton Town Hall

In Glasgow, they had to switch venues from The Electric Ballroom to Tiffany's. Sauchiehall Street was jammed end to end, and we needed a police escort to get us in, and out. It was unbelievable — we were so 'underground', so 'dangerous', people were turning up saying, 'Who is this band?' As word spread like wildfire and our concerts necessarily became associated with a police and dog presence, we began to change our whole pattern of behaviour at gigs. In times past, I played to audiences who would stay in seats, maybe getting up to dance around sometimes, but almost always well mannered and controlled. That changed with Deep Purple, and seating became redundant, removed (by promoters), as I invented 'headbanging'. In Gillan Band days (some time later), I'd define a 'headbanger' as a 'person with rhythm', but that aside, I believe that whole thing began as fans followed my example on stage, swaying the mane of hair I then had, which covered my face, while we all had a great party. There was no need for seats, as the crowd just wanted to be as close to the stage as possible, and share in the whole excitement. To quote from *Melody Maker* (24 October 1970): 'Now it's Purplemania. Deep Purple are the latest group to attract Beatlemania scenes in the north of England.'

Girls were flinging themselves at us and we played 'Black Night' to the backs of bouncers. Girls were fainting, crying and screaming at our feet on stage. We managed to get out all right, thanks to Jeff Docherty, the promoter, but they were screaming for the wrong reasons. It wasn't the music we played, it's just what we looked like that counted, because they were all very young. As one member of the band said, 'I suppose it is something we will have to face after appearing on *Top of the Pops*.'

We closed 1970 with a trip to Scandinavia and a tour of Germany, where we played Nuremburg, Wuzburg, Stuttgart, Hanover, Offenbach and Saarbrucken. It was a bad time, because the pressures of touring and our self-made lifestyle caught up with us in various ways, as the rioting intensified. On 8 December, fans ran amuck at Ludenscheid, and they hit the stage, smashing gear worth around £2,000. I guess it was partly due to the fact that we played as a quartet that night, because Ritchie had been taken ill, and was flown back to London for treatment. Two other members of the band were also taken ill, including me, so the rest of the German tour was cancelled.

It was all so different, and my first experience with Hell's Angels was in Switzerland, where the crowd went berserk. The next thing I knew was that we had about 15 of these guys on stage, their backs to us, chucking kids all over the place. It really pissed me off, and I attacked them with a mike stand until they left. However, after the show they waited for us to come out and chased us out of town! That was quite frightening, not least because whoever was driving took us into a field, where we got well and truly stuck!

Back home, I relaxed by playing football, and kept goal quite often for the local Pangbourne police team. They were great, but unfortunately many opposing pub and factory teams saw the games as a way to hand out legitimate violence, and included me in all of that. I've often found that, like many musicians, members of the police force have a wicked sense of humour, a great example being in my later Gillan Band days.

We did a show in Norwich, which was an end of tour gig. A party had been laid on with strippers, who were brilliant, and all went well until this twat tried to gate-crash. He was asked to leave and, as he went, he grabbed the tablecloth at the end of the buffet and dragged it along with him. I went absolutely mental, and raced out of the hotel to sort him out, but he'd got away. So I returned and ended up chatting to this guy, telling him what had happened, before going back to the party.

Unfortunately, Zoe and I had not been getting on very well, and she obviously thought I'd been out there with one of the strippers. And the more she went on about it, the more I wished I had been! Anyway, we had this huge argument on the way out to the car — we'd not had one for a couple of days — by which time I'd downed a few more scotches. As we drove out of the market square, I spotted a police car, which focused my mind quite clearly, and I drove very carefully down a one-way street, realising that he was looking to follow me. It was decision time and, without a map, I took the first available left turn and put my foot down. The thought of being caught horrified me, but however fast I seemed to be going, there he remained. After a couple of miles, I started to look for an exit — a farm gate, anything to get him off my back! But to no avail. Finally, he must have decided to end the game, and on came the blue light. It was a peep or two, and I thought, 'Oh well ... that's it,' and pulled over.

I got out and took a deep breath as he walked towards me. 'Nice bit of driving, Ian. No chance I could have your autograph is there?'

It was a brown-trouser job, but I most willingly signed, and then drove home — far too carefully. It was very stupid, and brought back my father's words that would caution me against momentary acts of lunacy, which could result in my being maimed — or killed. Or worse, doing it to somebody else. That said, it wasn't the first time the law had been kind to me in this country, and I realise that.

I've tried to compensate for moments of selfishness or insanity sometimes, and have come to realise I do have a responsibility to the public and, in particular, the millions of fans who come to my shows, buy my records and merchandise, and even have my picture on their wall. You can show that humility in various ways, beginning with the signing of autographs, which I've always tried to do as much as possible. Some artists like to get away from venues as quickly as possible, but others like myself are happy to hang out backstage, meet the fans, sign scraps of paper, records, even parts of their anatomy, if that's what they want. I enjoy doing that, as well as playing charity football, and sometimes a visit to a hospital allows me to show appreciation, and bring me back down to earth.

There was one such occasion when we were gigging at the Dome in Brighton, and after the sound check, someone told me about this young boy lying in a coma in hospital. He was a great fan, so I went to see his parents, and together we went to visit him. I just sat and held his hand, talking quietly, and left. When I got home, I made a tape and sent it to him. A short while later, I got a message that he'd come round, so I returned to the hospital. It was a choking experience just to see the look in his eyes. Although he'd suffered brain damage and couldn't feed, he seemed fully aware of what was going on, and it brought back to me those days in Beirut, where it takes another person's misfortune to make you look at your priorities.

There was no let up in our touring schedule, and 1971 saw us on a major UK tour, where we pulled capacity crowds, and were big box office. In February alone we did the Royal Albert Hall, Hull, Sheffield, Bournemouth, Portsmouth, Birmingham, Bristol, Plymouth, Manchester, Newcastle, Coventry, Leicester and Brighton. As such, our reputation preceded us, often to cause problems for all concerned.

For example, we'd had notice that we'd been banned from the Free Trade Hall, Manchester, because the authorities had decided that the band was 'not considered suitable for the hall', while Croydon's excuse was that the weight of the fans in the balcony might cause a collapse. Other venues found their own reasons to turn us down, but we carried on and March saw us in three shows for the BBC, before we went to Germany to do four dates, and then to Montreux for another two, followed by Brussels and Scandinavia where we did four more.

Our health should have alerted someone to question the routine, and we had some problems with Roger who'd been complaining about stomach pains, which were not improved by a £200 fee for a ten-minute consultation in London's Harley Street. It was a 'no win' situation for him really, because he was told there was nothing wrong, while if there had been, he'd have felt just as bad. More seriously, someone wasn't doing their job, because Rog became incapable of returning for several encores, and Chas Hodges (Heads, Hands and Feet, and now Chas and Dave) had to help out with the rock 'n' roll closer,

'Lucille'. Ritchie's helpful contribution to the bass player's agony was to suggest that if he had to die, he should do it on stage so we could cremate him as part of the act! Ritchie was in good form during that period, and went though a phase of using a catapult to brighten up long car journeys, off-loading peas at passers-by and men digging roads. Silly really, but better than the River Thames period.

A gig in Amsterdam, at the Concertgebow, I think, gave me the chance to do something different. We'd just driven from a show in Germany, and I had a severe bout of bronchitis, which I often used to get. I had a croaky voice, felt very unwell and knew I'd be going into a fight with one arm tied behind my back (in a manner of speaking). So I decided to help the cause in the backstage bar, and while dealing with a couple of large scotch and Cokes in a beer glass, I became aware of 'cue calls'. That meant the band were well into cranking up 'Highway Star', and the next thing I knew was that Ian Hansford was shouting at me, 'Get on stage, Ian ... get on stage!' Well, I guess I went into auto-pilot, and in my finest Dick Turpin boots, I walked through the door to what I thought was the stage. In fact, it was the entrance to the stage, but it was also at the top of a flight of carpeted stairs. Two balcony spots picked me out, and then brilliantly followed me as I performed all kinds of mid-air manouevres, before landing flat on my back, and raising a full glass of scotch and Coke to the cheering crowd! Not a drop was spilt, and the audience loved it. I don't think I could have done a thing wrong after that, and although I croaked my way through the show, nobody gave a toss!

Locked in our own bubble, nothing in the real world touched us, as we went from one town to the next. A few issues did get through, though: my Rolls Royce broke down, and 'hot pants' arrived, which the fat and thin wore alike. But apart from hearing that Mick Jagger had been married in the South of France, and that Chelsea had won the European Cup against

Real Madrid, life went on as usual, as we travelled wherever John and Tony sent us.

We also made *Fireball*, our last recording project at De Lane Lea and The Olympic Studio. It was also the last album we'd record for Warner Bros.

As with most progressive hard rock bands of that period, we avoided singles, but 'Strange Kind of Woman' ('I'm Alone' on the 'B' side) was released in February, and the album was on the shelves in time for our second American tour in September.

Opinions varied about *Fireball*, and I know Ritchie is quoted as saying, 'It was nothing, really.' He went on to (helpfully) add that being on tour was no way to write an album. In fact, he said the only time we got to write in Deep Purple was when someone was ill! Given that during this period most of us had been ill, including himself with appendicitis, I'm surprised he didn't feel better about the project. As for me, I thought we kept up our progressive standards with the album, and am proud of it. Songs like 'No No No', 'Demon's Eye', 'The Mule', 'Fools', 'Anyone's Daughter' and 'No One Came' which simply echoes my fears then (and thereafter) about the ultimate horror of an empty hall — well, those songs are fine by me! As for *Fireball*, we had found a new use for the central heating system at the studio — what you hear at the beginning, the 'whooshing' sound, is the system being switched on!

> *No one came from miles around*
> *And said, man your music's really hot*
> *Oh, I knew what they meant ...*

However, if I liked the album, I was definitely in the minority, because Jon, Roger and Ian Paice were pretty negative about it as well. Still, it can't have been that bad, because it went to the top of the UK charts in September, and made number 32 in the States. In July '71, we did a major tour of Canada and America, playing huge arenas — football stadiums and halls, in such places as St Lawrence, Toronto, Buffalo, New York, Hamilton (Ontario) and undertook a heavy schedule that took us through the whole of August as well. We crossed America, taking in Philadelphia, Cleveland, Ohio, Milwaukee, Chicago, Miami, New Orleans, Houston and Salt Lake City, to mention but a few.

Our fame was such that we'd later progress to travelling in a personal jet, with Deep Purple slashed across it. That was when we toured with Rod Stewart and the Faces — the real bad boys of rock 'n' roll'! To be honest, Rod was a flash bastard (look who's talking), but a great pro. He and the band had been doing this sort of thing for years, and they knew every trick in the book. Of course, they were fantastic, but the fact is they were so into enjoying themselves, they were arseholed all the time! Ron Wood, Ian McLagan, Ronnie Lane and Kenny Jones saw their job as one long party, while our hungry new band — out to impress — became a hard act for them to follow. But, my God, offstage they were even more amazing!

There was one gig at which Rod invited everybody back to his hotel, into which we were also booked. So about 3,000 youngsters turned up in the lobby, and it turned into one huge, long beach party, where all the straw shades were torched, a session upstairs involved Ritchie and Rod throwing food at everyone, and finally Russ Warner, from the label, came to calm things down, and was dumped in a bath. The hotel manager came up to complain, and Ritchie bundled him up in a fire hose, which prompted me to then start mooning, with a newspaper on fire wedged up my bum. Sadly, the police arrived to spoil our fun, but the record companies kindly picked up the bill for $25,000 of damage.

And so the show would move to the next venue, where the Faces would fall off the plane, be guided to the next concert hall, and entertain the fans, who had just had 45 minutes of Deep Purple! The transition from large halls in the UK to these ice hockey arenas and football pitches in America called on new reserves of nerve and energy — and alcohol. Apart from the fact we were touring with another band, who hardly set a great example in moderate consumption, I did find the whole thing daunting, and we'd all suffer in many ways.

At about lunchtime, I'd start to get superstitious, and would feel increasingly less inclined to chat to anybody. It was hard, and I'd go into my own little world, trying to focus on the night ahead. It wouldn't be a question of worrying about the words — they'd vary anyway. It wouldn't be a question of how I might dance or move around, or what I'd try and say to the audience. It would be about fears — fears that someone might not be well, that the show might be less than perfect — constant fears. And, finally, we'd arrive at the arena or 'bowl', hit the stage, and fall into a great groove! Before we went out with the Faces, we'd become aware that our show was possibly getting a bit stale, so we went to some lengths to look at it again, and material from *Fireball* was, of course, available to offer scope for change. We continued to be unafraid to ad lib, either with musical inputs, or the use of moving lyrics which we'd slot in.

My Aunt Nelly's got a big fat belly
And tits tied up with string
She sits in the grass with her finger up her arse
Singing 'Help, God save the King.'

We did, in fact, take our performances very seriously, and it mattered that we felt good at the end. As public property, a few media people tried to give us a hard time, often reading too much into what we were doing, and there was quite a lot of intellectual stuff written, which I can't stand! I was reported once as saying, 'We play for whoever wants to hear us. If the hall's full of heads smoking joints, that's OK. But if the next night it's all school kids dancing about and yelling 'Yeh ... Black Night ... Black Night' ... that's OK as well.'

And that sums up my approach to rock 'n' roll. And then our guitarist started to give us an increasingly bad time with encores, and we'd get to the end, not knowing if he was coming back on stage or not.

Frank Zappa once said that a musician can go crazy on tour — the hotel life, the concerts, the planes — and perhaps the tour with the Faces had that kind of effect on us.

It was important to get back to the UK to rediscover our perspective and sanity, and see whether we needed to change. Except Ritchie couldn't change, at least that's how it seemed. Recovery, so as far as our management was concerned, meant going straight back to work, and by 1 September we were in Germany doing a TV special. Then it was Vienna on the 4th, and eight more shows by the month end, in between other demands. Our appearance at the Royal Albert Hall on 4 October achieved two things: first, family and friends had the use of the Royal Box; and second, rock concerts were banned for some time to come. We chose that time to enhance our reputation further, by recording an entry in the Guinness Book of Records, as being the loudest band.

It was getting very tough; we hadn't had a break for 'years', but Newman Street still kept the 'Purple project' rolling. There were no other acts on their books, so while we couldn't complain for lack of undivided attention, we were still worked like dogs, and I think our health suffered because of the constant pressure. Arrangements were made for another American tour, and for us then to record a new album, *Machine Head*, at Montreux, Switzerland.

And so the moment has come for the story of the making of a song which would become so definitive of the band, and such a major rock anthem for generations to come. I'm talking (of course) about 'Smoke on the Water'.

The town of Montreux is nestled at the foot of the mountains, along the shoreline of Lake Geneva, and the old

Casino was the centrepiece, made entirely of wood — a building of great character. It was here in the Casino that we planned to make the follow up to *Fireball*. We arrived the night before, and checked into the Eden au Lac hotel nearby, just in time to catch the last show of the season before the place would be given over to our use.

On stage were Frank Zappa and The Mothers of Invention. I'd not long recovered from hepatitis, contracted during the tour of the States, and I was still a bit wobbly. Still, on 6 December 1971, the prospect of watching a Zappa show cheered me up no end. Flo and Eddie were with the 'Mothers' at this time, and everything was going great guns. As for the hall, because of its age and wooden structure, it needed constant refurbishment, which was usually done in the winter, when everybody had gone skiing to Zermat.

Although it was being used, its owner, Claude Nobs, was carrying out quite major improvements at the same time, including rewiring, as evident by the loose cables running along some of the cornices. Still, you only know these things in the aftermath of a disaster, which was about to happen.

During the show, I have this vague recollection of a guy of Mediterranean appearance walking in. I thought nothing of it, though, until the next thing I knew there was a flash of light caused by a flare gun, a sharp crack, and then the troubles began. It later emerged that the person I'd seen had apparently parked a Rolls Royce outside, and had come in simply to make a 'happening', to help the show along, I suppose! Apparently, no evil was intended, but never in his wildest imagination could he have expected his action to set off the tragic sequence of events which followed. A spark from his flare must have touched some exposed wiring around the covings, and then ... whoosh ... the whole lot went up like a firework display. It must have hit a soft spot because, within moments, the Casino was a raging inferno as the woodwork combusted instantaneously like kindling.

Zappa was brilliant, taking positive command of a situation which was rapidly turning to chaos around us. From his vantage point on stage, he directed and urged calm, as the audience began to leave, but there were corners of the Casino where the evacuation went badly wrong, with kids throwing themselves through huge plate-glass windows. Many suffered cuts and other injuries, but Zappa stayed as long as he possibly could, as the hall rapidly filled with acrid smoke. Eventually, he, too, had to leave, with us just ahead of him.

Strange things happen in situations like that, and cause strange reactions or priorities. For example, Zoe suddenly realised she'd left her coat behind, as if that was important in all the chaos. However, despite that, I went back into the building through the front entrance to find it, and what I saw was astonishing. Everybody was calling for Claude Nobs, because he was the man who knew all the answers, because he was in control ... because he *was* Montreux! Inside, there was nothing to see — no exit signs, no stage, no kids! All that could be heard was yelling and shrieks, but there was no sign of Claude — only smoke. People who saw me in there were shouting, 'Get out ... get out ... get out!' while others were calling, 'Where's Claude?' And then I was outside again, only to learn later what had happened to him.

It seems he'd gone to the kitchens which were underground, realising that some kids had gone through the doors that could only have led them that way, and they were trapped in smoke-filled spaces, which only he knew about. One by one, or in small groups, Claude led the youngsters to safety, repeating the journey until he was satisfied that nobody remained. Outside, and to my surprise, I realised I had Zoe's coat, but as for Claude — well, he's the 'Funky Claude, pulling kids out of the ground'.

We all came out to Montreux

On the Lake Geneva shoreline
To make records with a mobile
We didn't have much time
Frank Zappa and the Mothers
Were at the best place around
But some stupid with a flare gun
Burned the place to the ground

The emergency services don't need spectators, so we drifted back to the hotel, where we met up in the restaurant for a few drinks and a meal — for those who felt like it. And from there, we watched the Casino burn — flames high in the sky, smoke billowing. Some thought the brightness and intensity was caused by the downdraught from the mountains, but whatever the reason, the flames leaned majestically towards the lake, as smoke drifted across quiet water.

Two or three days later, Roger said he'd had this dream, and woke up sweating, saying the words, 'Smoke on the water.' He wrote it down, and suggested to me that we write a song about the disaster. It happened that another mind was working along similar lines; Ritchie had already found the riff, soon to become that classic rock intro, as Roger and I wrote the lyrics recalling how events unfolded. Twenty-one years later I travelled to Montreux to hand over a Harp Rock Plaque, to be fixed to the wall of either the Casino or the hotel where the song was written, and Claude was present. Quite where it ends up, we shall see, but I gather Claude's annual concerts are now held at a new venue — The Stravinsky Auditorium.

With our recording venue gone, rapid action was necessary, and taking time out from the mopping-up operations and his own problems, Claude managed to relocate us and the Rolling Stones' mobile we'd hired, arranging for us to use the Grand Hotel, which was vacant. It was also being redecorated, but they said we could use it, and Martin Birch went in to set things up. He parked the mobile outside, and went in to convert a corridor which had a 'T' shape layout into a studio. He put the drums on the T itself; the guitars and organ at one end — facing into a cupboard (filled with mattresses); and then showed us that to get to the truck, we had to go through the kitchen, then through a bathroom, out on to a balcony (in the freezing cold), back to the hotel via another bathroom, and finally out to where they were parked up. I rigged up a closed-circuit TV, but playbacks were terrible. Martin was brilliant and, one way or another, he adapted the place into something we could use. *Machine Head* was made, and would be a huge success.

It was at this time that the management came up with the idea that we set up our own record label, and we all convened for one of those chats, except, once again, I didn't like the idea. The concept was to set up 'Purple Records', and later 'Oyster'. Tony had already been in talks with Warner Bros, but I remembered one of Bill Reid's little talks about 'conflict of interest', and it annoyed me to see the gradual erosion by outsiders to what I saw as being against our interests as musicians. The management just seemed to want to do more and more themselves. First we saw the agency come 'in-house', then much of the promotion did the same. They had the publishing, and now we were to be a record label. So I asked them how seriously they thought they could manage us when they had the whole thing sewn up like that. How do you negotiate the best deal for your artist, when you are negotiating with yourself? It seemed so obvious, but the old 'divide and rule' act went into top gear, and the 'Purple Label' was formed to deal with *Machine Head* in the UK. The album topped the charts at home for three weeks, helped by a major TV advertising campaign (April 1972), and later made number 7 in America.

As for the new label, it went ahead despite my protests, and although I was offered shares, I refused. Still, there was no time to get bogged down with it all, because we were on our way to America, where we played three shows at New York, Virginia and Chicago, and it was at Chicago where it all nearly ended for me at the airport on 6 November.

I suddenly went yellow, and slid down a post. I'd been getting more and more ill as the touring went on, and had been throwing up regularly. I'd put it all down to the tension of going on stage, and the fact that perhaps I was drinking too much. It's just that I seemed to need the alcohol to keep me in control. So I was waiting for my bags to come through, when this appalling sensation came over me, a bit like leaping out of bed too quickly, and then I couldn't hear or see too well, or articulate to people who were moving very slowly around me, staring. It was Colin Hart's voice which came through, saying, 'Don't worry, Ian, we're getting you to hospital; you've gone a strange colour!'

When I came to, a doctor told me I was very ill, and diagnosed hepatitis. I tried to explain I needed to be on stage that night, but when he told me I was close to dying, I took that to mean he didn't think it would be that likely! At least Zoe — with whom I was at constant war — was with me, and I told her to organise some tickets home. She said there was no way I could travel, and when I looked into a mirror, I understood the score. I was yellow all over — including my eyes.

As I recall, some minion from the record company kept looking in, but nobody from management. I was poisoned to hell, and lost and lonely. The hospital people were very kind and attentive, and I was kept on a strict diet of boiled fish, water and cola. Any dairy product was guaranteed to kill me within the day, and the same went for fatty foods. Otherwise, there was this black guy, who seemed always to be walking around on his knees, and he kept coming over to inject me, invariably at four o'clock in the morning! Why always 4.00am? Could they not see I was upset enough? And why wouldn't he stand up!

Of course, it wasn't until my senses returned that I realised he was a dwarf, just doing his job.

After five days or so, I discharged myself, but the guy from the record company said there was no way they would let me on a plane, looking the colour I still was and being so ill. He said there would be a riot among the passengers, but my mind was set on home, so I covered myself with a scarf, and we flew out of Chicago. I have no memory of the journey at all, and vaguely recall the doctor coming to see me at Hyde House. Having access to wonderful English papers, and crossword puzzles which I love, was a great treat. In fact, just having *time* was an indescribable joy! The tour was obviously cancelled at a cost to the band of about $200,000, whatever that meant! What was it I said earlier about priorities? For me, it was a time for peace and gentle recovery and, after a few days, I got someone to take me to the saw mill, where we selected some planks of Japanese oak, which I had planed, and then I made a table, which I cherish to this day. Recovery from illness gave me the chance to look at life and try to find some kind of focus and sense of perspective and, as did the rest of the guys, I went into solo projects, including the producing of an album for a band called Jerusalem, and the development of a children's musical, called *Cher Kazoo*.

We were still Deep Purple, with a major programme ahead, but the cracks were there, both with the management and each other.

The main problem in the band had become centred on me and Ritchie, and because he was the more forceful of us, and better able to catch the attention of the management, I was seen as the problem. His growing interest in the mystical — castles and so forth — plus his total belief in the pre-eminence of the lead guitar, conspired to make our relationship increasingly difficult. Add to that our different attitudes towards the fans, and it's not surprising that relationships were strained. I'll admit to being often unyielding and pig-headed, but I only wanted to deliver Purple at its best, and we didn't seem to be doing that. I suspect Ritchie would say the same, but it's just that we saw things dogmatically differently.

Over a few beers at a pub in Stowe (Vermont) a few years later, he'd admit to never having been praised as a child, that his best could always be bettered. So perhaps this was at the heart of so much, and I choose to believe the man's infuriating attitude is sometimes not an act. I've seriously tried to work it out, and considered whether his progress through the business also lies at the root of his eccentricity. He had, by any stretch of the imagination, an incredible apprenticeship, going back to when he was 16 years old, and playing with Screaming, where he had to put up with the singer climbing out of a coffin and coming at him with a dagger, while the guitar player stood performing in a loin cloth. And then backing artists like Jerry Lee Lewis and Gene Vincent can't have been easy, and I know Vincent put him through hell.

In front of a packed house, the singer would go up to the audience and announce he'd just penned this little number 'which goes like this'. So while everybody's thinking 'Be Bop A Lulu', and Ritchie's keyed into E chord, he'd eye the guitar player, and Ritchie would cue him in again. This would go on for some time, until it dawned on Ritchie that this was one of those nights that Gene had been on the whisky bottle, and could not therefore remember the little number he'd just penned! The singer would then go to his agent, Don Arden, and complain that the guitarist was trying to screw things up for him, and that the crowd didn't like the way he dressed. Ritchie may have every reason to be how he is, but it's often a shame. As for *Machine Head*, it must have justified every single penny put into the new Purple label. We had made it with about two weeks' notice and, although I was still in recovery, it was our biggest album, with classics like 'Highway Star', 'Space Truckin' ', 'Never Before',

'Smoke on the Water', 'Maybe I'm A Leo', 'Lazy' and 'Pictures of Home'. It sold 3 million copies quite quickly, made Deep Purple one of the biggest-selling bands in the world and, as with so much of our work, it has been selling year in and year out, having recently been re-mastered and reissued, as has been the case with other albums. Touring was arranged to happen side by side with the album, and we were only spared another trip to the States when Ritchie became ill with hepatitis. Still, it was only a brief respite, and off we went to play non-stop, as the itinerary shows:

January

13th	Sportatorium, Hollywood
14th	Curtis Hixon, Tampa
15th	Climson, Florida
16th	Cumberland Fayetteville, North Carolina
17th	Buffalo, New York
18th	Must have had a cancellation!
19th	Detroit, Michigan
20th	Montreal, Canada
21st	Bloomington, Minnesota
22nd/23rd	Chicago
24th	Kiel Stadium
26th	Wichita, Kansas
28th	San Bernadino, California
29th	San Jose, California
30th	Long Beach, California
31st	Boise, Idaho

The whole thing was becoming a nightmare, and beginning to affect us very badly, like the time Ritchie didn't arrive in reception one morning, although Colin (Hart) had woken him in good time for our departure. We were well used to the guitarist doing things like this, but Colin went upstairs to gee him up, only to find him in floods of tears in the corridor.

It's difficult to put any real spark into this part of my life, because there was so little joy around. We were firmly stuck on the treadmill, trudging from venue to venue, and the downward spiral must have now been well and truly under way — except that nobody seemed to notice or care. Where was the smile, where was the glint in the eye, where was the spirit? Where was the rock 'n' roll? I'd have swapped all the money, the first-class hotels, the limos, the personal helpers and rock 'n' roll perks for just one gig in some club or pub!

Thankfully, I found relaxation and escape through meeting Buddy Miles with whose band we toured. With Buddy, there were many fine moments of nonsense, often at his expense, and it was so very different to what we were used to. On many occasions, Ritchie and I would behave like little kids, hiding behind pillars at the airport as Buddy waddled by — a man of large bottom, knees splayed out — on account of the fact that his thighs were so fat. As he passed us, we'd be cranking out a few bars of 'Them Changes', but done in a very irreverent way, and Buddy would swing round going, 'Who'zat? What'zat?' before giving up trying to source it, and checking into his flight.

With Buddy, I had my first introduction to the other world's peccadilloes, and it happened at one of the hotels where we arrived early, after three connecting flights. It was a Holiday Inn-type of place, and we turned up before noon. I went straight to my room, but simply could not get off to sleep. Somewhere across the hall, I became aware of the sound of Buddy and his band, doing what they seemed to do all the time — *party!* They partied all day and all night, and the whole tour continued like that for them — on stage and off! They showed no nerves at all, no pre-show butterflies — they just locked into their American groove, and stayed that way.

So I decided to go across to where the music was playing, wearing just a pair of jeans, no shirt, and barefoot. I whacked the door open, to be greeted by these wonderful smells coming out of the room. On the bed were these two chicks making love to each other, while this guy played his bone, as others just sat around talking and smoking joints. And then there was Buddy, lying out on a bed, all fat and hairy, talking music. It was all jive talk, which I didn't begin to understand, and they were all cracking up, having a great time.

Then Buddy saw me and said, 'What's up, boy?'

I told him I couldn't sleep.

'Well, maybe you should take a tote of this,' he said, and proceeded to roll a joint, which he passed to me — my first joint, really. I took a puff, and then another, and then again. And then there were all these hands reaching out, as I realised for the first time in my life that you were supposed to pass it round. Meanwhile, Buddy was rolling another spliff (I'm learning the jargon!), and this one was quite large. He handed it over, saying, 'Take this back to your bed, boy; that'll send you off to sleep.'

We had a show that night, so I drifted back to my room. Well, apart from one experience with a hubble-bubble in Beirut, this was the first time I'd touched anything certain people might not have approved of, as I turned on the TV, stretched out and lit the joint. Well, I slept all right! I had this incredible dream, which I remember in finest detail.

I was lying in a field in the wilderness, and this Amazonian-looking woman approached me. She was about 6ft tall, lean and quite small-breasted. However, the strange thing about her was that her sex was not between her legs, but on the pubic mound. She had no body hair, and these two swollen lips protruded vertically, inviting what was now my fierce erection. I got up from the grass and walked slowly towards her. My being then entered her, as I became aware of other women who looked the same. The experience would be a constantly recurring dream of immense sexuality and dignity and, when conscious, my condition was extremely painful, and I had to play four shows with a hard on. And then my alarm went, and reality kicked in!

We'd released a single in March called 'Never Before' ('When a Blind Man Cries'), and returned to the UK in early summer to find it had 'stiffed'. We all convened at the office to review things and look at the accounts with Bill, and when I asked what had gone wrong with the promotion of the single, John said, It was nothing to do with the promotion … it was just a duff record that nobody wanted to play or hear.'

I said, 'Well, John, as I see it, there was no promotion and people didn't even know it was out. It was a very low-key campaign.'

John then began to wind himself up, beginning with, 'There were full-page ads in all the music press, but of course you wouldn't know that, because you've been in America!'

Now it just so happened that Audrey had kept all the back numbers of the Melody Maker, NME and so forth, and I'd run through them before the meeting. So I challenged him with, 'That's not true, John,' and he must have realised I'd caught him with his pants down. It was all very embarrassing, as he got up, sweating, eyes blazing with hatred. I thought he was going to deck me, but instead he shouted, 'Gillan, you always were a supercilious bastard,' to which I replied, 'Well, if you're going to be formal, John, it's Mr Gillan,' before I took my leave to the sound of orchestrated muttering.

I later looked at one set of Profit and Loss Accounts for the Year End 1972, but the figures didn't really help much. Our collective royalties were £63,760.64, and income from the European and American tours came to £155,951.13, making a total of nearly £220,000. If I'd queried anything, I might have asked about the £6.73 postage that year, but things were stressed out enough, without me pushing my luck any further.

As the year progressed, the scale of gigs increased and we were in a routine which Ian Paice described as 'blurred together into one long stream, each one indistinguishable from the last'. I then decided to leave the financial side of things alone.

Ritchie came away from an internal flight in America where, having chatted to the boxer Joe Frazier, he promptly went down with hepatitis, for which the supremely fit and powerful boxer could not be held responsible! Because of cancellations when I'd been ill, every effort was made to work though this programme. We tried to use Al Cooper whom I thought was fine, but he called in sick soon after and we had to cast the net again. Randy California stepped in for the gig in Quebec City, and we included 'When a Blind Man Cries' that night. Randy played slide during 'Child in Time', and the audience went crazy. So, naturally enough, Randy was fired directly after the show, and the remainder of the Canadian dates were cancelled.

A show in Germany without Ritchie went down quite well, although we had previously offered refunds to the fans. However, most of them stayed, but unfortunately many also stayed on after the show ended and we'd gone. They smashed the place to smithereens, which made the authorities take our next gig at full band strength quite seriously. In fact, they brought in the army, which made me think, 'Is all this necessary, so five guys can do a concert?' The half-mile journey back to the hotel after that took two hours, reminding me of the adage that 'you know you've made it when you get stuck in your own traffic jam!'

Someone came on stage at Ludenscheid and announced we'd be coming back shortly to do another set and, when we didn't, the crowd wrecked our gear, leaving John and Tony to sue the City authorities successfully for damages.

All in all, I was beginning to find Deep Purple a machine over which I basically had no control, and I began to think about knocking it on the head. The Purple label was expanding to take in other artists, and Roger was showing an increasing interest (and skill) in the production side of things. He'd already cut his teeth on the album *Razamanaz* which he produced for Nazareth, but despite new artists on the label, and despite Ritchie not yet being recovered, we were soon on our way back to the States (May), before returning to Europe for more gigs and recording *Who Do We Think We Are!* That was an unhappy album in the making, because Ritchie and I had basically had enough of one another.

I often wonder whether the managers could have saved the inevitable happening by just calling a halt to the schedule and saying, 'OK lads, let's take a break for a few months.' But they didn't, and so the day came when I sat down to write that famous letter to Tony Edwards. We were doing a short tour of America, and I was at The Imperial Hotel, in Dayton, Ohio, whose notepaper had printed at the top, 'Where Every Guest is King'. It was a nice touch, although I didn't feel very 'kingly' then. I wrote:

Dear Tony,
Thank you for your telegram. Perhaps in my letter to you the word 'affiliation' misled you. I must now make clear that my doubts be in the direction of my own desires to perform as an artist. I am so depressed with my occupation at the moment as well as the circumstances and attitudes I have to work with that I felt it necessary to put on record my intentions to leave the group on 30th June 1973. This decision is not impulsive, but made after at least six months of thought. I am certainly not thinking of moving to any other companies for management etc. It is simply that if, after three months complete break, I decide to continue in the business, I shall find a new way of expressing my ideas, or at least a more varied way. I suppose I could sum up by saying that I think DP has become a stagnant, boring machine far removed from the fresh, innovative group it once was. I think this was

inevitable and that we should quit whilst we are ahead. Another advantage to deciding upon a date at least six months in advance, is that nobody will be able to take unfair advantage of the situation. You must admit that this is almost a probability were matters to follow an unguided course. I have almost formulated a basic pattern for the future and I shall obviously make you aware of my intentions when I reach London.
Yours sincerely, Ian

So when I met John and Tony, they said, 'Well, are you really leaving then?' and when I started to explain that I couldn't take any more, that I needed a break, John asked, 'How long can you stay?' So I told him I wasn't going to just walk out on them, that I'd stay long enough to see commitments honoured, and so on. They said they had just had the tour to Japan confirmed, and could I stay for that? I said, 'OK,' and that was it.

Not once was it suggested, 'Do you want to reconsider when you've had a rest?' or 'Is there some way we can approach this differently?' My God, I must have been an obnoxious, unapproachable creature for the end to come about like this. OK, so I know I'd been capable of arrogance, and the word 'supercilious' had been used from time to time, but it was only my way of looking after myself. Because I had the confidence to speak my mind didn't surely mean I was a loathsome prima donna. Could these people not see that not only had I lost respect for them, but that I'd also lost respect for myself? Could they not see that I'd spent months willing them to accept that this great band was in a decline of its own making? I mean, for heaven's sake, each member of the band had learned from their own experience about facing up to moments when it's time to call a halt, when the magic fades. I'd faced that situation with The Moonshiners, the Javelins, Episode Six and Wainwrights Gentlemen, but here there was no reflection, no self-analysis, just 'How long can you stay?' I admit now that I did not want to leave Deep Purple. I just didn't like the way things were going, and it was as simple as that. I didn't like the way the guys were worried about their futures, their lack of confidence, or the way they were looking retrogressively at the music we'd made two to three years before. Above all, I didn't know what I was looking for, and nobody had asked me. I was dying of frustration and nobody cared.

It doesn't matter how famous or successful you are, each one of us needs an arm around us sometimes. It's something I needed, and I didn't receive it in any form. My relationship with Zoe was unsuccessful, and I was faced with finishing *Who Do We Think We Are!*, plus a long period of touring, in isolation. We no longer seemed to be mates, and all conspired to cause the album to be deferred. The atmosphere in Rome was very bad, with the guitarist deciding not to be around the house when we were there; or should I say, when I was there, and it must have cost the record company a fortune. We gave them 'Rat Bat Blues', 'Place in Line', 'Our Lady', 'Mary Long' (Mary Whitehouse/Lord Longford swipe), 'Super Trouper', 'Woman from Tokyo' and 'Smooth Dancer'.

I admit taking my anger out on Ritchie in particular, and did so in the only way I knew best — hidden in the lyrics. 'Smooth Dancer' is an example of this, with frequent references to black suede, his favourite clothing. Unfortunately, I don't think he saw the subtlety, which made me even more angry!

As we struggled to produce that piece of vinyl, I know I wasn't the only one with thoughts of change in mind, and I believe Ritchie was cooking something up with Paicey and Phil Lynott. Paul Rodger's name was also thought to be in the frame somewhere, but as Deep Purple, we struggled through a hefty programme which was of such intensity, that it's hard to believe things were ending.

Now it was only place names: Southampton on 13

September; Leicester the next night; Brighton after that, and on through to November, where we criss-crossed America and Canada, and into December. We then started all over again in the new year.

Who Do We Think We Are! had been released in the States at the end of 1972, and came out in the UK in early 1973. It reached number 15 and 4 respectively in the charts, which posed a cruel dilemma for the management in Newman Street. The complete irony of all that was happening was while 'the greatest band in the world' was falling apart at the seams, its cashflow potential was bigger than ever!

Despite efforts to contain the fact I was leaving, the media and fans picked up on what was going on, and we toured to a bad press and increasing hostility. Some of it was justified, but other situations were plain stupid, such as when we refused to go on stage and play outdoors during a thunderstorm in New York. That event (with ZZ Top) caused fans to wreck our gear so we couldn't play Atlanta the next night, and one journal said of that farce, 'Deep Purple unwilling to die in order to sing a song.'

We arrived for the closing Japanese tour in August 1972, where we played Hiroshima, Nayago and two shows at Osaka. The concerts were recorded live for the *Made in Japan* (double) album, which was a huge success, and included 'Highway Star', 'Child in Time', 'Smoke on the Water', 'The Mule', 'Strange Kind of Woman', 'Lazy' and 'Space Truckin''. *Made in Japan* reached number 16 in the UK in January 1973, and 6 in America in April, reinforcing our world standing with *Who Do We Think We Are!* selling at the same time.

As most fans know, I've never personally been happy about live albums and would prefer to leave that side of things to the bootleggers. The thrill of the moment, and all that implies, means you have to be there, but I know and accept I'm in a minority on this subject.

I was leaving Deep Purple voluntarily, and Roger was also going, although at the time he didn't know it. When the concert was over, I kept my farewell to a simple 'Goodnight', and allowed myself to be swamped with relief. I flew home without a cloud on the horizon.

Chapter 6

Unlike most jobs when you leave, and move on to the next, it's not quite the same with a situation like Deep Purple. Of course I'd left the band, and it was of my choice, and fine. But when you are dealing with an organisation and business like that, there's more to it than meets the eye, and so I'd realise that although I'd gone, I had not gone completely. I had money tied up in royalties, and there was my stake in all sorts of deals the managers were into, such as the release of albums and compilations, which happened after I'd left, but had my name on them, and so it went on. So every time a record was released with my work on it, I had money tied up in it somewhere. There were a lot of situations like that: *Last Concert in Japan*, *Powerhouse*, *The Best of Deep Purple*, *Carat Purple*, *When We Rock We Roll* and *When We Roll We Rock*, *The Mark II Purple Singles* and *Deepest Purple*. And over the years, much more would follow.

However, in the early post-leaving period, the way our music was packaged and sold showed the brilliant marketing minds at Newman Street and, in particular, John's. The fact that his early background was in advertising was very obvious! The trouble from my point of view was that I had no idea what it all meant, how much money I had to take into the new era and, what was worse, it seems nobody at the office really knew either! As things would emerge, the whole thing was locked up inside the mercurial brain of Bill Reid, and he'd take all that knowledge with him when he sadly died a few years later.

It made perfect sense that Bill should remain as my financial adviser and mentor. We'd not fallen out and I continued to trust him, as I brought him into looking after the business side of my new whacky ventures. We'd both end up disappointed but, for much of the time, he gave his whole-hearted support. Having decided I'd never sing again professionally, I opted for a different kind of life. I had my hair cut quite short, dressed in a more conventional manner, and went out to find a building I could convert into the finest country hotel in the world. Having seen just about every hotel possible with Deep Purple, I figured I should have one myself, so Zoe and I toured the south-eastern home counties in the Roller, looking for the right opportunity. Despite my more restrained manner and appearance, my reputation travelled before me, and you could literally hear the fearful whispers when I started revisiting properties which might have been suitable. 'Oh God, we're going to have drugs and orgies in our village,' as the country folk braced themselves for their lives being thrown into chaos. In truth, they need not have worried, because all they were seeing was a demoralised, lost and quite hungry person in search of his own bar.

Eventually, our travels took us to North Stoke, near Oxford, where we found The Springs. It was a dilapidated building that had been used as a nursing home and, after talking to Bill about it, we paid around £100,000 in cash. I then set about having a great time ripping the place to pieces, stripping it back to the original fabric, at which point we found incredible oak panelling, fireplaces and such like. There was a terrace overlooking fields and a fantastic lake, but it was all very unsafe and needed a lot of work doing to it, as I set about designing the ultimate residential escape and business centre.

Within a few weeks, an annexe to the side had been done

up, and was running as a bar. Not surprisingly, it quickly began to do good business as all my mates turned up, as well as the curious locals, and I kept it open all day, and as late into the night as the last customer wanted. As for the main building, the hotel, that started to cost a lot more, as we found out just how insecure the structure was. Still, all I had to do was phone Bill, and he'd phone the bank, and I'd withdraw another chunk of money. It was gruelling work, but I put my heart and soul into it, and offered employment to all sorts of people who turned up saying they knew what they were doing, or just wanting to help the former singer of Deep Purple.

As time went by, many of these characters came and left, having screwed things up, or just having robbed me blind, while I was looking after guests at the bar.

Then I learned about things like needing a licence for the sale of alcohol, as well as planning permission to use the building as a hotel. Suddenly, there were people arriving from all sorts of official departments, and pointing at things I'd done. One of the best was this guy from The Forestry Commission or something like that. He arrived at the area where we were laying a fantastic driveway and car park, and shouted, 'Stop!' before going on to tell me that what I was doing was building a car park in a space where a few trees stood.

'That,' he said, pointing, 'is a mulberry bush,' to which I replied, 'Really, and very nice it is, too!' He said it would have to stay, and I told him it was right in the middle of my car park, and would be going! He repeated that it would be staying, going on to tell me they had something like the death penalty for even shouting at trees and shrubs in North Stoke.

Anyway, I said I'd leave it, at which point he went on to demand iron railings around the trees, in case one of the workmen should accidentally drive into it with a JCB, or something similar. I didn't give a monkeys what this guy thought; the job I was doing was being done with the experience of somebody who cared, and had seen good and bad taste in every corner of the globe. This guy had probably never left Oxfordshire.

Another feature I designed was the guitar-shaped swimming pool, with a fret board as the steps into it and an acoustic ring set in tiles beneath the clear water.

We made the interior of the building palatially elegant, with every whim anticipated. Each en suite bedroom had its own safe, and guests were asked not to steal things like the onyx lighters, but simply to take them.

The project, however, began to eat into my reserves, which Bill was continuing to top up as necessary at the local branch of Lloyds Bank. We had reached the stage where the hotel was short by just one en suite room — The Pool Suite — but it was not doing the business. A formal announcement read:

The Solarium at The Springs is now open. The Solarium, overlooking a beautiful spring-fed lake, is the dining room of The Springs, a country house being England moved graciously into this century. The menu is extensive, the food superb. With adequate notice, the chef will prepare any dish of your choice. The fine wines are a matter of course and the Solarium is also open for lunch seven days a week.

The restaurant and bars were brilliant, but the running costs were also quite high. On the ground, I was a lousy manager and, in any case, my mind was very pre-occupied by the fact the local authority said we didn't have permission to use the place as a Country Club. We were £300,000 into the venture, and they were telling me I couldn't trade!

It was pointed out that the odds on getting consent were pretty slim, so it was time to adopt the old 'thinking position' again. I decided to throw an official opening party for the entire village on Saturday 30 November 1974, and we went to the electoral register to find the names and addresses of every single person in North Stoke, including the vicar. The invitation referred to the occasion as a small 'cocktail party', lasting between 6.15pm and 8.00pm. Anyway, the whole village turned up, became paralytically drunk over a sustained period, and, as they gradually fell out, Zoe stood at the door asking if they'd had a good time, before asking them to sign a petition, which they most certainly couldn't read! So the village of North Stoke got behind the venture, and that sorted out at least one department at the local authority.

In the meantime, Bill wanted to keep a stricter eye on the business, because things were going missing. So he took on Jim Allen, and told him to report to him every day on income and expenditure. We were just beginning to look as if we could make the project profitable, but there were still some fairly large amounts owing, and one or two traders were starting to put stories about. Still, all I kept saying to Bill was, 'Can we afford it?' and he would say, 'Yes'.

A second venture I became involved in was the 'Mantis Motorcycles' project, which, just like The Springs, was something I started as a bit of fun, and then became totally wrapped up in. It began the day Zoe introduced me to a friend of hers' — Mike Egglington. Mike was a really nice guy, who used to own a small garage in Aylesbury, where he'd fix cars and such like to pay for his hobby — motor cycle racing.

The Springs was almost up and running when I went to see him race one day at Thruxton. It was unbelievable. There he was on this beaten-up old Norton, with no spares, and wearing ultra-cool, weathered black leathers. So he disappeared off round the first bend and, seconds later, we heard this crash, and saw the ambulance racing away. Sure enough, we saw no sign of Mike, and so began to fear the worst. When we got to the scene of the crash, it turned out that another rider had broken his legs in a collision with Mike, who was busy taking usable parts from the unfortunate competitor's bike and tying them around his machine (and himself) for future use.

He explained to me that he wasn't stealing the gear, because the other bloke knew he'd be out of the game for some time, and said Mike should help himself. This was the spirit and camaraderie of bikers!

Mike carried out repairs and improvements to his machine, using the new bits and pieces, before going out again a couple of races down the card, to come about third against riders on much better bikes, including Yamahas, which were beginning to come on to the market in a big way.

I fell head over heels in love with the sport, and decided to help finance my new pal's obsession. It was a fantastic period of my life, and we'd take our tents and camping gear to places like Snetterton and Brands Hatch, where we'd set things up in all kinds of horrendous weather. *Motor Cycle News* picked up on it all when they wrote on 3 September 1975: POP STAR QUITS FOR BIKES AND BACKS A NEW BRITISH ENGINE! It went on to say:

A pop star has entered the motor cycle world with plans to market an all-new British 4-stroke engine. This weekend he opens the first of a planned chain of motor cycle supermarkets, and at research premises he established two years ago, a prototype lightweight 4-stroke engine has been produced. The pop tycoon is Ian Gillan, 29, former lead singer with Deep Purple, a rock group which made a small fortune each time it toured America. He left the group two years ago to pursue business adventures, which also include a small hotel and music recording and publishing companies. He is currently making a solo album. On Saturday, he opens his supermarket under the company name World on Wheels in Mangotsfield in Bristol. The premises were originally built as a natural supermarket. Meanwhile, at his research shop, Mantis Motorcycles in Salisbury, Jack Williams, father of bike racer, Peter, and former road-racer, Mike Egglington, are working on the smaller of the two projected engines. 87cc, it is based on one cylinder from a 350-stroke originally designed by Mr Egglington. Plans to develop the 350cc are also reported to be in hand.

We quickly moved on to buy an old removal truck for about £250, and then found enough farings and general gear to make up three bikes. I basically became Mike's grease monkey, helping him hold things together for welding, finding out how you 'do this and that'. I started staying with him while he worked on cars during the day, and then we'd roll them into the street, and start on the bikes at night. We'd work on the machines until about 3.00am, ending up with a couple of production Norton 750 Commandos and a bored-out 997, which we put in for the Open Class. Mike built a special frame for that, made out of Reynolds tubing, and welded it together in a criss-cross pattern that was 'state-of-the-art'! It was brilliant, and he started to win races, although he fell off many times, a misfortune we'd put down to the fact that he drove to the limit, and sometimes past it!

Then came the day when we wondered whether we should go up a grade or two and buy a quicker Japanese model, to which Mike said, 'Why don't I build one?' We sat down to look at the idea seriously. It was based around an engine concept he'd had in the back of his mind for years. We took a great old boy, Jack Williams, on board, who used to design aircraft for Vickers at Bristol, and he started preparing working drawings for us. Others joined in to help fashion gear boxes and cooling systems, and Dunlop were happy to give us all the tyres we needed. Girling gave support for the braking system, and Lucas came in with the electricals.

We had basically tapped into all the A and R departments at the factories, and bought a house next to the garage, which we turned into offices. An advert went out for a production manager, and the whole thing snowballed into a company with ambition — and apparently of financial substance. With about 15 people on board, we dug out the basement in Salisbury to make room for the test bed and benches, and the happy day arrived when all the newly-made castings, bearings and assorted components came together to make a working machine. We all got obliterated on champagne!

The decision had been made that we'd take on the Japanese, so the Bristol showroom became our sales and PR centre, while plans were made to open a similar facility in Coventry. We set an initial target to make about 10 machines a week, increasing to around 25 after three years or so. The whole operation was put in the hands of Ted Wood, with the instruction that he kept Bill Reid closely involved. In fact, it was hard to keep Bill away from the enterprise as he loved the whole idea, and was a great admirer of Jack Williams. The two of them — one a pipe smoker, and the other a cigar man — would end up nattering away into the early hours about what we were doing.

We then opened in Edinburgh, and were looking at Dublin, on a roll of excitement and ambition. Each unit looked to be self-supporting, and it even got to the stage where I'd turn up to races in a helicopter. And then the bubble burst — or rather the British motorcycle industry did, mainly around NV Triumph.

Tony Benn, the then Minister for Trade and Industry, pumped 'millions' into the ailing company, and hired a Chairman to make sure the money was well spent. But it seems the priorities were to redecorate the factories and replace worn manually-operated gear, while everybody else was converting to automation and focusing on technology for the future. Eventually, the money came to an end, and the great leaky model of British machine excellence collapsed, leaving a group of people trying to set up a partnership out of the wreckage. Today, it's called a 'management buy-out', and it was an incredible thing to see, as Ted, Zoe, Dixie (her father) and I went to find out what was going on. What we discovered was a workforce in gloves and coats, without electricity or gas, trying to see how they could somehow save this great national heritage in a market where people like Lord Hesketh were moving into the game, much along our lines at Mantis. However, the sad fact was that with the Japanese stranglehold, companies like BSA (who'd already gone) and NVT just weren't in good enough shape to compete, and the knock-on effect meant that people like Lucas, Dunlop and Girling had to diversify their activities. That, in turn, meant our company lost valuable sources and resources for R and D and, even if they had remained, the morale and enthusiasm was no longer there to support us.

In desperation, we went to meet an MP at the House of Commons, and it turned out to be a disaster, since all he was interested in was where best to invest his money, and what did I know (from my travels) about tax havens like Jersey, the Cayman Islands and so forth. Whenever I steered the meeting back to the collapsing bike industry, he ducked the issue by blaming it on some report the Government had commissioned (*The Boston Report*, as I recall), which looked into alternative strategies, while basically passing the death sentence on the industry, its support companies and services. Finally, at the bottom of the pile of ambition, my own fine project, Mantis. From that moment, my whole world began slowly and cynically to collapse, as phone calls only meant 'pay up' or 'sorry, but we're no longer in business'. When Mantis closed, all that was left in the factory at Salisbury were a few plans and an engine with no bike!

I took Ted Wood with me to another venture closer to my area of skill — the studio I'd bought from De Lane Lea in Holborn, London. As mentioned, my leaving Deep Purple did not mean that I had cut myself off from the many people I'd been with during that period, and neither had I really fallen out with everybody. I would still visit Bill at his offices in Wallington, and it was quite early on (before The Springs Hotel) that Martin Birch, Lou Austin and Terry Eden had come to see me. They told me the De Lane Lea Studio we'd used for our early projects had moved their operation to Wembley, and that the lads didn't like the new set-up. De Lane had left Holborn with all its gear in place, and apart from still paying the rent of about £25,000 a year, they had basically locked the doors and thrown away the key.

Martin, along with half the world, was convinced I was a millionaire, and he asked if I'd be interested in buying the place, and putting them into it.

So with Bill's help, we began negotiations for the whole thing, beginning at around £100,000, but then being offered it for £40,000, which was considered a 'give-away'! Finally, I bought the basement studio and some car parking spaces for £15,000.

I changed the name to Kingsway, because that was the name of the main street outside, and thought the whole thing pretty neat — except it wasn't, as we ran straight into problems.

When Deep Purple used the studios, the upper floors were used by an advertising agency, and they were a great bunch. Next to musicians, those guys drink the most, and we had some memorable sessions in The Newton Arms nearby. However, by the time I took over, they had sold their interest to the Civil Aviation Authority, who put their computer room directly above the studio. That room had a slight bass leak that seemed to travel through the building, and emerged upstairs as a quite serious thumping sound. The CAA tried to have our use stopped, and we had people over from Southampton University to do reports on what was reasonable, tolerable and all that. But in the end, I had to use the studio more for fun than for a serious business concern, while still being liable for the rent of £25,000 a year.

Restrictions meant that we could only record after 6.00pm, unless we had a very quiet string quartet in! It left us to use the place as a planning office during the day. It was not what I needed. In fact, it was a stupid thing to embark on in the first place, because I'd never been in the least bit interested in the technical side of making records, and that didn't change with taking on Kingsway.

Martin and the lads had told me it was a really funky studio, and having settled into that idea — by which I mean after about four days — Martin came in to see me. He was very sheepish, and told me he'd just been offered £40,000 a year to go on permanent retainer with Deep Purple. It was an offer he couldn't refuse, having just married, and that left me with Lou Austin, who'd barely cut his teeth as an engineer, and under Lou came Terry, Bob, George and Chas. In fact, Chas Watkins stayed with things for some time to come.

With my contacts, I was able to bring in a number of artists and bands, and we did make some good records for people like Leo Sayer and The Sweet. Roger also used it to make *The Butterfly Ball* in 1974, and I'd use it for making my own records at a later date. I suppose it was Roger's project that reminded me of what I'd walked away from and, although I don't feature on his album, I was glad to help him with the live production of *The Butterfly Ball* at the Royal Albert Hall on 16 October 1974, when Ronnie Dio had to pull out at the last minute.

Putting that show together in aid of Bud Flanagan's Leukaemia Fund and Action Research for Crippled Children was a major effort by Rog, and it brought together a lot of old mates. Jon Lord was there, as well as Tony Ashton, Twiggy, Al Matthews, David Coverdale and Glenn Hughes from the current Deep Purple.

For me, horribly unfulfilled in my various ventures, the show was one of great emotion, surprise and joy. I thought that with the passing of time and the ongoing Deep Purple, I'd be a forgotten star. At the announcement of my name for my song, the audience rose and gave me a standing ovation! 'Welcome home, Ian' they seemed to say, and Vincent Price had to pause in his narration from a peacock chair in the organ loft, as the applause and cheering grew and grew. Singing to a crib sheet, that experience was overwhelming.

Back in the world of cash flow, which meant money going out, I struggled to maintain some form of dignity in the tidal wave of collapsing business ventures, but it was difficult, particularly with Zoe, who showed an incredible tendency to lay the blame on everybody but the two of us. I'd given a job at Mantis to my old mate, Barry Higgins, after he'd made it known he was fed up working at the Inland Revenue in Hammersmith. In fact, he called me once he'd left and, after chatting to Ted, Mike and Dixie, we gave him a job, caring for the paperwork.

Well, none of them seemed to get on too well, so I asked Barry to get involved in a solo piece of work, something I'd dreamed up in the days when Barry Dass was alongside me. I explained my idea to Barry (Higgins). It was to design and build an entirely new engine. I could see the end approaching for the internal combustion engine, which was dirty, noisy and heavy on oil, and it seemed electricity was the best alternative, and the way forward. I'd thought about the complications of recharging units in a vehicle, where the search for perpetual motion was paramount, or at least getting as near to it as possible, and eventually I found a solution for achieving this through the use of the long-forgotten clockwork engine. Of course, I wasn't thinking of having winding-up keys; instead, this mechanism would work on a combination system, which used brake power to engage a winding movement on the springs.

So while one of the cogs would be driving the vehicle, the application of brakes would prepare the other for taking over when the previous one had used its full drive power. And the whole process would begin all over again. Of course, this system would need to be augmented in some way, but that would come later. I never heard from Barry again! You never lose the inventive spirit, and some years later I'd actually design and make a household product of great potential. It was assembled with Graham Underwood ('Squiffy'), and is known as the 'Motorised Garden Fork Mark II, with Optional Strimmer'. It is precisely what its name suggests, consisting of an engine mounted on a garden fork, and fuelled via a whisky bottle!

Beware of the chair that isn't there
A furniture illusion
If you ever squat on a chair that's not
You'll suffer some confusion.

Chapter 7

With the roofs of several ventures falling in on top of me, various people still seemed to want me to keep them employed, and Zoe's dad, Dixie, was one of them. An ex-RAF officer, Dixie approached me one day with an idea — that he'd open a travel agency which specialised in making arrangements for rock bands.

So we found ways of setting it up. I said, 'OK, Dixie, go ahead, use my house, my table and my name ... and over to you!'

Well, all I remember about all that is being woken up in the middle of the night, with one of the Stranglers screaming down the line at Dixie. It seemed they had arrived at some destination a considerable distance away from where they should be, and it is sufficient to say that Dixie didn't like being spoken to like that.

So he went to work at his grandparents' health shop, at which point Bill Reid called to say we should have a chat. When we met, he was not the Bill 'of old', and it was clear he'd been trying hard to come to terms with a very difficult situation, one that had been rumbling around for some time. He told me things were not good, and that the only solution caused by the collapse of my various ventures was to go and live in Paris.

He explained that the nucleus of the Deep Purple business (which was a source of income) had been located 'off shore', through Deep Purple Overseas Limited, and I was assured that it was a perfectly legitimate way for the management and its advisers to run the affairs of the company and, subsequently, the musicians. However, there were moves afoot by the Government of the day to close a loophole, which meant establishing a fine line between what was legal and what was not. Bill used two words to make the point — 'avoidance' and 'evasion' — the first meaning permissible, and the second meaning illegal.

So the situation was explained like this; that despite the fact I'd apparently gone through vast amounts of money, Deep Purple were still selling records, their music was earning royalties, and so forth. The only way to protect myself was to live abroad, with just 60 days allowed when I could be in the UK. He said John Coletta and Tony Edwards had already bought homes in Paris and, despite the past, he thought I should go there quite quickly – and even meet them again! Once out of the way, things could be sorted out at home, by which he meant The Springs, because the other projects were dead ducks anyway. As for The Springs, Bill said he'd find a full-time manager.

In later months, it would dawn on me just how much pressure Bill had found himself under, as the Inland Revenue gave him and our business affairs a very thorough 'going over', and I began to wonder just how well thought through this change in the game plan really was. I know it took a lot out of his poor wife, May, who I don't think was too well but, in the final analysis, I don't know if the authorities ever got to understand what secrets Bill may or may not have had.

By that time the Purple account had multiplied itself many times, as the band had spread out to become Rainbow, Whitesnake, Paice Ashton Lord — each with new musicians and friends. The entire network of arrangements in the UK and abroad, lay stored in Bill's brilliant, but now clouded and tired, mind, and he would take it with him to his grave.

Still, I went to Paris, and Bill found this guy, a Swiss hotelier, who took control of the running of The Springs. His pedigree and references were immaculate, and we showed him over the premises of my brainchild with hope and enthusiasm. He seemed happy, and only wanted to make a few changes, mainly to his quarters, so he could have his family with him. We also took on new staff, and bought a couple of small houses and cottages in the area for their accommodation.

Despite all these efforts, I was forced to watch the whole thing collapse, without even being able to return from Paris to help out. I began to give up on the idea of running my own business. If only somebody had told me I'd be fucking useless at it! But then again, if they had, I wonder if I would have listened.

And so the call finally came from Bill, saying 'Ian ... I don't know how to tell you this, but you are in trouble.'

I said, 'What is it, Bill?'

'Well, the overdraft at the bank is on the limit, I cannot let you have any more money. I've got just about enough to cover the mortgage, and for your living expenses, but after three days of toiling with the situation, the only thing I can recommend is "voluntary liquidation".'

It was a terrible situation to face up to, and arrangements had to be made for me to sign papers, without technically coming on to British soil. With Zoe alongside as a Director and single shareholder, we did the necessary, and I later learned that the liquidators sold my hotel for about £100,000 — that was just enough to pay everybody off, including the bank (of course), with all its fees and commissions. One of my mates later took my car to the local garage for petrol — I'd had an account there for some time. As he started filling up, this guy came screaming out, shouting, 'Take it out. Don't put petrol in ... that's Gillan's car, and he's bankrupt!'

Back in Paris, I turned my mind back to the idea of singing again. In fact, the germ of the idea was planted back in

England, when I found myself at some meeting or other at The Springs, sitting with people I just couldn't relate to. So I shut myself away for a few days, wrote some songs and decided to make a record. I needed to think about a lot of things, and an early issue was who should manage me. Bruce Payne came to mind, since I knew he'd been doing a great job for Ritchie and Roger. But I found myself going to see John Coletta to discuss the album, its label and my ideas for the new band. I was still in touch with the 'Godfather' of Purple, Bill Reid, and he thought it a good idea. In fact, the meeting took place in London, at John's house in Wilton Crescent, near Hyde Park. It had once been owned by Rex Harrison, and John showed me around — his gun collection, the snooker room and so forth. After a few frames, we settled down to business. John lit a cigar and gave me his shopping list of terms. It was high percentages all round, but I thought 'better the devil you know' and we agreed.

I introduced John, Tony and Bill Reid to my new band — The Ian Gillan Band — in Paris. Initially intended to be called 'Ian Gillan's Shand Grenade', we came together in September 1975 with my old mate, John Gustafson, bass (Hard Stuff and Quatermass); Ray Fenwick, guitar (After Tea and Spencer Davis Group); Mike Moran, keyboard; and Mark Nauseef, drummer (Elf). In fact, Roger (Glover) was part of the early set up, but this one wasn't to be, although he produced our first album (*Child in Time*). As I recall (and I may now be incorrect), we all met up at La Coupole in the artists' quarter. It was a place of great character, with high ceilings, bright lights and wall to wall with characters drinking coffee and enjoying brandy (as only the French know how); the air was thick with 'wacky baccy'! The waiters were immaculate, and although there were dogs roaming around eating tit-bits, this place was definitely a class joint!

So there was John, with Sherry on his arm; Tony with his 'complex'; Bill with his cigar; my friend and roadie Dennis, and a lady journalist from *Music Week*. And, of course, my band were also there, since the idea had been to launch us that night in the public eye. So it was a pity that only one journalist turned up, and she seemed to find John more interesting anyway! As time went by, my band started to drink quite a lot, and Bill — ever the diplomat — said he thought it might be a good idea if he went over and kept the lads company, so I could field the questions, so to speak. That left me sitting next to Dennis (now sadly dead), but then with the habit of being easily overwhelmed by events, and showing this with a nervous 'Ooooh ... ooooh!' As John Coletta held the attention of the journalist, so my attention wandered through the tiny gap in the tables — just wide enough to allow a waiter to squeeze through. And there I could see Sherry, sitting in a stunning white (and expensive) skintight outfit, through which you could see every part of her anatomy. My eyes then picked out John Gustafson, moving across in the famous 'Gustafson lurch', one eye fixed in the approximate direction of his destination; head firm, but body ... not so! He intended to give Dennis his dirty plates and, on doing so, said, 'Hang on a minute.' With lots of oooh-ings, Dennis made the fatal mistake of taking the offering in both hands, which meant he'd committed himself to Gus for the whole table. And so he began to disappear as 25 to 30 plates were rapidly stacked up. The 'Ooohs' became more laboured, as John Coletta tried to concentrate on the interview, while also trying to see that Sherry was all right, and trying to look unconcerned. It was difficult, because Sherry was now hidden from sight by the plates, to which Gus was now adding the condiments. The careful placing of the mustard pot was the final straw as, with a final 'Oooh', Dennis dropped the lot! The mustard pot exploded into life, turning Sherry's immaculate catsuit a horrific yellow! John ended his interview to scream at Gus, 'You fucking animal ... You've fucking covered my lady in mustard!' In reply he got, 'Mustard? No thanks, mate ... can't stand the stuff!' And Gus sauntered off. What a hero!

Eventually, and not for the last time, The Ian Gillan Band (and friends) were thrown out, and we returned to the apartment I was sharing with the band. John and the journalist came as well, and we arrived to find some of the lads already there, reclining among the priceless antiques and rugs. Given the advanced state of drunkenness of just about everyone in the room, it probably isn't surprising that the evening ended on a sour note.

After the guests had gone, Gus and I decided to have a screaming match, and this went on for two to three hours. I vaguely remember Zoe saying she was going to bed, and Mark also disappearing, as Paris came to life. Through the noise came the sound of police sirens, but I didn't imagine they could be anything to do with us. However, Gus was much wiser in these matters, and has an amazing sixth sense, which tells him when something is about to go terribly wrong. So he stopped screaming and went to his room. Unfortunately, he'd forgotten how we'd rearranged things to cope with more people, and he stumbled over a mattress on the floor by the window. To recover his balance, he grabbed the curtain, wrapped himself round it a few times, lost his footing and smashed the window to pieces, sending a million pieces of glass to street level about three floors below. He then collapsed into oblivion as the police arrived, called, it seems, by the dreadful concierge, who was convinced murder was afoot.

Arriving at the block of flats, and seeing shattered glass on the pavement, as well as the sight of curtains billowing from upper floor windows, it's easy to understand why the police behaved as they did. They battered our door down, and entered with guns cocked — real movie stuff! They found me whistling away, and dusting the table.

After a stunned silence they asked, 'What the fuck's going on?'

'What do you mean?' I replied.

The lead policeman was babbling on about somebody being dead, and they started rushing into rooms, which woke up Zoe. Finally, they found Gus, wrapped in a curtain, lying in the glass. I picked up a bottle of whisky, and with much 'tuttings', explained that the wretched fellow was hopelessly drunk, and they left.

Now, it hadn't occured to me that some of the visitors were plain clothes officers, so having thought I'd got rid of them, one, who'd been hanging back, said most firmly 'Come with me.'

'Hey,' I said, 'I thought everything was cool here,' but he was determined. All I was wearing was a very short, brightly-coloured kimono dressing gown (which was very much the 'thing' at the time) and the article barely covered my 'privates'. I said, 'Shall I go and throw something else on?' but that was not allowed. So I was led past this grinning concierge to the street, where the guy pointed to the pavement debris and said, 'Pick it up!' By now it was about 8.00am, and the city was going to work. It was also true of Paris then that, of all the world's major cities, it was top of the dog crap league — I mean, it was everywhere! Watched by this copper, I had to bend down in my scanty clothing, and pick up very single piece of broken glass from among the dog shit. And then a lady from the cheese shop opposite came over with a newspaper for me to put everything in. Upstairs, the cause of all the chaos and misery lay fast asleep!

Take me to the preacher
Take me to your god
You got me thinking like you
And you're thinking like a dog 'Shame'

We made our first album with Oyster (Polydor), with the songs 'Lay Me Down', 'You Make Me Feel So Good', 'Shame', 'Down the Road', 'My Baby Loves Me', 'Let It Slide' and the title track, 'Child in Time'. We went to Musicland Studio (Munich) to write most of the material and record it, and then Mountain Studio in Montreux for the mix. It was strange to see the name HEC on the album credits.

In fact, we were quite lucky to make it to Munich in the first place, because the band were arrested at the airport, having behaved badly on the flight. But we got over that problem, and the album came out in July 1976, charting at number 56, just behind *Wish You Were Here* (Pink Floyd), and one ahead of Led Zeppelin's *Four Seasons*. Rod Stewart topped the charts, and Thin Lizzy were there, plus Nana Mouskouri, Doctor Hook, the Beatles, Genesis — and *The Very Best of Roger Whittaker!* *Penthouse Tapes* by The Sensational Alex Harvey Band was also in, and more about one or two of those guys later!

While recording in Munich, we stayed at Arabellahaus, where Mack and Hans used to be. Mack was the engineer for Queen and, on this particular occasion, we were hanging around the cocktail lounge, when a bunch of hookers turned up. In fact, we got to know them quite well — as friends — and, after a few minutes, this old boy turned up with one of the girls in tow. He was quite diminutive, and had this big cigar. So Gus and Ray started taking the piss out of him, but he took the whole thing in his stride. I told them to leave him alone, though, and in a moment of extravagance, and because I wanted to get their minds off the old geezer and his pleasure, I said to Dennis, 'Look, why don't you take the Roller and the lads out. Here's some money ... just have fun!' I realised as I said it what a gross mistake this was, but I made it clear to Dennis (and Zoe's brother, Paul) that I wanted no screwing in my car. And no damage either!

So it turned out that they found their way to a disco/bar, and who should turn up, but the old geezer and his hooker, who, by the way, looked a million dollars! So they sat down, and were quietly enjoying champagne and canapés, when Ray decided to get involved. Now it's one of the facts of rock trivia that Ray has one of the hairiest arses in the world, and he decided to approach the table, drop his strides and sit in the plate of canapés. Having pulled himself off the plate, pieces of cucumber and carrot were still attached to his bum and, to the distress of onlookers, Ray then proceeded to waggle this unpleasant sight in front of the old fellow. A bit like a weapon! Without taking the slightest offence, the guy took a nice long drag on his cigar and stuck it very firmly up the rectum of my guitar player and vocal sidekick! There was quite a lot of leaping around, before they went on to better things! In fact, Ray, John, Mark and poor Dennis went on to a bar, and there they started mooning the joint, before going behind the counter where the wall was decorated and shelved. One of them leapt for it but, because his trousers were down, he didn't have complete co-ordination, and ended up bringing the whole lot to the ground, along with most of the booze.

I took the rabble on tour, where we were a great success, particularly in South East Asia, Japan and France, and a number of singles were put out, and did quite well. Fairly early on, Mike Moran was replaced by Mickey Lee Soule (ex-Rainbow), then to be replaced by Colin Towns, who would stay with me for some time to come.

The American tour continued to experience the high spirits of this line up and, because of that, I travelled separately. Not out of self-importance, but because the chaos was too much to handle on a full-time basis. They quickly ran out of drivers, and it fell to one of the lighting engineers to take on that role as well. It was a move he thought quite smart, and got him out of the crew bus. But he was wrong and, after three days, he pulled the car to the side of the freeway and walked off into the sunset — never to be seen again!

It seems it was the 'in-car tennis' that was the final straw, a game which involved ripping out the interior lighting, taking a coat hanger, straightening the wiring out, and wrapping an end around a ball of scrunched up newspaper. The surplus length was stuck back into the interior lights, and the newspaper was then set on fire. The two front headrests were taken out for use as tennis racquets, and whoever scored the most points won. Just like Wimbledon, really!

We organised our own baggage delivery, which worked best at motels. It went wrong the day Mark and Gus were in charge of the roof of the station wagon. All I heard was an approaching vehicle, followed by a crashing of windows as the gear was delivered!

The relationship with Polydor/Oyster was not a great success, so we signed to Island Records. In fact, the decision to go was made 'absolute' the day I played a charity football game with George Best, Dave Dee and Patrick Mower, after which we went to Tramp. A guy from Polydor came over and said 'Hi' to George, and Dave Dee then said, 'This is Ian Gillan,' to which he said, 'Hi, Ian,' before going back to George, and then moving on. A bit later, he came back over and was really nice. Somebody had obviously told him I was with the label, so he should 'go and make your peace with Ian'.

I laid it on the line to him. 'I tell you what ... nothing personal, but you and everybody at your company can go and stuff themselves, because you are not getting another album out of me.'

If I'm making it all seem very simple and joyful, nothing could be further from the truth. I still had some sort of relationship with John (Coletta) and Tony (Edwards), and lived in Paris, when not in the studios or touring. I'd often be invited to Tony's flat, and it seemed that he and John were not getting on too well. Tony and I would sometimes go to the cafés, where he'd get very drunk — and that wasn't his style. Neither was picking fights, and I'd often find myself apologising for situations that began with, 'What are you staring at?'

Tony was a gentleman, so it was quite difficult when he started slagging off Bill Reid. Then, when I saw John, he'd do the same, and both would tell me that Bill was 'out', which closed another 'glory days' period. Bill was so wise, so perceptive all the time, both before and after shows, when the different women in our lives caused trouble. But then it also became clear that in treating me as a capable and businesslike person, he was mistaken. n going along with my every request for more money, I might have thought he was the only person I could blame for the collapse of my various endeavours. I lashed out at Bill, and, yet again, found revenge in my music through a song on *Clear Air Turbulence*, our first album for Island. About that, and with the benefit of hindsight and maturity, I am deeply sad.

Chapter 8

In truth, I had not a single reason to feel bad about Bill. I needed a new manager, and Zoe knew a guy called Gerry Black, who first took an interest in my problems, and then took over the papers and negotiations which would eventually disentangle me from Purple, Oyster and so forth. It was Gerry who set up the deal with Island Records, and whatever documents were put in front of me, I signed. I've lived with that ever since, but I can see now that I was ill and unpleasant — and whoever stood in my way took the brunt of all that.

I could have re-financed The Springs, instead of letting it go at a knock-down price to people who, I believe, have since turned it into a country club and golf course. But I didn't.

As we began to record *Clear Air Turbulence*, I'd frequently wander off into the production department, the art room, the A and R section, and generally keep in touch with progress. Many a morning I'd play pool with Bob Marley.

Island Records was owned by Chris Blackwell, and it would turn out that his heart wasn't really into rock music. Chris built his fine reputation and organisation on his love for the Caribbean, its culture and its music, and apart from artists working in that field, he also signed people like Steve Winwood and David Byron. My band was really not his 'catalogue', and we were signed for 'not a lot'.

Still, it was OK, and we worked with Chris Fosse on the cover design — the bumble bee spaceship — and they were great people to be with. I still had Kingsway, and the album was produced there. I wanted it to be different to Purple, different even to *Child in Time*, and that came across in the music, which was more aggressive, more jazz-rock than was expected by some fans.

The tracks on the album were 'Clear Air Turbulence', 'Five Moons', 'Over the Hill', 'Goodhand Liza' and two which dealt with some areas of my past, 'Angel Manchenio' and 'Money Lender'. The album came out on 5 April 1977, and a UK tour was scheduled, including the London Rainbow. It was short, but intensive:

April

29th	Cardiff University
30th	Bradford University

May

3rd	Sheffield City Hall
4th	Liverpool Empire
6th	Fortune Theatre, Bury St Edmunds
7th	Southampton University
8th	Queensway Hall, Dunstable
10th	Whitla Hall, Belfast
11th	Dublin Stadium
13th	Bristol University
14th	London Rainbow
15th	Middlesbrough Town Hall
17th	Aberdeen Music Hall
18th	Glasgow Playhouse
19th	Edinburgh Playhouse
20th	Newcastle Mayfair
21st	Manchester Apollo
22nd	Birmingham Odeon
23rd	Liverpool Empire

We played a set that mixed new material with stuff from Deep Purple days, things like 'Child in Time', 'Woman from Tokyo' and ending usually with 'Smoke on the Water' as an encore. Under our own management, things were fine (most of the time), but some decisions, made with the best business intentions, did go wrong.

One was my idea to buy a car for the band, because the taxi bill was becoming ridiculous. They would use taxis to find cigarettes, go to the clubs or just buy strings with, so I thought we should get something like a Ford Cortina Estate, which we could use to transport gear as well. After the recording, we could always flog it, so the whole thing made sense.

Dennis went out to find one, and when he returned, he parked it in my space at the studio. When I went out there and saw it, I thought, 'That's well out of order,' and as I passed by, I noticed something strange about it. It was not until I was in the corridor of the studio that I decided to take another look. It still seemed all right, but when I got closer and peered inside, there was nothing there — no seats, no steering wheel, no dashboard. Nothing! Not a bloody thing! My car was a shell. The band explained that they didn't like Dennis' choice of colour, which pretty well summed up how life was in that period.

They were a great band and we did a short tour of France, going later to Japan in February 1978, where an album *Live at the Budokan (Vol 1 & 2)* was recorded, but was not released in the UK.

We were filmed at London's Rainbow, featuring 'Money Lender', 'Clear Air Turbulence', 'Child in Time', 'Smoke on the Water' and 'Woman from Tokyo'. After *Clear Air Turbulence*, we recorded *Scarabus*, a more straightforward rock album, which came out in October 1977. 'Mercury High', 'Twin Exhausted', 'Slags to Bitches' all seemed to be popular, but we were being tagged with styles like 'jazz fusion' and concepts like that.

You've got the money
I've got the need
So, baby, I will stand with you
There's no way you can stop it
You've got my heart in your pocket.

It gradually began to dawn on me that although I was with fine musicians and great mates, the one thing they didn't seem to take seriously was rock 'n' roll. Mark, in particular, was a great jazz enthusiast, and the whole group seemed to be about making music in a complicated and tricky way, instead of dealing with rock as it should be — simple. I respected them a great deal, but I'd not got back into the swing of things enough to focus minds and take control of direction and the band.

And anyway, how could I ever get angry with someone like Gus! I mean, I'd admired the man from my earliest days in music when he was with the Merseybeats, and later recording 'Bumper to Bumper' and 'Take Me For a Little While', and I'd always remember how it came about when I first met him.

It was at a party during the days of Episode Six, when the door opened and this guy came in — unshaven, and looking as if he'd just crawled out from under a park bench. He took himself off to a corner and sat there scowling all night, drinking and clutching this small attaché case — the little brown sort you see the Jewish tailors carrying around. In the end, I went over and spoke to him for a while, but he was very down, and explained that he had some appointment or other the next day. In the end, he slept on the floor, and when he got up in the morning, I peeped from under my covers to see him go into the bathroom with his little case.

After about 45 minutes, he came out, and I just went, 'Wow!' Gus had transformed himself from a tramp to a superstar — it was incredible. He'd shaved, washed his hair and put on these superb clothes that somehow had fitted into his case. He looked so cool, so excessive — wonderful! Here, then, was the man responsible for the bass line in 'Love Is the Drug' by Roxy Music.

Gus made a big impression on me, but I'd come to learn that he's a complex guy, who doesn't like things to be steady for too long.

A lot of people had warned me against getting too involved with Gus; some would come up and say that he just ruins things and so forth, but I've never seen it that way. We're all excessive people in the business, and I think Gus went about things the same as most of us, but with a bit more style!

He wasn't with me for very long, but he came to Japan, and is on *Live at the Budokan*. In fact, we headlined in Japan — it's always nice to creep up the bill — so we all felt pretty good!

The first show was at the Osaka Kosei Nenkin Hall, where we opened with some music Colin had written for the film *Full Circle*, starring Mia Farrow. It was an eerie piece, which he'd over-dubbed with 200 voices, and we'd then follow with 'Clear Air Turbulence', 'Money Lender' and 'Child in Time'.

Gus would then do something from his solo project, 'What's Your Game', and we'd carry on with more from *CAT* and *Scarabus*, before ending with a rock 'n' roll medley. We played the next night at Kyoto Kaiken Dai-Ichi Hall, and took the next day off to go sightseeing.

During that trip, Ray was asked to autograph a baby, and we were followed all day by a group of fans who'd hired five taxis. We spent the next day at Hiroshima, which was a sobering moment, but the gig at the Yubin Chokin Hall went brilliantly, and brought back memories of the visit I made with Deep Purple, which didn't compare. We had time off to enjoy the visit, in complete contrast to the old days, when we'd lurch from gig to gig without rest. We finished at the Budokan, where the promoter, Mr Udo, resplendent in a fine suit and a constant smile, said he'd have us back any time we wanted.

After seeing us off, he wandered off to welcome Eric Clapton who was soon to arrive. His name crops up again later.

This is another period when it all seems to be ticking along nicely, but in truth there were underlying problems, beginning with the manager, Gerry Black.

Island Records had not taken up their option after *Scarabus*, and the band and I should have picked up on the vibes much earlier. Still, it's always easy to say that with the benefit of hindsight. After the Budokan show, Gerry came in and said, 'Well, lads, that's Japan ... now the world!'

It was so awful, we just curled up with laughter. I mean, could he not see what a mess we were in? OK, maybe I should have seen it, but I didn't expect the manager to be so naïve.

As for Island, they really weren't too pleased with what we were doing. They were good people to be with, but they couldn't sell our records, nor could they get us into America. Part of the deal in leaving was that I recovered my catalogue, which I put into Clear Air Music Publishing, but we were suddenly exposed and with no position. It all reached boiling point at Birmingham.

I could feel that people were confused by the music, having come to see me for a great night of rock 'n' roll, only to hear us play something quite different, and I'd get the reaction from the fans backstage, which finally got through to me.

So I had words with the guys and said, 'Look, we're not getting down. All this "itty bitty jangly" stuff's really putting people off. Why aren't we doing rock 'n' roll? Remind yourselves of Louie Louie!'

So I was in the dressing room, when I suddenly heard its intro. It sounded great, and I rushed out thinking, 'Yes!' only to realise they were taking the piss.

The end was approaching, and it came to a head in the studio, when we were working on new material — more fusion shit, and at the time that punk was showing the way. Colin came in, and I could hear lots of laughter and piss-taking going on. So I said, 'What's the matter?'

'Oh, it's alright,' he said.

But I persisted and, seeing Colin was near to tears, I said, 'What's going on?'

'Oh, I don't know,' Colin replied, 'it's just that I've got this song ...'

The others were muttering, 'You just hear this ... God Almighty, and it's big yawn stuff.'

'Alright,' I said, 'let's here it then.'

Colin sat down and said, 'It's called "Fighting Man",' and started, 'There is a man ...'

It made me sit up and think, 'Wow, this guy remembers "rock 'n' roll", so we set the studio up to record it, but the others weren't too impressed. So I gave it to them straight. I said I was sick to death with all this fusion shit. It was crap, we were English, and we couldn't deal with that gear any longer. And even if we could, who wanted to listen to it anyway? I reminded them that we'd played to about 200 people at Slough recently, and asked if that didn't tell them something!

So I played back a couple of rough tracks to show them what we were going to do, and said, 'Well, guys, that's it ... that's the end!' They asked why, and I told them I was not going to carry on with another album; in fact, I was not going to carry on with the band. I put it down to working in different directions, and ended by saying, 'Oh, by the way, Colin, I think we should start work on the new material this afternoon!' I said this deliberately, because I figured they'd been giving him a lousy time.

So Colin and I rolled up our sleeves and found musicians to work on the project, which we simply called 'Gillan'. It was August 1978, and the initial line-up was Colin Towns (keyboard), John McCoy (bass), Liam Genocky (drums) — replaced by Pete Barnacle soon after — and Steve Byrd on guitar. An early gig was the Reading Festival on 27 August, and between us we looked for a return to 'roots and rock', which found itself with stuff like 'Secret of the Dance', 'Fighting Man', 'Message from a Bottle' (which, as the title suggests, deals with booze) and 'Back in the Game'.

After a while, Pete was replaced by my old mate, Mick Underwood, who'd been with Strapps and, of course, we'd been together in Episode Six. I put the musicians on equal shares, and we ran a sort of democratic management with Ted Wood as our central organiser. Ted had, of course, been with me on the ill-fated Mantis venture, and the idea was that he'd bring some discipline and organisation to Gillan. He took up the challenge, making it clear he wouldn't stand sloppy attitudes, and it quickly became apparent that he was not well suited to the studio!

It wasn't long before noses were put out of joint, and one or two key technical people left, moaning about the organisation. While all these people were coming and going in an atmosphere of complete chaos — of my own making, I suppose — I came to the decision to part with Zoe after all our years together. It wasn't her fault that things hadn't worked out, but we were simply incompatible, and had been for many years. I honestly believe I gave the relationship every chance, particularly in the bizarre world of rock 'n' roll, and I'd done so because I desperately wanted stability.

The idea of settling down and having children was not on Zoe's agenda, and she'd refused to marry me on several occasions, because she'd seen so many marriages fail in the business. She was forever suspicious of the people I mixed with, to the extent that it sometimes caused friction with the musicians and others I associated with.

Zoe basically never let me out of her sight, and so came the moment when I sat her down and said, 'Zoe, I'm going. I've finished with the band, and I've finished with you. I don't want this to be a mucky, horrible thing, but I can't take any more, and I'm going.'

She wouldn't believe me, and when I left, she was in tears. It was very, very sad. She ended up with the house and contents, which was about all that remained anyway after the collapse of the various projects, while I was left with the table!

Because she'd been a director of various companies, she took me to a tribunal on the grounds of unfair dismissal. But it all came to nothing really, and another chapter of my life closed without glamour or satisfaction.

Been so many words, so much to say.'

Top: Episode Six – my first record deal.
Bottom: Home comforts help on the road.

op: Backstreet heroes.

set: Hard at work with the 'Incredible Bard', David Cohen

Top: Roadies must have personality and intellect!

Bottom left: Training Squiffy's dog Kevin to eat properly.

Bottom right: My motorised garden fork – a Gillan invention.

Top: Live with Deep Purple, 1994.

Bottom: Live in Russia with the Gillan Band.

Top: With Jon Lord, George Harrison and Phil 'Bung 'Em In' Banfield. When they told me to put something on, I found a sock.

Bottom: With Bron and Deep Purple.

Top: At an early age I chose between singing and drumming – no contest – and then came the congas.

Bottom: The Ian Gillan Tour.

Top: It's not the shows that give life to a tour – it's the company you keep. With Brett Bloomfield, Lenny 'Mayor of Hell' Haze and Dean Howard.

Bottom: The smile is there, the glint in the eye is back – as is the spirit and rock n' roll.

Chapter 9

With so much change going on, another was under way. I had been using a booking agent, Phil Banfield, and after the Ian Gillan Band show at the Queensway Hall, Dunstable, he caught me backstage, and when asked what he thought, he told me! He said he thought it was 'horrible', that he'd been watching the looks on the faces of the audience, that I was a rock singer and not a jazz performer, and that all this 'tweedle dee' stuff for 'Smoke' just wasn't on!

When he later heard I was putting Gillan together, he called and said we could now think in terms of places like The Marquee, and start to build things up, and that's what he began to do.

We started by playing the clubs, universities and so forth. We went to Spain and elsewhere in Europe, and were going down well. What we didn't have was a record deal, and Phil talked to our then manager, Dave Hanfield, asking why that was.

It turned out that Dave had been going to the different labels asking for 'telephone numbers', and then finding himself on the street with the door closed very firmly behind him. It's hard to go back to people after that, but in March 1978, I asked Phil to be my manager. Once again, I knew I was putting my career into the hands of someone who had no track record in this kind of work. I agreed with Phil that he should continue as my booking agent as well, and met him at his office at 10 Sutherland Avenue in London, with his partner Carl Leighton Pope. There, we decided to phone every single record company in the country until we got a deal, and eventually, we arrived at the doorstep of Acrobat, who had been recommended to us, because they'd done such a great job for Roger Chapman.

I spoke to the people personally, and although it began with a singles deal, it was still a great start.

For the first time in years, I felt there was focus and direction. Bernie Tormé had joined the band, and now we had Phil Banfield on board. Raw energy returned as we recorded 'Vengeance' for the new label ('Smoke' on the 'B' side), and I got my first taste of working with Phil.

The two of us went to the south coast to get a picture for the record sleeve, and generally to figure out what to do. I was roaming around in the freezing water, in wellies, when Phil hit on an idea. He wanted a picture of me with only water in the background. And to get the effect, he said I'd have to jump. So it came about that when my manager said I had to jump, I'd jump! He made me do it quite often.

1979 was a year of great hope, as Phil started to put us in front of audiences in a big way. One of the people I greatly admire is Jack Barrie, who for many years was responsible for the booking policy that made The Marquee world famous. As mentioned earlier, he also looked after bookings at the Reading Rock Festival, and now he offered us a spot on the same bill as Steve Hackett, Thin Lizzy and Rory Gallagher — now, sadly, no longer with us. I suspect we were only used as padding, and we were told there would be no time for an encore. However, we went down so well, we had to do one, and played an unrehearsed medley of rock 'n' roll, which the audience loved.

It was good to see the reviews, with *Melody Maker* saying that it was only when we hit the stage that the audience could really get down to any kind of serious headbanging, and that

'Gillan rocks with force'. Playing to 30,000 people was good for morale, and brought back memories of how it was before, and could be again.

As an aside, I used this period to define certain words in the dictionary of rock 'n' roll. First to deal with is a 'headbanger'; that's a 'person with rhythm'. Then there's a 'headmaster' — he's an 'ex-headcase'! A headcase is an 'ex-person with rhythm', and there are many other important terms worth checking out!

Anyhow, this was it — we had Acrobat committed to an album, *Mr Universe*, which came out in October, as Phil worked on setting up a major UK/European tour, to be followed by Japan, Australia and America.

In the UK, we promoted the records supported by Randy California of Spirit (and very short-term Purple experience) in Canada. Samson were also there with Bruce Dickinson, and it was another intensive short tour.

October

2nd	Guildhall, Preston
3rd	Market Hall, Carlisle
4th	Town Hall, Middlesbrough
5th	Mayfair, Newcastle
6th	Cricket Ground, Northampton
7th	Odeon, Birmingham
8th	Winter Gardens, Cleethorpes
9th	Apollo, Manchester
11th	De Montfort Hall, Leicester
12th	Victoria Hall, Hanley
13th	City Hall, Sheffield
15th	City Hall, St Albans
16th	Tiffanys, Scunthorpe
18th	Capitol, Aberdeen
19th	Edinburgh University
20th	Glasgow University

21st	Caird Hall, Dundee
22nd	Pavilion, Ayr
23rd	St George's Hall, Bradford
24th	The Rainbow, London
26th	Pavilion, West Runton.

Why do I schedule these dates so fully from time to time? I guess one reason is because many of my fans have followed tours, coming to see me on more than just a visit to one venue, so perhaps it's a nice reminder of 'what we've all done'. It's happened to me worldwide — even in Russia, where familiar faces have appeared somehow at different shows. How you manage it — particularly in territories like that, where distances are so great, I cannot begin to know, but wherever it has happened — here, or over there — it's great. So I know there are friends who like this kind of information, as fully as can be remembered, but for absolute completeness, Simon Robinson's *Darker than Blue* (*Deep Purple*) magazine, is the key reference point. But then I guess you know that!

Mr Universe made number 11 in the UK charts (on 11 November), and included a number of tracks on the withdrawn Gillan import from Japan: 'Secret of the Dance', 'Roller' and 'Vengeance' showed we meant business and 'Puget Sound' was reflective of that trip I did so many years ago with Audrey and Pauline.

I loved the band; Bernie and John grabbed audiences with their electrifying stage presence — they oozed rock 'n' roll, and in John's case, he was even described by one reviewer as a 'walking absurdity'. It was fantastic!

Of course, people always wanted to know how I felt about Purple, particularly as the management had put out a compilation, and they also wanted to know what I thought about Rainbow. The question of a reunion would often raise its head, but I steered well clear of any talk that could be misinterpreted or get me into trouble. That said, I did have an unusual surprise one Christmas, when Ritchie turned up on my doorstep.

It was quite late at night, I went to the door, and peered into the darkness. The snow was falling. There, standing about two or three paces back, stood the guitar player with his silly pilgrim's hat.

'What do you want?' I asked.

'I'm looking for a singer,' he said.

'Oh well, come in then!'

'Do you mind if I bring the girlfriend in?' he asked.

'Where is she?'

He said she was standing at the end of the drive, and when I asked why, he replied that he was worried I might hit him!

They came in, and Ritchie started knocking back the vodka, which was surprising really, because I knew him as a scotch and beer man. After a few hours, he said, 'Do you want to join Rainbow then?'

'No,' I said, going on to ask if he wanted to join Gillan. I was looking at the time for someone to fill the place Bernie would take. He said, 'No ... No, Ian, you're doing it all wrong — you should be playing the big stadiums.'

Well, I knew what he was saying, because Rainbow were cutting it quite big, but they weren't doing as many shows as we were, and they weren't going into some of the more far-flung countries, the names of which he'd probably never even heard!

In the end, it got to the point where we obviously weren't going to do a reunion, but I asked, 'Why don't you come to The Marquee on Boxing Day, and play with us?'

In fact, we had three nights there and, to give Ritchie his due, he did turn up and joined us on stage. John chose that occasion to display a side of his character that would cause problems, because when Ritchie came up, he started ruffling his hair, and generally being a bit stupid. John could be very boorish sometimes, and he didn't take it kindly when I started to question the wisdom of opening a rock show with a bass solo.

Anyway, Ritchie departed as quietly and strangely as he arrived, and it would be a long time before we'd meet again.

I was happy with Gillan and its potential, and the idea of joining the 'whiz pops' in America didn't interest me, just as gigging around Britain wouldn't have appealed to Ritchie. Once again, the UK was where it was all happening.

It would have been around that time that I also had a call from Tim Rice. It was 'Hello, dear boy, how are you?' to which he got 'All the better for hearing from you, Tim!'

He's a lovely man, and his purpose was to tell me about a new project he and Andrew were putting together. The show was called *Evita*, and I could guess what was coming. He asked, 'Would you like to play the part of General Peron? I'd really love you to do it!'

We talked about *Jesus Christ Superstar*, how alive and rock 'n' roll it had been, as well as how I was able to relate it to my situation with Deep Purple at the time. It all then seemed to be part of some wider scheme of things, but when I called him back about *Evita*, I said, 'No.' The Gillan band was my priority. Of course, *Evita* was another huge hit for them, and it was another great offer I refused. I hope Tim wasn't too upset by my decision then — I've really learned so much from him.

The chemistry was just right with Gillan, and I was happy to be quoted that way often. We became a serious force to be reckoned with, and went into 1980 with a settled band and a change of label to Virgin. That situation came about as a result of moderate success with Acrobat, who, to our horror, ran out of money! They said they couldn't pay us, but would do all they could to give us high profile so we could find another label. They were pretty nice about it, but what good is success without pay, and the band immediately started on the tack that we were being ripped off, leaving me and Phil to try and persuade them that getting blood out of a stone was a waste of time and energy. I'd say to them, 'What the fuck do you want me to do? Go round and beat these people up? It's not going to get us any money!'

It was a bitter blow. We'd fronted the cost of *Mr Universe* before signing with Acrobat, so our signing-on fee with Virgin just about squared the decks, before we started on *Glory Road*. We were locked into what's called a cash-flow problem, in which our advance on the first album went to pay off *Mr Universe*. That meant we had just enough for the new project in terms of production costs, but with nothing as such to live on. We'd have to wait a long time until royalties came through to ease things, but the band didn't seem to see it that way. They saw *Glory Road* become a huge success — going to number 3 in the UK charts, and 183 in America — and this, together with the fact that our single 'Sleeping on the Job' made number 55, encouraged them to press for money.

At the same time, they will have known that Deep Purple material was in the charts, with *Deepest Purple* being number 1 for a week, whilst 'Black Night' was re-released. It's understandable; I guess they thought I was holding back.

The fact is, we were equal shareholders in Gillan, something I'd later vow never to do again (until the next time), and there were some serious band politics flying around.

There were also lighter moments, even with John, and when he was in a good mood, he was simply brilliant and tolerant. We were now selling out concerts within hours of tickets being available, and doing dates like the Hammersmith Odeon, where a second night was added. It was 'non stop' — literally.

September

| 26th | New Theatre, Oxford |
| 27th | Dome, Brighton |

| 28th | De Montfort Hall, Leicester |
| 29th | St George's Hall, Bradford |

October

1st/2nd	Mayfair, Newcastle
3rd	Town Hall, Middlesbrough
4th	Guildhall, Preston
5th	Empire, Liverpool

And on to Sheffield City Hall (6th); Manchester Apollo (7th); Hanley Victoria hall (8th); Birmingham Odeon (10th); Derby Assembly Hall (11th); Coventry Theatre (12th); Hemel Hempstead Pavilion (13th); Hammersmith Odeon (14th/15th); Bristol Colston Hall (16th); Southampton Gaumont (17th); Bracknell Sports Centre (18th); Cardiff Top Rank (19th); Ipswich Gaumont (21st); Edinburgh Odeon (23rd); Glasgow Apollo (24th); Dundee Caird Hall (25th); Carlisle Market Hall (26th); and Hull City Hall (27th).

For me, *Glory Road*, with 'Unchain Your Brain', 'No Easy Way', 'Sleeping on the Job', 'Are You Sure?', 'Time and Again', 'If You Believe Me', 'On the Rocks', 'Running White Face City Boy' and 'Nervous', was my best piece of work since *Machine Head*, and we gave away a freebie with the first 15,000 copies. That included a crack at Samson's *Vice Versa* (listen to 'Egg Timer'), all of which they took in good part. (In fact, the freebie was upped by public demand to 25,000, and still people were disappointed.)

You tell me what you're never gonna be
And I'll show you what you just can't see
If you want good livin' gotta grab it with your hands
If you don't then don't bother makin' no plans

Of course, there was the Purple material in the charts, so everybody was asking whether a reunion was on the cards, but it was a subject to be steered away from as much as possible. I used to say they may just as well ask David Coverdale of Whitesnake the same question. Anyhow, the logistics would be horrific. I mean, here I was with a major band, under management I trusted completely, with Phil. So what was the point in getting involved with a situation which needed about 15 agents, 10 managers, 2,000 road managers, 9 private jets and all that? OK, so I'm prone to exaggeration sometimes, but you get the drift?

But still people would not let go, and I heard that Tommy Vance had been given the nod that I was set to join up again, and dates were being booked in America. It pissed me off, not least because that kind of talk is bad for all concerned — particularly in my band. I went on record as saying, 'My band is so tight, you couldn't prise us apart with a razor.'

The situation on the ground was often difficult, though, and the question of money continued to fester. The band started wanting increasing pay every week, plus shares when royalties were released. Unfortunately, you cannot have it both ways, and the niggling extended to arguments and suspicions as we then argued who should produce *Trouble*, which we were rehearsing. It's the old story; you begin something with excitement and a belief that you all understand the game, and so it's done informally. Who wants to show cynicism by asking for water-tight contracts, when you are all in apparent total agreement, and sharing direction? It was another of my misjudgements, and maybe I wasn't in the greatest shape. I felt it, but I know Phil was concerned, more about my smoking than anything else, and there was certainly a period when shows were cancelled because of infection and illness.

Of course, the media and others preferred to put the situation down to drink, but it wasn't the case. One of Phil's tasks was to explain many things and set various records straight. He took on board difficulties with the band, he sorted the various closing difficulties I had with Zoe (who had put herself forward as my manager) and, above all, he sorted out a few people who seemed to be ripping me off, telling me who was and who was not.

The amazing but sad irony about what was going on around me, was this idea that I was a millionaire, and no amount of denial would change that. It wasn't paranoia, because I could see how things appeared, particularly since there were two albums doing the business in the charts — *Deepest Purple* and *Glory Road*. There must have been moments when even the most loyal musician, associate or observer must have wondered if I was taking the piss!

Anyway, Virgin were great, and planned to keep our profile high with singles and albums that sold. So 'Trouble', an old Elvis favourite, was recorded, and went to number 3 in the UK charts, and the 'bearded one' Richard Branson gave a party for us all in a curry house in Hammersmith, attended by my old mate, Tommy Vance. Richard chose the occasion to add to the gold and other discs that hang on the walls of my home, and spoke some good words about *Glory Road* (that had earned the award), and about the value of Gillan to the label. A lot of people don't like the idea of these awards, but when they are given in the setting of a curry house, and in the company of people from all sections of the label — the art section, secretaries and so forth, it's brilliant and worth having. Awards are a confirmation of fan approval and a mark of achievement, and I'm not embarrassed by either.

Our 1981 UK schedule was arranged around the release of *Mutually Assured Destruction* in February, and set around a nuclear idiocy theme. It would make number 32 in the UK charts, and we backed it with a tour, taking in Nottingham Rock City on 4 March, and then going to the London Rainbow, Newcastle City Hall (for a charity gig), Middlesbrough Town Hall, St George's Hall, Bradford and the Apollo, Manchester. Venues at places like Bournemouth and Blackburn were slipped into gaps. Good old Phil — or 'Bung 'em in' Banfield as we call him sometimes! By the by, I was voted in the charts (again) for best male singer (*Sounds*), and *Mutually Assured Destruction* stayed around for quite a while.

From where I stand
I can see mushrooms in the sky
From where I stand
I can watch the bleeding children cry
And they will die
And you who have no wings will fly
From where I stand
I know what they are planning
I know they're planning one big bang
And they call it mutually assured destruction

We played to full houses wherever we went and did a European tour, plus a few other venues like the AEK Stadium in Greece, where I believe we broke the audience record set by The Rolling Stones, and then just topped by The Police. The place was packed, and we got the vibe that they had not expected that kind of turnout. As we came on stage, they were literally pouring over the high security wall, and dropping to the ground like flies. Many must have suffered terrible injuries.

We kicked off with 'Unchain Your Brain', with the fans becoming instantly hysterical. I turned to grab a towel, only to witness one of the most frightening sights in my life. There, through the backstage area, and across the pitch behind it, were a couple of hundred storm troopers in full riot gear. Whatever was going down had been planned, and these guys meant serious business as they broke into a phalanx and assaulted the audience. Kids were beaten up, and I ended the show immediately.

On stage, this was a great band to be with. Although Mick and Colin kept a low profile, they were experienced and fine musicians, as were John and Bernie, who added a huge dynamic to our performance, with John's awesome appearance, and his rolling, lumbering stage manner, sometimes given an extra dimension when he'd dismantle his guitar and stage gear. Bernie's guitar heroics and hyperactivity around the stage, plus my own way of projecting my music, made sure the fans 'got off' on Gillan. And they did!

The humour was there as well, both on and off stage. For example, there were the ritual birthday celebrations rock musicians take so seriously! Why is it that bald heads are so attractive to cake? Yet behind his fearsome appearance, John could be very generous, as fans who collected the European Tour brochure would discover by his competition. For those who impressed him with the most ridiculous photo, he was giving away a signed album,with a rare cassette of silly bits we couldn't fit on — for Gillan fans only. As second prize he gave away a backstage pass from The American *Glory Road* Tour 1980, plus a tin of baked beans, but he made it clear that the snaps could not be returned, because John had made it known that he would be eating some of them!

Bernie was a more reflective guy, and his contribution to the brochure offered no prizes, but a crossword puzzle he'd devised. Clue One (across) asked for 'the greatest guitarist alive' (6,5). Colin and Mick just lent their portraits, while I gave revival to thoughts of infinity.

Seldom if ever are we knocked off our perches
with the threatening 'beginningless'
Time goes forward doesn't it?
Endless we can cope with,
after all we understand procreation
and humanity's determination to be around forever
let alone any personal plans for the hereafter
'Beginningless', that's another story

It never started?
Ha, that surely means we're not here
Well here we are, so that can't be right ...

In between the demands of rock 'n' roll, I still kept up with my old mates, and played as much football as possible, often for charity. Because of Jonathan Crisp's connection with the sport — he was very involved with advertising and sponsorships at clubs such as Ipswich Town FC — I got to meet a number of my heroes, such as Terry Butcher, Russell Osmond and Paul Mariner.

I know football managers hate it, but these guys like to party as much as musicians do, and there was one famous occasion when Jonathan arranged that we get together at a party on a sea-going barge, which was moored up on the Orwell Estuary. Although we started in the pub, he'd ordered tons of booze for the vessel, but forgot to supply food. So a few of us went to the fish and chip shop and ordered fifty packs of fish and chips and a barrel of pickled onions.

After a while, I felt a bit hot — indeed, a bit strange — and decided on a swim. I began to strip down, but they all started shouting, 'No, no, Ian, you can't do that!' But it was too late, as I dived into the Orwell, and swam round to the bow end, beneath the gaze of the drunken partygoers.

The vessel was moored by chain, and so I clawed my way up, to arrive back on board, furious — and caked in slime and grease. I was furious because I'd gone over without a knife between my teeth. I mean, how can you possibly climb back on board a ship without a knife between your teeth? The only thing I could lay my hands on was this plastic knife we'd brought back from the fish shop, so I put it in my mouth and was about to return to the mud, when Russell and Terry grabbed hold of me, and said, 'No way — that river's dangerous; it's littered with disease and God knows what else!' At that point I had to tell them that I didn't get diseases, I only gave them! With the amount of alcohol inside us all, plus my ridiculous appearance, it gave us all a good laugh. It wasn't so funny the next morning when I looked at where I'd been swimming — a flat calm of oily water and a load of dead fish. As I said earlier, I only give diseases!

Back on tour, we wrote new songs and, in April 1981, Virgin brought out *Future Shock*, so called after the book by Alvin Toffler. On *Future Shock*, I think we played some of the best material I have ever written with Colin, and the band were fantastic. We were at our peak, and Virgin were putting a lot of energy into making sure the album and our singles sold. They offered a 16-page colour booklet with the first 60,000 sales, and alongside the touring, it wasn't surprising that this project was a success, making number 2 in the UK charts with songs like 'Future Shock', 'Nightride out of Phoenix', '(The Ballad of) The Lucitania Express', 'No Laughing in Heaven', 'Sacre Bleu', 'Bite the Bullet', 'If I Sing Softly', 'Don't Want the Truth' and 'For Your Dreams'.

Gone were the days when Phil had to beg to have me at the Reading Festival — that was now in the dim and distant past. That year we topped the bill. 'No Laughing in Heaven' is a song from the album of which I am particularly proud. It tells the story of a guy who has been a sinner all his life, but then decides he'd better reform if he wants to get to heaven. So he does a lot of obnoxious and cynical things to find his way there:

> *I decided to reform and pray,*
> *Beg mercy for my soul, I prayed in Church,*
> *Threw away my bad habits,*
> *Prayed out of Church,*
> *Adopted an entirely different role,*
> *I gave money to the poor,*
> *Until I was poor,*
> *But at least I ensured,*

That I would go up there,
Instead of down below,
To the inferno.

On arrival in heaven he is so chuffed, he starts laughing and jumping around, enjoying himself, only to get arrested. He's told that if he wants to do that sort of thing — have fun — he would be better off in hell, and it ends with him screaming:

Let me out of Heaven,
I've got it wrong, no I can't stay in here,
No laughing in Heaven
Oh God it's awful here,
Going crazy in Heaven,
Take me out, let me go to Hell,
No laughing in Heaven,
Don't laugh this place is Hell.

Chapter 10

This was a fantastic period, and I felt great. For the first time since the heyday of Purple, I was back in the vanguard of rock music, with strong and confident material. Although I'd never seen myself as a singles artist, Virgin's policy for lifting a track from the album made sense, and my cover version of Gary U S Bonds' 1960 hit, 'New Orleans', was released and made number 17 in the UK charts.

We were enjoying going to work, playing flat out, and the fans could see it. Unfortunately, as with a lot of major acts, we couldn't crack America, and our tour there was not a success. We lost money, not helped either by the fact that Virgin seemed to be having problems breaking their label over there as well. It's a complicated business, that side of things, so we decided to concentrate on the UK, Europe and then the Far East, where Phil was beginning to have serious negotiations, in which the length of my hair was proving to be a stumbling block.

While all that was going on, we went back to Kingsway to follow up *Future Shock* as quickly as possible. We were brimming with ideas, and *Double Trouble* was the outcome. However, it didn't feature Bernie.

Beneath part of the façade of success, there were still problems in the band, and John was being quite difficult. Bernie's departure came while we were in Germany, and among all the personal appearances (PAs) we were booked for, one was *Top of the Pops*, which we needed to fly back for.

John was dead against that, and it seemed Bernie shared his opinion as he failed to arrive at the airport. We were all clock-watching, and going, 'Where the fuck's Bernie?' and eventually getting round to 'That's it ... he's out,' and so on. Finally, we boarded and flew out. On the journey, we discussed who could take his place, to help finish the tour at least, and Janick Gers of White Spirit (and, later, Iron Maiden) came to mind. I called Janick to explain the situation, and although we did *TOTP* as a four-piece, he started learning the songs, and agreed to help out.

In the meantime, there was a call from Bernie, asking what had been going down, to which I replied, 'We're in bloody England ... we've done *Top of the Pops* as a four-piece! That's what's going down!' I then told him he was out. He vehemently denied the fact that he'd deliberately let us down, and John also denied any complicity.

Anyhow, we settled down to consolidate with Janick, who quickly fitted into the band. Bernie put out stories saying he was furious with the way he'd been treated, saying things like Gillan was really a band backing its singer, that it wasn't as democratic as it should have been, but adding that although he was disappointed, he didn't hold me entirely responsible. It is true he offered to complete the German tour, but I'd now settled the new situation, and wished Bernie well with the solo album on which he immediately started work.

Double Trouble was a double album, released by Virgin in October 1981. Part of the work was based on live recordings taken at the Reading Festival on 29th August, and it went to number 12 in the UK charts. We rehearsed the material in Lyme Regis, Dorset, using a place called Drake Hall, named after Sir Francis, the sailor; Steve Smith produced and mixed it. Early on, I remember taking a copy of it with me in the car on the drive to

London, listening to it and then ditching it somewhere. I hated it, and left it to rot!

A few weeks later, I listened to the tapes again, and realised that I'd completely missed the point. How stupid I'd been, because it was a fine piece of progressive rock, and I don't think I'd ever felt that way since the early Purple days. Songs like 'Restless', 'I'll Rip Your Spine Out', 'Hadley Bop Bop', 'No Easy Way' and the single, 'Nightmare', all jumped out at me. Who said you couldn't make a good album while on the road? Gillan were doing it with consistency, while playing 200 shows a year. 'Nightmare' was released at about the same time as the album, and went to number 36, as we approached the year end having toured Greece, Japan, Hong Kong, Australia and a 42-date programme in the UK.

Janick turned out to be a brilliant find and, yet again, we were pleased with our record company. Songs on the album continued my commitment to hard-edged rock, and kept us in the front line. Constant touring, for which I live and breathe, was guaranteed for months ahead.

Setting up tours in new territories is always a major challenge for management and the artists, and I've learned not to be too surprised by demands and expectations. The first time I went to Kuala Lumpur was with Gillan, and we did three nights there, and another three in Manila. We played to big audiences — between 12,000 and 18,000 at a time. Phil's people checked for every point of protocol, our lyrics were dissected by the authorities for possible messages of insurrection or revolt, and everything was set to go. And then we received an extra rider which went something along the lines of: 'The boys in the band shall not allow their hair to fall upon their shoulders'!

So Phil said, 'How do we deal with this?' and I told him we'd deal with it when we got there, one way or another!

We were being sponsored by Pepsi Cola who were making big efforts to catch up with Coca Cola, and so part of the deal was that we'd do some promo conferences in a hotel. The guy in charge, Jack, kept saying he'd feed me the lines to questions, but I quickly got into my stride. He reminded me that he had the answers for me, but I told him I'd say what I thought, which miffed him a bit.

It was an incredible gathering of people from radio, television, cultural departments, the papers and so forth. The questions were very wide ranging — they wanted my political views, ideas on religion and much else besides. It was quite difficult, and lasted about two hours.

Throughout the whole business, I had my hair tied back, and wrapped in a shawl of neutral colours, as I patiently tried to explain the emergence of music like the Beatles, and then my own approach to rock 'n' roll. We then took to the stage and, as usual for a first night in a new country, the first five rows would be reserved for ministers, trade big wigs and privileged guests — all dressed in suits, ties and evening gowns. Behind the dignified formality of the five rows, you'd then see the kids going crazy, and so our first appearance in Kuala Lumpur was a great success, capped perfectly by the closing moments of the evening.

The dignitaries all filed backstage, and a spokesman came over and said, 'If your headdress should fall off tomorrow night after the third song, forget about it ... you can just be natural. We understand a lot more now, and it's been great!'

It was a wonderful moment, and we had a brilliant time over there. As it happens, the headdress did fall off the following night, and the whole place went 'Wow!' They had never seen hair like it before. Remember, Cliff Richard had been refused entry to Singapore because of the length of his, so this was something else!

I believe the audience had travelled from far and wide, by all means of transport, to see us, and it was sensational. We spent the first few days making everybody comfortable with our work, and received unbelievable hospitality.

One night went a little bit 'off the rails' *differently* — when we were taken to this club where a great blues band was playing. We had a few drinks and then, around midnight, a party of strippers and hookers turned up, off duty, to relax a little. About an hour later they closed the bar, and the girls all said, 'Let's go party ... let's go party,' which sounded fine by me.

I thought they were off to another club, or to someone's house, so off we went, walking down the streets in the tourist area, where we passed the hotels, shops, cafés and restaurants. Everywhere, the place was lit up by neon lights. Mick was with us, a bit reluctantly, as we moved to another part of town — the banking area. It wasn't like New York or Tokyo, but just a load of average-height buildings — six or seven storeys maybe, but modern and with a lot of glass. The streets struck me as spotless, as we trooped into this alleyway alongside an office building, and then followed the girls up a fire escape, thinking maybe they lived on the top floor. They did!

We finally arrived on the roof, where there was a mini condominium of little shacks among the lift houses and air-conditioning enclosures. It was astonishing as we took in the sight of about 15 girls sitting around a fire, or asleep in the nooks and crannies. There was a delicious smell of food wafting around, and under the beautiful moonlit night, we started to party. The girls started to strip off, and I started to get intimate with one of them, as I gradually removed my clothes — or had them removed.

Mick departed the way we'd come, leaving me to enjoy myself with the girls. Eventually, I was invited to eat with them, and there I lay, propped on one elbow, being fed food and wine by this beautiful Eurasian girl, who moved alongside. It was like being on a magic carpet, flying somewhere, and I became drowsy.

I must have fallen asleep in the middle of eating my rice,

because the next thing I remember is being woken by the early morning sun beating into my eyes. I couldn't breathe or suck in air and realised, to my horror, that my mouth was full of clogged and congealed rice. Commuting between my open orifice and my rice bowl, now on its side next to me, were three or four cockroaches. As one crawled out of my mouth, I spat the whole lot out with as much force as possible, and reached for a bottle of wine. It tasted like warm vinegar, as my gaze wandered across the fire to see this ugly, fat, bloated, toothless horror, who'd just a few hours ago been a beautiful girl with whom I was sharing pleasure!

There I was, on the roof of a bank, confronted by a load of naked old whores, and naked myself from the waist down. I eventually found the rest of my clothes, dressed and climbed down the fire escape — and beginning now to chuckle. It was seven, maybe eight in the morning, and the business community was on its way to work. So there I was, walking through the streets with rice-smeared, wine-stained and crumpled clothes, looking like something that had just crawled out of a trash can. I got some very strange looks from the local workforce. And even stranger ones as I walked into the hotel lobby!

I don't know if the sheer pressure of touring gave added weight and stress to the problems bubbling around in the band, and I thought (for example) that it may have been one of the reasons why Bernie had got fed up. It's my way of life, and I seem to have the constitution to keep going. Having said that, I was beginning to suffer more than usual from throat problems, and was diagnosed as having enlarged nodules.

A single in January 1982, 'Restless', kept us in the public eye, and made number 25 in the UK charts, and 'Living for the City' reached number 55 in September that year.

We were a good band with a great image and appeal, such

that fans — men and women — were even turning up to shows looking like John, with their heads shaved and with stick-on beards! We'd climbed from the bottom to the top, and stayed with our label for over 10 releases, most of which were successful. Colin had become a transformed character from that tearful day at Kingsway, when we'd said goodbye to rock fusion, and on stage his flashing tie was great. Janick became an instant favourite with the fans, although Bernie's departure still cropped up from time to time, and seemed to rankle a bit. Mick and I had known each other for so long, it was magic to be having such a good time (most of the time).

As for John, well, John on stage was his usual bumbling, cruising self, but there were problems brewing, not helped by suspicions that I had been talking to Ritchie about a reunion. Well, it was true that there would be a visit to America during June 1982, but apart from the fact that it was a hopeless journey, I was also entitled to moments of personal disappointment, concern and career re-evaluation. Still, the media picked up on the possibility and gave it full coverage.

The only way to deal with situations like that is to get back on the road, and Phil planned a huge schedule, including 37 shows in the autumn. We were booked to support Status Quo at Donnington Park on 21 August, with other acts like Hawkwind, Saxon and Uriah Heep on the bill. Tommy Vance — who else? — ran the proceedings in a year when, at the grand old age of 37, I was voted top male singer. Colin was voted second best keyboard player — after Jon Lord (then with Whitesnake) — and we came in sixth, one above Rainbow in terms of top band according to *Sounds*.

In the early part of the year, we'd been overseas, returning to the Far East, and otherwise preparing for the last album we'd make for Virgin. *Magic* would make number 17 in the UK charts during October 1982, while 'Living for the City' was still there, and 'Long Gone' did pretty well. It was recorded at Kingsway and mixed by Mike Glossop at the Townhouse. It's an album I'm proud of — 'Bluesy Blue Sea', 'Long Gone', 'Driving Me Wild' and 'Demon Driver' are all a credit to the often bickering musicians.

In terms of shows, we were perhaps getting a bit stale, and maybe that's down (in part) to the sheer amount of touring we'd been doing, including a return to the Far East, where our star shone bright. Still, it was there, in Bangkok, that I witnessed a scene later to emerge in one of my songs on *The House of Blue Light* (Deep Purple).

A few of us went to this place I knew about, where you could see shows which were pretty well down to the knuckle. We went in, and there was this strip routine. After everybody had left, we slipped into a room behind the kitchen, where there was an altogether different cabaret going on. It was highly skilled and very, very rude, but without being smutty. What these girls were doing with their bodies — double-edged razor blades tied with cotton; signing autographs without using their hands; opening bottles of Coke — well, the whole thing was astonishing!

The highlight of the evening was one particular lady, and how she entertained a table of about five Italian business people. They were sitting in amazement at the spectacle before them, each with a wine glass on the table. Then the lady bent over backwards, in a crab-like position, and from between her legs she fired five ping-pong balls in rapid succession, each one landing in a wine glass. Apparently, it's a high form of art over there, and before table tennis was invented, they used eggs! Not the sort of thing to promote in England, however, which is where the final tour by Gillan was planned, and performed to full houses. The idea for the song 'Mitzi Dupree', was planted, but it needed a later incident before it would be written.

October

22nd	Civic Hall, Guildford
23rd	Oasis Centre, Swindon
24th	Guildhall, Portsmouth
27th	Rock City, Nottingham
28th	Civic Hall, Wolverhampton
29th	Guildhall, Preston
30th	City Hall, Newcastle

November

4th	Capitol Theatre, Aberdeen
5th	Caird Hall, Dundee
6th	Apollo, Glasgow
7th	Playhouse, Edinburgh
8th	Market Hall, Carlisle
10th	Victoria Hall, Hanley
11th	Liverpool Empire
13th	Apollo, Manchester
15th	Brangwyn Hall, Swansea
16th	Top Rank, Cardiff
17th	The Leisure Centre, Ebbw Vale
19th	St George's Hall, Bradford
20th	Leeds University
21st	Festival Hall, Corby
22nd	City Hall, Hull
25th	The Leisure Centre, Gloucester
26th	Colston Hall, Bristol
27th	The Colosseum, Cornwall
30th	Cliffs Pavilion, Southend

December

3rd	The Arts Centre, Poole
4th	The Gaumont, Southampton
5th	The Apollo, Oxford

6th	The Brighton Dome
8th	The Assembly Rooms, Derby
9th	City Hall, Sheffield
11th	The Odeon, Birmingham
14th	De Montfort Hall, Leicester
15th	The Gaumont, Ipswich
17th	Wembley Arena (London)

After a schedule such as this, one of a few reasons for disbanding Gillan was to give my voice a much-needed break. In fact, it was the main one. However, no sooner had that been made known, when rumours of a Purple reunion resurfaced.

They began with moves by Ritchie to bring us all together again, and I was perfectly happy to listen and make myself available. By the time everything would be in place, my voice would be recovered, and the idea was attractive. Ritchie and Roger could do it, because they were in Rainbow, Paicey was at a loose end having just left Whitesnake, but it turned out that Jon, who was very close to David Coverdale in that band, said he was staying there. So the idea fizzled out, having caused its own public intrigue. However, while that was happening, a more unlikely opportunity emerged in the form of Black Sabbath. They had also just disbanded, with the departure of Ronnie James Dio and Vinnie Appice, which left Tony Iommi and Geezer Butler to decide what to do next. They signed with Don Arden's management, and asked Bill Ward to come back and me to join, so that *Born Again* could be recorded. Although Bill would do the album, ill health (the excess of rock 'n' roll) meant that he would not tour, and Bev Bevan was brought in from the 'resting' ELO.

The announcement, so soon after the disbanding of Gillan (for health reasons), caused a huge uproar with the band, and gave the press a lot to write about. The *Magic* album was one of my favourite projects, and it was sad that circumstances conspired to make the closing period such an acrimonious business.

In fact, the request to join Black Sabbath came initially from Don and David Arden, who had the creation of a 'supergroup' in mind, with Tony, Geezer, Bill and me. The first meeting with the lads took place at a pub in Oxford, where we drank a great deal and got to know one another.

It really was a meeting
The bottle took a beating
The ladies of the manor
Watched me climb into my car ...

Of course, we'd all met before on the festival and rock circuit, but our music backgrounds and the fans we appealed to were very different. Still, Don's idea was fair enough, and things started well, until we all (I think) began to question the wisdom of going out as Black Sabbath. It's true that three-quarters of the line up were from Sabbath, but it raised early questions about my position. Anyway, the official announcement was made on 6 April 1983 at a press conference at Le Beat Route Club in London's Soho, and we began rehearsals immediately.

In May, we went into The Manor Studio at Shipton on Cherwell, in Oxfordshire, where the band and Robin Black produced the album for the Vertigo label, marketed by Phonogram, for what would become a cult project. Songs included 'Disturbing the Priest', 'Trashed', 'The Dark', 'Stonehenge' and the title track, 'Born Again', were the result, with the distinctive cover of the baby. Plans were made for us to headline at Reading Festival in August, and then go to America, where the band had a formidable reputation. On the road, I soon found it quite difficult. In many ways, the lads almost directed me, which was not at all what I'd been used to, and when it came to songs, of course, they wanted to do old stuff, *their* old stuff, so as not to upset their fans. The only concession was that we'd close with 'Smoke on the Water', which puzzled a lot of people. I had also heard that Rainbow were also closing with that song, and Ritchie was very pissed off with what we were doing.

With Sabbath, I had to learn the lyrics from their catalogue — stuff like 'Paranoid' and 'War Pigs' — plus the new material, and unfortunately I'd never really paid close attention to the detail of singing 'to the letter', even with my own songs, as many of you will know. So that would turn out to be an early problem.

Then there would be the question of clothes, since it was impressed on me (by Geezer) that I'd be expected to dress in black, typical of the Sabbath culture. Well, as most band photos show, I refused to do that, but almost certainly the greatest difficulty of all was facing up to the fans themselves, each one a devoted follower of Ozzy Osbourne.

Although I'd taken over from Ronnie, Ozzy *was* Black Sabbath — as I suppose I *am* Deep Purple — so this was a whole new experience for me, and on stage I was often uncomfortable. Before we started the European and American tour, I realised that I really had to do something about the lyrics, and so Bron ('B', my wife) sat up with me for half the night writing crib notes in large felt pen. Key lines were highlighted, and the whole show was then put into a perspex folder, which I put on the floor and learned how to turn over with my foot. I spent hours in the kitchen practising the technique, so that when it came to the first gig, I told the crew to set up a couple of wedges (I never use monitors), so I could hide the book.

We began the opening song and, to my horror, I saw clouds of dry ice billowing across the stage — knee high! As my precious crib sheet started to disappear from sight, I was reduced to falling on hands and knees to clear the smoke with huge wafting motions. It must have looked incredible to the audience, because all they will have seen would be this three-foot tall, demented singer peering every now and again over the wedges, bellowing whatever lines seemed right. My misery was completed to damnation when some bright spark in the front shouted, 'It's Ronnie Dio!'

I didn't dare catch the eyes of Tony or Geezer, because I knew they'd be mad, but I occasionally caught Bev Bevan's silly grin from behind the drum stack.

The tour, under management supremo, Don Arden, was incredible. Apart from only occasional interference with our music, he basically left us to get on with it, while he concentrated on his own input, about which he was irrepressible, and over the top. We did the world tour to a backdrop of Stonehenge, and the model was almost as big as the real thing.

Don had booked us into The Maple Leaf Gardens in Toronto for three or four days, prior to our first show, so we could take delivery of his masterpiece and rehearse with it. The monoliths came in about four articulated lorries, and were made of fibreglass. When laid out on the floor it was huge, but what Don and his design enthusiasts had forgotten was that, on stage, the structures took on a massive dimension. From floor level, you looked up to the stage, and then began ... Stonehenge! In fact, we couldn't get half of it in for most of the shows, and we were playing mostly ice hockey arenas and football stadiums! Still, Don was totally nonplussed at the situation, and gave us a lecture about not knowing about entertainment, showbiz and so on. As if to make the point, he then upped the stakes by adding thunder flashes and all sorts of other nonsense — taped music from the bowels of hell — until Bev came up to me with news on his latest idea. He said he'd seen this dwarf hanging around the set all day, so we went to see. Well, sure enough, there was this little guy roaming around, and we started saying unkind things, like 'Maybe he's Ronnie Dio's hairdresser,' and 'Someone had forgotten to say Ronnie had left the band,' miserable things like that.

But when we started for the sound check, the guy climbed into this red costume, and attached horns and long finger nails. Of course, we realised then it was the baby from the album cover, and there was a rush to stop Don from allowing this madness. No such luck! As the tape rolled, and the moaning and screaming of a distorted baby's voice was mixed in, he started crawling along the top of one of the structures. So there we were, with these putrid noises and the horrible sight crawling over Stonehenge, screaming, and then, all of a sudden, he stood up, screamed and screamed, and fell off backwards to the safety of a mattress below.

Then the roadies came on dressed as druids, cowls and all, to the sound of deep tolling bells. At this point, we were supposed to rush on and start playing, but instead we found Don and said, 'We can't have this — it's in appalling bad taste!'

We received a vintage Arden reply: 'You lads play, I'll provide the showbusiness ... Give them what they love!'

Well, I looked at Bev, he looked at me, we both looked at Tony and Geezer, and it was clear that nobody was very happy. So we had this argument about the dwarf with Don, but he's not really the sort of guy you mess with and, in the end, we shrugged our shoulders.

We went on stage that night, the show opened with the smoke, the cannon, the explosion of red light, and in this eerie atmosphere, the Devil's baby started to crawl along the top of Stonehenge; screaming its head off. It then stood up and fell off as we rushed on, and started playing. Except the screaming kept going on and on — right through to the end of the first number. It seemed that someone had taken the mattress away. He wasn't there the next night.

As for the album, it went to number 4 in the UK during October, and 39 in America. About the cover, I had some people design something, but it was rejected out of hand as being not nearly dangerous enough, and Don arranged for the final product. We all thought it pretty unfortunate, but I quickly learned that Don tended to get what he wanted! Still that could be a 'plus' when a guy of that calibre is looking after you as an artist.

Talking of artistry, I know Tony (Iommi) learned a few things from me, as I brought my own way of approaching life on the road to the band. I first gave him the clue at an early get together at his local pub, where I got very drunk, dropped my trousers, and encouraged a lady to let me wear her tights, and then got her to let me have all her clothes. Well, that's what I've done from time to time — a sort of challenge, if you like. Deep Purple understood!

However, I think what really irritated the band was that after a session I'd be up first thing, fresh as a daisy, doing the crossword while they came down looking like shit!

And then there would be the occasional party where various substances were passed round, and people were 'pinged' to walls. At one, a roadie came up and pushed something under my nose, but it didn't do anything for me. So (I am told), I asked him to run it by me again, and the result was the same. He wandered off looking very puzzled. Hmm ...

If I didn't much like the shows, I did enjoy the social side of Sabbath, as we went from one crisis to another. We were arrested in Barcelona, after I'd apparently set fire to a waiter's jacket, and Don had to send some people out from Germany to take care of us. They were told to stay with the band everywhere after that incident, and I mean everywhere! Don also deducted the cost of our behaviour from our earnings!

The American tour was bigger than anything I'd ever experienced, even when we toured with The Faces. It was a masterpiece of organisation, handled by Cal Star Travel, who were based in California. A typical day sheet of information would summarise how we'd travel, how our crew would travel, where we'd be staying, and where the crew would stay. We'd know who the drivers would be and have their addresses and phone numbers, as well as exact details of each venue, the time for travel to each show, how many were expected and who was promoting, handling backstage and so forth. Our 'load in' time would be mentioned, and when we'd be on stage and off.

I was used to good organisation before, but 'Sabs' had it well sorted out. I also thought I'd toured Canada, but with this band I did it as if we were gigging with the Gillan band in the UK. City to city over there means huge distances, but we did it, effortlessly.

January

| 29th | Salt Palace, Salt Lake City |
| 30th/31st | The Ice Arena, Denver County |

February

1st	Civic Centre, Amarillo, Texas
3rd	Colosseum, Corpus Christi, Texas
4th	The Convention Centre, San Antonio, Texas
5th	The Convention Centre, Houston, Texas

And so it continued, through to Beaumont, Little Rock, Lakeland, Hollywood, Savannah, Atlanta, St Louis, Toledo, Dayton and more besides. October and November saw us in Quebec City, Montreal, Ottowa, Sudbury, Toronto, Buffalo, New York and on to yet more major cities.

And so we come to a moment where the past catches up. It happened on a flight between Los Angeles and Salt Lake City, and I was travelling ahead of the band, in the only seat you will get me to travel in — 3A — which is normally by the window. When I turned up to settle in, there was this lady sitting in my place, and the stewardess said she'd ask her to move if I wanted. I said not to bother, and took an aisle seat next to her.

Well, we fell into conversation, and she said she was on her way to one of the mining towns to do a show. She explained that she was an entertainer, and for the full story, it's best you listen to the track 'Mitzi Dupree' on *The House of Blue Light*. Anyway, it turned out that the highlight of her act was the ping-pong trick I'd seen in Bangkok, and when I told her I'd seen the routine behind the kitchen at this club, she became very agitated, and made it quite clear that whoever I'd seen doing it had stolen her act. Well, it wasn't for me to discuss how many generations of artists had beaten her to it, but she was a great character.

Flying to Salt Lake City
Seats 3A and 3B
I was down and I needed a window
But in 3A sat Mitzi Dupree
Hi, I am Mitzi
Queen of the ping pong
Where are you going boy
I said, nowhere — I'm moving on!

Born Again made number 4 in the UK charts and 39 in America, but I had decided that Black Sabbath could not be a long-term situation for me, and gave Don my notice before the second American trip. It just wasn't me, and I suppose the most memorable legacy we left from that collaboration was the inspiration to the makers of the film *Spinal Tap*. Since that experience, I've always avoided driving past Stonehenge if at all possible!

Chapter 11

I'm aware that I am constantly observed for my drinking habits, and that my enjoyment of scotch is frequently seen as the reason for something not going according to plan. I've never made any secret of that pleasure, which I've taken in moments of prolonged stress, but also out of sheer enjoyment. It's something I got into in the early days, and it's something I know how to deal with. I know when I've nearly had enough, and I've never blamed alcohol for any part of my life going wrong. Apart from one incident, it has never affected my ability to perform as a professional artist, although it has certainly helped me cause considerable embarrassment from time to time. However, it's not my fault if people can't take a joke!

I have my own pub sign, 'Gillan's Inn', and that, plus my pool table, is frequently with me on tour.

Of the one incident in question, Bron (then my wife of just a few months) and I had spent the day at the Grand National, courtesy of Radio City, and after that we'd been invited as guests to the Battle of the Bands competition, where I was to be one of the judges. (That took me back a few years — The Essoldo, to be precise.) Each year they'd have a 'top' band to close the evening and, on this occasion, it was my old mates, The Climax Blues Band. Present also was 'rock jock' and dear friend, Phil Easton.

Anyway, some of the guys had their wives or girlfriends with them, and these Grand National ladies moaned constantly about the cold and everything under the sun. So while Phil and I went backstage to decide how we'd cast the votes, his lady went and bought a bottle of vodka, to encourage the girls to stop complaining. So they got pissed, we judged the competition, and then The Climax Blues Band came on.

At this stage, two of the guys left to take their 'other halves' home, but on the way back, the girls, being much the worse for drink, ran into difficulties. One of them was sitting in the back, with the nearside window open, and the other sat in the front, with the window also open. The one in front decided to throw up, and the whole lot came straight back through the open rear window. So everybody was now moaning, but it was poetic justice for the girls being such a pain.

In the meantime, I did something I rarely do, and came on stage to guest with the band, and I'm afraid the song went on for a very long time, on account of the fact I was now incapably drunk. As I sang this great blues number, the venue started to empty and the musicians also started to lay down their instruments. The drummer then left, so I thought I'd have a little go at that. Then I went back to singing, and next, I picked up a guitar. I also decided that B should sing as well, but she was in the wings shouting 'enough is enough', and very definitely wanted to go home. So I picked her up and threw her over my shoulder, and continued to entertain, until satisfied there was nobody left. By then, I was a roaring Oliver Reed character, and I felt so great, I just wanted to share it with everyone. Unfortunately, there was only one person left, and he was outside the venue (the Royal Court Theatre), packing up his hot-dog stand. In fact, he was packing up very quickly as I approached, but I got alongside him, and asked if he'd like my autograph. He indicated that not only was he not too keen, but he didn't know who the fuck I was anyway, and would I get out of his face! He kept calling me a 'fockin' yeti', which I took exception to, and grabbed him by the throat.

I think it was Bron who hit me over the head with something heavy, and we eventually returned to the hotel, where we emptied the lounge bar of late night drinkers!

I met Bron when I was with Virgin, making the *Magic* album. She and a couple of other girls joined the UK section of the tour, travelling as backing singers, called The Cucumbers. One of the other girls later married Phil (Banfield). At the time, Bron was going through a divorce, and I was at a pretty low period of my life. We went to live in Westbourne Grove (in London), and she then became pregnant with our daughter, Grace.

Quite a few people seemed to give her a hard time about our relationship, asking her why she was marrying Gillan, that he'd dump her and so forth, but we talked things through in every detail, and she understood the kind of lifestyle that goes with my work. Bron will sit alongside me at some meetings, but she knows my manager is Phil Banfield, and leaves our business affairs to him.

When it comes to my health, she is more forthright, and during the period when the band was coming to an end after the *Magic* tour, she picked up on the fact I was throwing up before and after shows, and told me I was a mess. I also had broken ribs from a football mishap, and my hair was falling out. She said it needed to be cut, to which I agreed. It was, after all, getting in the way of my beer!

It was about that time, we decided we needed a motto. It became *'Oh Dear, Never Mind'* With a child on the way, and a commitment to Bron, there's a need for many things to be understood. Of course, that goes for everybody, but in rock 'n' roll, we lead different lives, and a lot of musicians find mine even more different than the norm. Bron knows that when I'm on the road I like to party, but I'm truthful to her, and the most I ever get up to is a bit of fiddling and twiddling. I love her more than life itself, and any girl I meet knows I'm the happiest married man in the world.

I suspect that friends like Roger, Phil and others (who have to share my company) find it all strange and sometimes embarrassing, but that's how it is. Bron's mother, Sheila, and sister, Julie, once asked me what I'd think if I heard Bron was behaving like me while I was away. I think my reply surprised them. This is not the reply, but it's about the one I love.

I love you darling
When you're feeling sad and lonely
I love you darling
When you put your arms around me
When we talk on the phone
You make me feel like coming home.

It's a measure of the love, support and sometimes very stretched tolerance shown by B, Phil and those close to me, that my peccadilloes are under much more control these days. I still drink and like a cigarette, but most days you'll find me with a cup of tea in my hand and, as for smokes ... well, I can take them or leave them. I do get rampant now and then, but it's mostly when I 'rock 'n' roll'.

I'm a proud father now, with a growing teenage daughter, and I shall never forget, after a particularly heavy night some years ago, when my darling little girl, Grace, whispered into the cloud on my pillow, 'Daddy, your head smells terrible.' That sort of thing stops you in your tracks!

The last time I'd seen Purple was when Phil Banfield and I went to America to meet the band and Ritchie's manager, Bruce Payne. On that occasion, I gather I behaved very badly, got extremely drunk, poured a pint over my head and went mooning in the streets, returning to find that Ritchie and Roger had left. A little while later, around Christmas 1983, Bruce called Phil to see how things were with me. He knew I was with Sabbath, but just wanted to check out to see if the reunion idea was worth another try. Because I'd already seen the end of my time with Tony and the guys approaching, it seemed worth giving it a go, and negotiations began.

The next thing I heard from Phil was that Ritchie was after 50% of the band, and willing to leave it up to the rest of us to work out how we wanted to share the remaining 50%. I told Phil to tell Ritchie to fuck off — it was equal shares or no reunion. I did this without consulting the others, but expected them to take whatever was sorted out. So straight away it was back to the 'good old days', with Gillan being an awkward sod! This time, however, my stand worked, whether because of record company pressure or whatever.

Ritchie agreed to the equal shares deal, and even began writing in the New Year. He planned the winding up of Rainbow after their shows in Japan that spring, and Jon also made arrangements to leave Whitesnake. We all came together for a civilised and progressive meeting in April, after which Tommy Vance made the news public on his *Friday Rock Show*.

From then on, the news spread like wildfire, as Deep Purple came together again under two managers, with Bruce representing everything except my interest, which Phil looked after.

That part of the reunion caused early difficulties, since Bruce obviously saw himself in the driving seat, which in many ways was, I suppose, the case. However, the initial idea was that it would be run on a sort of joint basis, but when it came to commission on royalties and other matters, Bruce said that the band had screwed him down too hard, and Phil agreed to take a knock in everybody's interest.

It wasn't easy for him, and he quite rightly came and discussed the matter with me. I told him not to worry, that he was still my manager, and that he'd earn from everything I was making with Purple. While the main effort then went to Bruce's office in America (Thames Talent Limited), Phil spread his wings in the UK and developed what is now Miracle Prestige

International Limited (MPI) in London, tying up with Miles Copeland, the manager of The Police and Sting.

We began rehearsals for *Perfect Strangers*, although I must tell you that rumours of a $2 million advance for that album were grossly exaggerated, the figure being nearer half that amount. Most of the advance necessarily went on making the record for the Polydor label, as well as the organisational costs incurred in setting up the touring.

As in the earlier days when Bill Reid was around, I could always have asked about the details, but didn't, and it was much the same now. Had I wanted to know, I suppose I could always have asked Ian Paice, who was as interested in matters of money as ever. He was still the only one of us with any grasp on the subject. The story goes that he used to go window shopping at the Nat West Bank, just to watch them change the rates of exchange! I just left it for Bruce to report to Phil as necessary.

So Roger and I spent some time together putting ideas down and we then went to Bass Lodge in North Vermont to rehearse. It was a great location, owned by the Von Trapp family, and set in many acres of mountain landscape. Ritchie had been there before to work on the album *Bent out of Shape*, and he now came up with the idea that we should have the speakers out in the natural environment, and play the sound back through Le Mobile (our studio on wheels). However, the State Authorities didn't think it was such a great idea, and we soon needed to find an alternative location and facility.

Very early on, we discovered The Pub in Stowe (Vermont), and more importantly, its owner, the Englishman Richard Hughes — larger than life and a future friend. With Richard, everything is possible, and he soon found us a place called Horizons, where we set up, and put Le Mobile outside. Once settled in, we started jamming in the basement and, in those early days, I didn't do anything but listen to the guys putting ideas down. It all sounded so good, and brought a smile to my face. Engineered by Nick Blagona, the whole album came together quite easily in a mood of good vibes, a lot of momentum and with very few problems. So much so, that we were only there for about a month, from July 1984, which isn't long for a Deep Purple album. It was mixed at Tennessee Tonstudio, in Hamburg (Germany), and mastered by Greg Calbri at Sterling Sound in New York. It was great to be together again!

Can you remember, remember my name
As I flow through your life
A thousand oceans I have flown
And cold spirits of ice
All of my life
I am an echo of your past ...

We played a lot of football, and made many friends, although nothing had really changed so far as Ritchie's competitive attitude was concerned. The lengths the guy will go to to win are incredible — take football, for example. We'd always start a game with a sort of Deep Purple team — engineers, roadies and so forth — only for Ritchie to spot some player on the opposing local factory team who looked a bit good. So he'd say to Colin (Hart), 'I want that player in our team,' and Colin would somehow arrange for a swap with Ian Paice, or me, or Roger. Not only that, but Ritchie would then tell the opposing captain where he wanted us to play in their defence, and the game would go on and on, until the right side won — preferably with the guitar player scoring the winning goal!

Ritchie is a competitive person, and it shows a lot in the music as well. There was a time when he approached me at a rehearsal, and said something like, 'If you start putting on a good show, really doing well, then I'm going to try and blow you off stage, and that will make you do better, and it will make me do better!' So despite the everpresent and underlying tension between us, there was still the potential for a creative collaboration, and I think it came out on *Perfect Strangers*, with songs like 'Knocking on Your Back Door', 'Under the Gun', 'A Gypsy's Kiss' and the title track itself.

At the close of 1984, *Perfect Strangers* made number 5 in the UK charts, and went to 17 in the States (Mercury label). In February 1985, the title track came out as a single (number 48 in the UK), and 'Knocking on Your Back Door' reached number 61 in America. In June it made 68 'at home', while the double compilation album, *The Anthology*, reached 50 in the UK charts.

During that project, Roger introduced me to his friend, Chet King and, over a period of time, we became great mates. Chet, in turn, introduced me to serious scuba diving, as a sport and means of relaxation, away from the music business. I'd already done a little of it and had the bug, but Chet showed me the more demanding challenges, with a dive on the *Carrie Lea*, a sunken vessel which was sitting on the edge of a reef about 200 feet down, and thought to be ready to topple into the depths of the Caribbean. Just before leaving, Chet asked if I'd ever 'narked out', which brought my enthusiasm to a temporary halt. I said, 'Do you mean, "nitrogen narcosis"?'

'Yes,', he said, adding, 'well, you are going to get it today!'

He explained that we'd be dealing with some fearsome currents, and to make it to the vessel, we'd be dropping down like the clappers on an anchor line, with the air supply turned off in order to decompress on the way up. To be honest, I don't remember the full detail of what it all really entailed, but it's sufficient to say that we didn't drink or smoke the night before, and come the morning, my excitement was tinged with a little concern. At the start of the dive, four of us bombed down, and reached 100 feet in seconds. Once down, we continued on a 'buddy basis' to drift through the cabins of the *Carrie Lea* — the sight was fantastic! There were still bicycles lashed to the deck, and as we glided towards the stern section, I looped a Deep Purple pendant on a lanyard over the bow rail in a symbolic gesture. The dive was inspirational, and appears in my music on the song 'Cayman Island'. I didn't 'nark out', though, because it was decided that people who drink on a regular basis shouldn't do it!

Chet is one of those people who have a special quality which is impossible to describe. But people like him (my buddy Mike Curle in England is another) exude a calm nature, which touches me deeply.

Back at Vermont, there was a lot of ballooning done, and plenty of wining and dining, which we're all pretty good at. We'd all find our favourite restaurant, and generally enjoy drifting around together, having a good time. I suppose they soon realised that I'd not changed that much, which was confirmed (I guess) the night I emptied my trousers of various things, including a candelabra! There was also quite a lot of 'afterburning' going on, and seeing how quickly you could get a girl to get her clothes off and do a swap. It's just something I like to do from time to time, and I think the fastest I managed at Stowe was 20 seconds!

On one occasion, Bruce brought his girlfriend to the restaurant we were meeting at and, at that time, she'd not met any of the band. He'd left me at the table to go and collect her, and by the time they had returned, I had moved to another spot. So they came in, and she was saying, 'Well, what does he look like?' So Bruce looked around the bar, and there sitting in the corner in a blue dress, high heels and with long black hair, was his singer! He turned to his girlfriend and said, 'You see that girl over there in the blue dress ...' — she nodded — '... well, he looks remarkably like that!'

Things like that happened quite a lot, and the band took it all in good spirit. In fact, the reunion was working, and Polydor

Records were very happy with what was going on. (Did I once say I'd never make another album with them?)

It seemed to me we'd captured that chemistry of what Roger once referred to as an 'old love affair', where 'love can be very close to hate'. Well, that chemistry was in *Perfect Strangers* — it felt wrapped up in warmth, care and love, which was how our best work always happened.

We rehearsed for the world tour in The Attico Room at Bedford, and worked on a set which included our old material such as 'Lazy', 'Space Truckin'', 'Child in Time' and 'Woman from Tokyo', and we then worked on stuff from the new album. Tommy Vance was an early interview for the BBC, as well as Phil Easton at Radio City. In fact, the media willingly picked up on most of the project, and the whole world seemed delighted we'd got together again.

We kicked off the *Perfect Strangers* tour in New Zealand and Australia, travelling via Los Angeles, where we rehearsed for a few days. After that, the gear was shipped out, and we took a more leisurely flight, stopping off in Tahiti. Here, then, was a chance to further enhance my knowledge of different cultures, and I contemplated the old colonies.

Basically, it seemed to me that the British and the French were raving expansionists in the early days, and here was another territory touched upon by these great countries. I mentally ran through the list of 'fortunates' — America, Guadeloupe, India, Algeria, Malaysia, Vietnam, Australia, Lebanon and so it goes on. Who ended where and why is beyond me ... it surely couldn't have been because of the food!

I've always enjoyed French cuisine — I ate it all the time during my year in Paris — but I suspect its reputation travels somewhat better than its substance. Talking of France and substance, we went to this French restaurant in Tahiti, where the meal was ordered, made up of bits the cooks usually throw away. It looked, smelt and then tasted appalling, with fish heads and all sorts of rubbish swimming around in the soup, like swill. In fact, it brought back memories of my swim in the River Orwell, but this was called *bouillabaisse*. So while we spent time discussing the merits — or not — of French food, Bruce (Payne), who was eating next to me, said, 'Well, what did you order for the main course?'

'Duck,' I said.

Unfortunately, he didn't, and so he got my hand round the back of his head, about which he was not amused. In fact, he was furious, shouting, 'What the fuck did you do that for?'

Well, I said "duck," didn't I?'

And so the band continued on its happy way to Australia. I'll say one thing for Purple, they do many things in style, and on long-haul trips, it would usually be first class. Apart from the fact that it's a great way to travel — extravagant, of course, but comfortable — it does help keep you in shape, which is important when you're hauling yourself out of bed in the morning to get to another city, and doing that routine day in and day out. The peace and quiet of first-class airport lounges help make the downside of rock 'n' roll seem worthwhile. Our road manager Colin Hart, who'd been with the organisation since we nicked him from Rod Stewart's crew, always looked after the detail (and still does!) and is very good at that sort of thing. He'd pick up the smallest details, saying such things as, 'You spent a long time on the phone last night, Ian?'

'I know Colin,' I'd say, 'I was talking to B.'

'Yes,' he'd say, 'I recognised the number!'

Or after we'd checked out of a hotel, he'd say something like, 'The bar bill's a bit high this morning.'

'Yes,' I'd say, 'had a bit of a bender last night, Colin!'

He'd never query the figure, but you knew that if you tried to fool him, by pretending you hadn't used the mini-bar or whatever, he'd have quietly checked it out!

Despite the constant talk and rumour about the millions of

dollars sloshing around, it's never quite that way, and the managers have to keep some sort of grip on budgets, however famous and successful the band is. Looking through the logistics of touring with Deep Purple, it might interest some readers to get a feel for just what goes on behind the scenes of a show. Here's an example taken from a more recent tour schedule, The *Perpendicular* Tour 1996 (Japan leg).

Setting aside the management (Bruce Payne's office and Phil Banfield's), a world tour has a back up of 'thousands'! There's Colin Hart (Tour Manager); Charlie Lewis (Production Manager); Rick Taylor (Tour Accountant); technicians like Mickey Lee Soule (keyboard, former Ian Gillan Band), Scott 'Porno' Porterfield (drums), Warren Lyndon (guitar), Michael Ager (bass), Moray McMillan (house sound technician), Xavier Theys and Ton Maesen. Then there's Steve Arch, Andrew Mills and Craig McDonald on lighting; John Dall (rigger); Patricia Tervit (wardrobe); Sally Hogg, Mary Caird and Graeme Morrison (catering); and last, but by no means least, people like Ron Tasker (band bus driver), Steve Howson and Ken Atkinson (crew drivers) and Steve Elsey, Les Martin and Nigel Hudson, all truck drivers.

Many others are involved, and then, of course, there's the cost of studios, where you can pay a fortune, and also have to be right for the project. I've worked in the best and, at the other extreme, the most basic. Both can work for you, and it also depends on the advance available and the label behind the album, but perhaps the point is made!

Perfect Strangers in Australia was one long party; the shows sold out and went down well. The vibe in the band was fine and, in Brisbane, I had a surprise call from B.

'Where are you?' I asked.

'I'm at The Townhouse,' she said, which struck me as strange, because the Townhouse is a studio in London, and I couldn't figure out why she should be there. So when I said that, she said, 'No, The Sebel Townhouse Hotel in Sydney,' where we were heading for our next show!

There are long separations in this business, so it was a great call, and we had a good time. The Sebel Townhouse is one of those party hotels, and did we party! There was one member on the tour who was feeling very horny when we arrived at the hotel, so I fixed him up. I told the girl to pretend she was my friend, gave her the money, and said, 'Just give him a good time.' A bit later, my 'girlfriend' returned, followed soon after by a grinning colleague, who gave me a very quizzical look. He'll know who he is and will, at last, have his suspicions confirmed!

One of the highlights of that tour was the arrival at The Sydney Entertainment Centre of a friend of Jon's and Ian Paice — George Harrison. He came on stage with us to do a version of 'Lucille'. Now, as fans know, I've recorded 'Lucille' many times, so when it was suggested we do it, Ritchie said, 'What key?' to which I replied, 'No problem ... any key you like. I can yell that song any way you want!' What I wasn't expecting was the Everly Brothers' version, which is a very slow treatment. And then they chose the worst possible key of all! I introduced George as 'Arnold from Liverpool' and, of course, as quickly as the crowd realised who was on stage, they went potty! A prized possession is the photo with Phil Banfield, Jon Lord, George Harrison and myself after the show. I was in the shower when the idea of a photo came up, so when they told me to put something on, I found a sock!

That Australian leg brought back memories of a Purple tour 'down under' many years before, the first show being just after Mick Underwood's wedding, at which I'd been best man. Then we went out with Manfred Mann and Free, so it was a very strong package, promoted by Sammy Lee.

I arrived on the morning of the show in Perth, where we were playing The Olympic Pool. I came in at about 5.00am, and dozed off, to be woken by a spider creeping across my eye and

down the bridge of my nose. I gently closed my mouth and, as
the spider got to it, I blew it across the room. I then looked at it,
and noticed it had a very bright orange spot on the middle of its
back. I then went down to the desk, to organise a cold beer.
When asked if I was having any problems sleeping, I said to the
porter, 'Just a few,' and mentioned the spider on my face. When
I described it, he identified it as a kind that had killed three or
four people quite recently.

And on the subject of danger, I came to meet our promoter,
Sammy Lee, who came across ... well, let's just say quite strong!
Sammy was from Melbourne — short, busy and very
charismatic. He also wanted to be associated with me, and
'blew out' the rest of the band. Remember, we're looking back
at early Purple days, when *Jesus Christ Superstar* was so big.
And so, in Sammy's book, I was somebody 'to be seen with'. He
was an amazing character, with a penchant for big sweaters,
and alongside him travelled Jake, who carried an attaché case
full of guns. Once, when the press were advancing towards
me, Sammy extended his arm up, reaching quite a long way up
to my shoulder, and said in this unmistakable Aussie twang
(and with a husky voice), 'Hey, boys, this is the greatest singer
since rock was invented ... this is the greatest singer in the
world!' He then paused, looked up at me and said, 'What's your
name, boy?'

Sammy was truly amazing, and so enjoyed the visit by these
three great bands from the UK, that he told us he'd added
another show at just one day's notice! Not surprisingly, because
nobody knew about it, only about a hundred people came
along, and it then turned out that the deal was 'cash up front'.
When it wasn't there, Manfred's manager phoned Sammy from
the hotel, asking for payment before the band left. That caused
Sammy to get very indignant — he didn't like being thought of
as a crook — and so he arrived with his cohorts, whom he left
around the hotel lobby, taking just a couple upstairs to give

Manfred's manager a serious hiding. The noise was unbelievable, but the hotel refused to do anything about it. I eventually thought enough was enough, and walked in to find Sammy almost having a heart attack with rage as they beat shit out of the manager.

It also happened that Sammy liked me (aside from the *Superstar* bit), so when I said, 'Hang on, Sammy, this isn't very good for your image,' he backed off. Sammy paid up, we did the show to the handful of punters, and flew out. I believe Sammy later died of a heart attack, but that was my first introduction to Australia, and I've gone back there as often as possible.

Back with the more recent *Perfect Strangers* tour, nothing dramatic like that happened, and we moved on to America. That leg was huge, and progressed along similar lines to the Black Sabbath visit I had so much respect for. Except now I was with my people and playing to audiences who were glad to see us back. The tour schedule began at Ector County Colosseum in Odessa, Texas, and then incorporated:

January

19th	Amarillo, Texas
20th	Wichita, Texas
24th	The Summit, Houston, Texas
25th	The Reunion Arena, Dallas, Texas
26th	The Convention Centre, San Antonio, Texas
28th	El Paso County Colosseum, El Paso, Texas

And so it continued — Arizona, San Diego, Colorado, St Louis and Kansas. Deep Purple has always been a working band, and the touring went through to the end of March, when we flew into Canada for shows that took in Montreal, Quebec, Toronto and Vancouver. As we travelled, so more shows were added, and apparently we took in $7million for that section alone.

As the tour ground to a halt, what else but another album! Except now I 'accidentally' made two! This is what happened. Roger and I did a great deal of preparation for what would become *The House of Blue Light*, only to discover that Ritchie wasn't really interested in listening to us. After trying out a couple of studios, we ended up back at Stowe, Vermont, where we set up in the Playhouse. This time it was going to be a struggle. There was no spirit, no cohesion — it reminded me of Rome all those years ago, and making *Who Do We Think We Are!*, when Ritchie vetoed 'Painted Horse', which he hated.

Now for *The House of Blue Light*, we had 'Mitzi Dupree', the story about my airline flight during the Sabbath period. Roger and I had worked on this, giving lyrics to the rough backing tracks but, once again, Ritchie hated it so much, he refused to record it. So what you hear on the album is the original demo!

That sort of thing used to piss me off big time, until I began to realise that's what Ritchie seems to get off on. So Roger and I set up camp in the Playhouse, working in a tiny room with no windows. In no time at all, the walls were covered with bits of paper, song titles and lyrical themes, as we kept ourselves busy trying to turn the arrangements into songs. It's an arse-about-face way of writing, but there it is — what else can you do?

Well, for one thing, I went to the pub in Stowe to enjoy the company of Richard Hughes, and we spent many a happy hour — sometimes at work, and sometimes not!

The album was far from finished when everybody packed up and left, so Rog and I took the mobile, and parked it at the back of his house in Greenwich. There, away from the Prince of Darkness, as Ritchie is affectionately known, the mood lightened, and we made some progress — 'Mad Dog', 'The Spanish Archer', 'Bad Attitude' and 'The Unwritten Law' were all finished off in Roger's basement studio, with the aristocratic Russian/Canadian hippy-cum-teddy bear of an engineer, the amazing Nick Blagona, helping to make it happen.

Take a look at these dirty hands
Take a look at this face, these blazing eyes,
Do you see me as a broken man,
Tell me are you really that blind ...

Other songs on the album were 'Call of the Wild', 'Hard Lovin' Woman', 'Strangeways', 'Dead or Alive' and, of course, 'Mitzi Dupree'. Roger then went to Germany to mix the thing, and when he got back, his brains were like scrambled eggs!

I've already made comparison to this album and *Who Do We Think We Are!* and, you know, it's a funny thing. If you look at a top athlete or, in fact, anybody at the top of their tree, the wizardry seems effortless, while others struggle to emulate them. And it's the same with Deep Purple. If the chemistry isn't right, if the spirit isn't there, then an album can sound like a struggle, and I think *The House of Blue Light* (and *Who Do We Think We Are!*) fall into that category, while albums like *Deep Purple In Rock* and *Machine Head* show a band at ease with itself.

And so came the day when the final touches had been put to the mix, and our work was over. I looked at Roger and said, 'You look fucking drained!' He said he was, so I came back with, 'I tell you what ... I've got an idea. Let's go and make a record!'

He just stood and looked at me, so I followed it up with, 'Look, Rog. We've just finished a record, and it's like a bad fuck.'

So we got hold of Nick Blagona, and took off for the Air Monserrat studio in the Caribbean to write and record something joyous — *Accidentally on Purpose*.

We arrived and immediately went over to the studio, where we arranged for a little 'inspiration' to be delivered. As we shook out the bag of marjuana on to the table to make into a conical pyramid. I remember saying to Roger, 'This is going to be a great album!' We went and put down the acoustic and bass to 'Dislocated', had some food, climbed into our cars — Hillman Avengers, I believe — and found our way into town, and a bar called The Plantation. We walked in and went upstairs, and the first thing I noticed was a fan turning slowly. I'd never seen a fan with such a rotation, but this was very slow. It was hot and sultry, there were shutters for windows, and a lot of dust on the floor. And then my eyes picked out this very large Teutonic sort of woman swaying about on her stool, and about to fall off. I went over to help her, but everybody said, 'No ... go away!'

There were a fair number of ex-pat types sitting around, and so we just watched what happened until, finally, she fell off. There was a huge crash, the dust flew, and as we again moved to pick her up, two or three guys pushed us away, as some others were seen to be setting their diving watches, and looking down on her.

After what seemed an eternity, they started going, 'No ... no ... *now!*' Watches clicked, and they went back to the bar, leaving her on the floor. They were roaring with laughter, and then a couple of them hauled her to her feet, and she was taken home. It turned out that she was some kind of travel agent, who had settled out there, and that every Friday she'd turn up at the bar and get completely wrecked, and fall off her stool. It seemed that the lads had picked up on the fact that, due to her large and independent breasts, when she crashed to the floor, her bosom continued to move for some considerable time afterwards, until it settled down, so to speak. So the Friday night wager was on just how long it would be until all was still. On the evening of our arrival, I believe it was 45 seconds.

With order restored, I moved across to the bar, and ordered drinks from this guy, who had an immaculate Oxford accent. He greeted me with, 'Hello, my name is English!' To which I replied, as so many must have before me, 'Would you mind telling me why you are called English?' Well, it turned out that English was sent to England for a fine education, and he then became a barrister. Walking through Lincoln's Inn one miserable January morning, the thought crossed his mind, 'What the fuck am I doing here? I'd rather be in Monserrat, my home, serving rum punch!' So he jacked it all in, returned, and started working behind the bar — getting drunk, smoking a little, writing a bit, usually for people who needed legal advice such as letters, that sort of thing. And he was as happy as ... well, English!

Since the volcano disaster, I've often wondered what became of English. He was such an inspiration — I mean, what a fine life choice to make, from being a barrister in London, to serving B52s to visitors on that wonderful sub-tropical idyll. So we smoked a little, and then Roger said he wanted to get back, and I offered Nick a lift with me.

Now, Nick trusts me to drive with care — I drive slowly — so we got into the car, rolled a couple of large ones, and off we went. We were cruising along, saying how great this song was that we'd started on, and playing with the melody: 'Dang de dang ... Dang de dang,' when suddenly we happened upon a cow lying in the middle of the road. In fact, it was fast asleep with its back to us so, after a polite pause, I tooted my horn a few times, then leaned out of the car and coughed, and finally called out, 'Excuse me, but I need to get home now!'

Well, it reluctantly got up, gave me a baleful stare, stepped to the side, and looked at me, as if to say, 'Sorry, pal. On your way then.' I thanked the beast, let out the clutch, and we continued, 'Dang de dang.'

Everything was fine for several minutes, and then I happened to glance at Nick, who'd gone very pale. He was looking past me out of the window.

'Nick, what is it?' I said.

'Look,' he replied in a hushed voice. So I turned to look, and there was the cow walking along, and now overtaking the car! As Nick will confirm, I'm a very slow driver!

Ears are screaming
Vase a leaning tower
On my plate at the party
There was no party
There was no suitcase
There was no back seat
There was no car
Dislocated, dislocated, dislocated, dislocated.

About half the album was done in the Caribbean, but we had to stop to pick up on touring with Purple. Although *The House of Blue Light* would not set the world on fire — it was released in January 1987 — and made number 10 in the UK and 34 in America.

The tour started well, and got better. Rog and I decided to travel by bus, while the others flew, the idea being that we'd be better able to write for *Accidentally on Purpose*. And so we just cruised through the countryside, took in the scenery — there was no rush, no airport lounges, no irritating packing and unpacking — we'd party when we felt like it, and sleep it off in the bunks. It was the only way to go.

Chet King flew up from the Cayman Islands to spend a few days with us — he loves his rock 'n' roll! One day, he picked up the internal phone in the toilet, poked his head out of the door, and said, 'Can I call home from here?'

'Who wants to live in a telephone box?' came the reply. It was a pretty odd exchange, but I picked up the guitar, and the song 'Telephone Box' was born. It sounded good on the radio a year or so later. And 'Lonely Avenue' sounded good on *Rain Man*, the Dustin Hoffman movie!

Back on tour with Purple, we did a show at Phoenix, and the band was performing at its best. Ritchie threw his guitar in the air, and temporarily forgot where he put it. Too late, he reached into the 'spot', mis-timed his catch, and broke one of his more important fingers! The tour was cancelled, and Roger and I went to Minot Studios in New York, and then The Power Station, to finish *Accidentally on Purpose*.

We brought in some great musicians, including Doctor John, Randy Brecker, Joe Mennonna and the exquisite Vaneese Thomas. We are still chuffed with the results! However, due to politics or whatever, the record was almost completely unsupported by Virgin. The Managing Director at Virgin/Ten was Richard Griffiths, and his enthusiasm had been fantastic, right from the beginning. He really stuck his neck out for us, but sadly left the organisation just before release, so it floundered in the market.

I have to say that everybody I know who has a copy of that album, tells me it's their favourite, and of all the records I've made, it's the one I play the most. As for Roger, well, he has been an inspiration to me, and the nearest I've ever had to having a brother. I love him.

Accidentally on Purpose was released in 1988, and is a clutch of songs: 'Clouds and Rain', 'Evil Eye', 'She Took My Breath Away', 'Dislocated', 'Via Miami', 'I Can't Dance To That', 'Can't Believe You Want To Leave', 'Lonely Avenue', 'Telephone Box' and 'I Thought No'.

Once Ritchie's finger had mended, the Purple tour picked up again in Europe, but the spark had gone; tensions were back! There was an incident in Italy, when I said at a press conference (in reply to a question about why the routing was so strange), "The problem is that our manager, Bruce Payne, is a dickhead!' Or something like that. It was a cruel remark, born out of frustration. I think I'd just heard Paicey say he never went near his drum kit between tours. It got me thinking, 'it's all going down the tubes again,' but I apologised to Bruce, and guess I'm forgiven. Bruce Payne is actually a very funny guy, and we have been together long enough now to have learned the ropes — at least as far as we are both concerned.

As the tour struggled on, there was a dressing room incident towards the close, after a UK date. I had a cold, and was sitting quietly, when Ritchie burst in, eyes blazing, and with a china plate in his hand. On it was spaghetti, and someone had smothered it in tomato ketchup. He charged over to me, and said, 'Did you do this?' but without waiting for my answer, he then smashed the plate into my face as if it were a custard pie. I slowly stood up, and he started dancing around me, fists raised, saying, 'Come on then ... come on!'

'I don't want to hit you, Ritchie,' I said, and turned away to go into the bathroom to clean up. Once there, I cried with rage and frustration, and said to myself, 'I quit.' But then I changed my mind, since I realised how pleased he would have been. But it was downhill all the way from that moment. The next album, *Nobody's Perfect* would complete the three projects for Polydor Records, and it included stuff we'd recorded on our tour, live, such as 'Perfect Strangers' (California, May 1987), 'Hard Lovin' Woman' and 'Black Night' (Oslo, August 1987), 'Lazy' (Phoenix, Arizona, May 1987), and even 'Hush', taken from a jam session at Hook End Manor in 1988! Although my views on this kind of project are well known, I still approached it with a positive and ambitious approach, saying, 'Let's make this as good as we can.'

However, when we took the material into the studio at Hook End Manor for post-production, the difficulties became obvious. OK, you can use a studio to make bum notes come out right, but other issues, which are more problematic, need to be addressed. For example, what happens when the tape runs out in the middle of a song, or when there are crackles and screeches? We didn't seem to go into that project with the absolute will to make a great live album, otherwise I suppose we'd have taken more than one tape recorder!

In addition, the band wanted to use a lot of the *Made in Japan* stuff, and add newer songs, to show how we had changed. Sadly, it was clear that we'd hardly changed at all, we'd just become more slick, and adding 'Hush' was the strangest decision of all! Nobody has yet owned up to that idea, although I did try to get it across that Rod Evans could have done a much better job than I could with the newer version. An original is always best.

At some time I ventured the idea that we make the album in New York, which provoked Jon's memorable reply, 'The thought of recording in New York fills me with dread!'

I tried to explain the logic behind the idea, that the management were there, Ritchie lived there, as did Roger, he had a studio we could use, that the equipment was kept there, and the tour manager and many of the crew lived in the city, and so on. Anyway, it was all rejected, so Los Angeles was then proposed, only for Ritchie to knock it down. The atmosphere in the Deep Purple camp was very difficult!

Bruce then came up with the thought that maybe we should get some studio brochures together, and I found that unbelievable! I started to ask if he'd not realised that most decent studios were long since booked out, before falling back on the 'dickhead' description for which he'd forgiven me first time around. I said, 'Bruce, you are supposed to be picking the stones from out of our path, and instead all I hear is, "I don't want to do this" or "That's not possible."' I told him it was driving me crazy, being with a 'band I'd die for', when all I got was 'negatives'. Finally, I said, 'You are fucking useless,' at which point Ritchie walked out without saying a word. Jon said something I didn't quite catch, and left, with Bruce not far behind. That left Roger. Roger, my dear friend of all those years, leaned forward across the table, knuckles bunched, and stared me in the face.

'Ian,' he said, 'you have gone too far this time.'

The snow was down in Stowe, and I began drinking more and more heavily — my presence was not really required.

One night, I arrived back to find my door locked. For some reason I was naked, except for two bin liners tied below the knees to keep my feet dry. So I moved across to where Ritchie was, and kicked the door down. My arrival was greeted by an open-mouthed tableau — there was Ritchie, his girlfriend and Colin Hart, who I think was trying to help sort out a domestic between the guitar player and his lady. Somebody else was also there, but it mattered not, as I realised that the momentum caused by kicking in the door had become an unstoppable force. And so I lurched forward, mouthing silent words, eventually to hit the settee, which I crashed over, bringing down a couple of glass shelves and the cut-glass contents. And so, naked and dressed in my improvised 'wellies', I fell asleep at Ritchie's place.

I was sitting at home in England, when I got a call from Phil Banfield, saying I'd been fired.

Chapter 12

So Phil's on the other end of the line, with that tone of voice that tells me something terrible has happened, and this was not a good moment for him. After the brief and hollow pleasantries, he came to the point.

'Ian, we've got problems,' and, of course, I knew exactly what was coming.

'It's Purple, isn't it?' I said. 'They fired me, didn't they?'

'Yes.'

At the time, I was sitting in the small studio which was part of our house, and from that room, I could look over a small lake, over which I've seen the seasons pass, or sat around on warm summer days and evenings in solitude, or with friends. How strange it seemed then, as I watched carefree wildlife and movement on the water, while hearing Phil's voice from hectic Soho, as he spoke about musical differences, the band looking for another singer, and running by me his thoughts on how we should deal with the media. I've little recollection of taking much of it in, as I struggled with my situation.

On the one hand, I knew I'd not been coming up with great ideas for Purple, but I knew it was in me to do so. *Accidentally on Purpose* proved that. OK, so *The House of Blue Light* had been a struggle, but my efforts to contribute had been worth nothing more than a drowning-out session, mostly by guitar! Suggestions and half-worked ideas had been strangled; so long as Ritchie was happy with his parts, then the lads were happy with the project. Well fuck it, I wasn't happy, and said so. Perhaps my own way of dealing with my frustration gave them the chance to think me a nuisance, but could they not see my difficulties?

In the meantime, Phil was bravely continuing with the crap gossip which had been going around the business; that I didn't really want to be with Deep Purple any more, and was looking to revive my alter ego, Garth Rockett and The Moonshiners.

To this day, I have no idea how it all got so totally out of hand, although the buzz was that Ian Paice had something to do with it. Anyway, whoever it was, he or she added fuel to the fire, and people were able to say, 'Well, Ian doesn't really like Purple any more, and Garth Rockett had always been his first love.'

It was quite convenient, and I know Simon Robinson from our fan club, Darker Than Blue, had a call along those lines.

So all this is going through my head, and then I saw B standing in the studio doorway.

'What's wrong?' she asked.

'The bastards have fired me,' I said.

After a pause — just a lingering moment, when you wonder what's going to happen next — a great big grin crossed her face, she ran across the studio and threw herself at me, arms around my neck, legs around my waist and cried happily into my ear, 'Gubbins, now you can do what you really want!'

Looking back on it all, it must have sounded a little strange to Phil, who was still on the other end of the phone. Here was my manager firstly giving me the depressing news, but getting no feedback, and the next thing he's hearing is a celebration party! I eventually returned to the phone to say I thought the

Garth Rockett project a great idea, and fuck Deep Purple. I may also then have used the words I'd have to explain a few years later, that 'I'd rather slit my throat than sing with that band again!' (Never say never again!)

So having fired me, Purple hired Joe Lynn Turner, and started work on *Slaves and Masters*. Of course, those wicked journalists naturally asked him for his thoughts about me, and one of his stock-in-trade answers was, 'Ian Gillan? Let's not speak ill of the dead!'

I picked up with The Moonshiners project, and planned a single concert at the Southport Floral Hall, which Phil Easton promoted.

There were early doubts about the venue, which had got the place booked out for a disco on the night in question — hosted by Phil. When *Raw* magazine eventually traced me, I simply said they should call Garth Rockett! The idea was to find a bunch of musicians who would work with me for the sheer fun of playing rock 'n' roll on the club circuit, and I found them in Mark Buckle (keyboards), Keith Mulholland (bass/vocals), Lou Rosenthal (drums), Harry Shaw (guitar/vocals) and Steve Morris who came along as guitarist and musical director. The band all came from the Liverpool area, and had been recommended by Phil Easton.

We rehearsed for a couple of weeks at the Cumberland Tavern in Liverpool, and the Southport gig was just great, a quantum leap from my lifestyle of just a few weeks before, but fine, nevertheless. Inevitably, a number of fans had made the Garth connection, and we had a constant party, playing songs like 'I'll Rip Your Spine Out', 'No Laughing in Heaven', 'Living for the City', 'Ain't That Loving', 'I Thought No', 'No Easy Way', 'New Orleans', and a slow lament which I'd perform a lot, 'No More Cane on the Brazos' — or just 'Brazos' as it became known.

It's a song Roger reminded me of, and is variously credited, usually to Lonnie Donegan. Although there was no money in this for Phil (Banfield) — in fact there was no more than pocket money for us all — he still backed the project, and it turned into a mini tour. It was early 1989, we were working flat out; we were accessible, affordable (tickets at the Tivoli, Buckley cost just £2.50) and the shows were good. We toured to;

May

14th	Sheffield University
15th	Birmingham Edwards No. 8
16th	The Ritz, Manchester
17th	Leeds Irish Centre
19th	Civic Centre, Wolverhampton
20th	Nottingham Trent Polytechnic
22nd	Mayfair, Newcastle
23rd	Mayfair, Glasgow
24th	Fat Sams, Dundee
25th	The Venue, Edinburgh
27th	Stairways, Birkenhead
28th	The Bierkeller, Bristol.

Although we made a video *Live at the Ritz '89*, it was never my intention to make records with The Moonshiners, nor to develop from that format into something bigger. The idea was to have fun and tour out of a suitcase, and I think we did all that.

Various old mates looked in at the gigs, people like Tony Iommi, Cozy Powell and Bev Bevan, and we'd usually end up in the early hours at some club, or just keeping the hotel bar open.

Perhaps the lads in the band were hoping things would lead to something else, and although I'd made my position very clear, we all still have our dreams. Maybe I'd let my attitude that I don't close doors on anything seem misleading, but then I think it's only human nature that we all pick out what we want to hear, and dismiss the rest. And that's dangerous.

So when I began to formulate plans to make the album *Naked Thunder*, and rediscover my career as a major artist, there was some disappointment and a few harsh words, when all but Steve Morris had no serious place in the next stage.

At around that time, I'd also become friendly with Graham Underwood — drinking buddy, deadly pool opponent, car fixer, anything fixer, non-stop piss-taker and general partner in crime. Graham easily slipped into the role of tour manager and general listener, trouble-shooter and so on. Our first meeting was at some pub or other (where else?) and I realised I had no money on me to stand my round. I asked Graham if he could lend me some, and he bought me two! I then asked again if he could help me out with a note, to which he said, 'What do you want to drink?' So I thought I'd better deal with this, and said, 'Triple scotch and Coke, please,' which prompted him to lend me the money!

It was towards the end of the Garth Rockett dates that I mentioned to Steve I was going to do an album, and he just quietly said, 'Oh, I write songs, actually.'

'Well, feel free to send some down to me ... I have people sending me tapes all the time,' I said. And I promised to give his work a listen.

So one morning, I was having my cereal and doing the crossword, while also separating my mail into two piles; one for the bin, and the other to deal with, and there was one package in a brown envelope. It had no return address on it and was sealed with almost an entire roll of sticky tape. After fighting it for a while, I chucked it in the bin.

A short while later, I was playing pool with Graham, when I heard this great backing track come on the speakers, so I said to Graham, 'Where the hell did you get that from?'

'Your bin!' he replied.

Of the four tracks on that tape, three ended up on the album, *Naked Thunder*. That was the first tape Steve sent me, and I had thrown it away!

Steve would then start to come down and work with me, or we'd send stuff backwards and forwards by post, building up a project I decided for various reasons I'd finance myself. Looking back on that decision, it was a mistake, and as far as the album was concerned, there are things which could have been done better. Quite honestly, the Garth Rockett tour had been a most welcome distraction from the Purple business, but it had not found me reserves of energy and neither had I rediscovered my touch. I should have come out on *Naked Thunder* with both fists flying, but I didn't want to be undignified, nor to be seen to be in a corner.

What I was dealing with was equivalent to a traumatic divorce, in which the parties should have been able to work something out, to stay together. The first divorce had been bad enough, but in that case, I'd been the one who walked out. This time I'd been thrown out, and my band was continuing without me, making a Deep Purple album, *Slaves and Masters*.

So that was going on as we worked out the material for *Naked Thunder*, for which I brought in Leif Mases as producer. Leif came with great credentials, having just finished a project with Jeff Beck but, nice as he is, and with his obvious ability, he came to work with an artist, me, who had very few positive ideas, apart from ordering another drink!

So how do I look back on that period in terms of a creative statement? Well, I guess I summed it up myself in the studio one day while we made the album, realising that I was crafting my songs by taking Steve's material, and singing along with a scribbling pad in a 'hum dee hum' fashion. The other way is when I get hold of a multi-track, set the tapes out, crank the volume up full throttle and start 'Whoooaaooing', and rock 'n' rolling. *Naked Thunder* was a 'hum dee hum' album, and while there's a lot about it I'm very happy with, I can see that it disappointed some people.

I'm gonna build a bridge
To take my train of thought
I'm gonna break the law
And spread my wings across the water
You think you're something special
But you don't know what you're doing
I've got news for you, babe
What you're doin's gonna ruin you.

Perhaps the only real moment of contentment and reunion with my past was when I got involved in the aftermath of the Armenian tragedy, when a few of us came together to make 'Smoke on the Water' in a benefit for victims. A lot of mates were involved, including Bruce Dickinson, Bryan Adams, Dave Gilmore, Tony Iommi, Roger Taylor, Paul Rodgers, and uncle Tom Cobbly an' all! Quite a line up. Ritchie came in on a separate occasion to record his contribution — when no one was around. Later that year, we'd all be awarded gold discs and thanks for our contribution to that cause, although it was not necessary. You don't do a thing like that to add to the collection of mementoes, but the gesture was still appreciated. A lot of people don't bother to thank you at all.

We made *Naked Thunder* at Duncansby Crescent Studios in Warrington, Woodcray Studio near Bracknell and Amazon Studio, Liverpool. It features several respected musicians. Steve was, of course, there, and so, too, were Peter Robinson (synth/piano), Tommy Eyre (also on synth and Hammond), Simon Phillips (drums), and other great players like Bev Bevan, John Gustafson (that man again!), Dave Lloyd, Harry Shaw and Carol Kenyan. They worked enthusiastically on stuff like 'Gut Reaction', 'Nothing But the Best', 'Love Gun', 'Brazos' and the rest.

But then I realised just how hard the business is, how it changes, and how quickly it forgets you, as finding a record deal became a demoralising experience. Suddenly, it was a far cry from the days when there were record companies all over the place. Now the whole business seemed to be owned by people who also sold washing machines, televisions and other useful objects. I had to go through the whole experience again, knocking on doors, playing tapes to a new generation, some of whom hadn't been conceived when my career began!

Finally, we signed to Teldec/East West, and the album was set for release in July 1990 (a little before *Slaves and Masters* came out). *Naked Thunder* would not sell very well, but on the back of it, I could make plans to do what I like doing best — touring. While the Ian Gillan Band Tour was being put together, beginning in the former USSR the following May, I set about finding a seasoned bunch of travellers, who needed two essential qualities — playing skills and endurance! I ended up with much, much more.

For a tour like this, it was out of the question to ask the likes of Simon Phillips along. People like Simon and Pete Robinson can earn more in a few hours in the States than they'd take home after months on a tour like the one I had in mind. They work with top artists frequently, and earn big money. We had to settle for lesser mortals, and with no disrespect at all, they were Steve 'Navajo' Morris (lead guitar); Chris Glenn (bass) — known as 'Big Bad'; Ted McKenna (drums) — known as 'Big Mental'; Tommy Eyre (keyboard); Dave Lloyd, great singer; and Mick O'Donoghue, also on guitar (rhythm). Ted and Chris were out of MSG, and go back further to The Sensational Alex Harvey Band, while Mick became known as O'Duff, except, of course, the night we played Odense!

And so we left for the vastness of Russia, where everybody seemed to be called Sasha. After rehearsals at Nomis studio near Earls Court in London, we travelled to Moscow, where we played four shows at the Olympiiskyl, and where I had a little confrontation with a guy who wanted me to sign an anti-drugs petition. I basically put it to him that I couldn't do as he asked, believing that it wasn't the way to deal with this thing.

He replied, 'Ah, so you are in favour of drugs then?'

Knowing Moscow had — and still has, I guess — a growing and worrying drug problem, I tried to explain that the day you ask a Scotsman not to have another whisky, a German not to drink another beer, a Frenchman not to have another glass of wine, or even a Russian not to have another vodka, that's the day I'll ask a Jamaican not to smoke his ganja, a North African not to touch hashish or a Bolivian not to chew his coca leaves.

The arrogance of one society to judge the customs of another as uncool astounds me, but having said that, I've seen close friends come to grief because of drug abuse, and I do not condone the use of opiates, heroin, cocaine and the shit the gangsters try to get people into. Neither do I have any intention of sticking a needle in myself, and hate to hear of situations where food, drink or cigarettes have been interfered with. It's a subject I can best deal with in my music, and 'No Easy Way' is an example. It looks at the tragic end of two friends of mine, one a hooker, the other a junkie.

Little John took the easy way he said
Bye bye to the light of day
He didn't need a gun at all
He went flying and took a fall

Little Ann took the easy way she said
Take the money and run away
Lie down and look away
Save the money for a rainy day.

Back in the USSR, we went to Yerevan for another four gigs,

before going to Tbilisi for five more. The programme continued across that huge territory of Ordzonikidze, Grozny, Nalczyk, Volgograd, Mahatchkallah in Tjaistan on the Caspian sea and, finally, back to Moscow, for a return to London. At all venues we performed a number of shows, and tasted many experiences. This was a tour by plane and bus, and we were taking our music to places no British or American band had ever visited.

Al Dutton was the tour manager, and Graham (Squiffy) Underwood also came along. It was one long drunken party out there, with many misunderstandings but a lot of good shows. We took the 'Gillan's Inn' pub sign, and the pool table came as well, just in case anybody became disorientated! We also took my spare washing machine, but despite the attention to home comforts, there were moments of personality clashes and grief, and Tommy and Al fell out quite early on.

We dealt with liquor by the crate, quickly running out of Heineken, then to find Becks and so it continued as the convoy of vehicles moved along, a bit like a mobile brewery with guitars!

On one occasion, we'd been on the road for about eight hours, when we came across the largest gathering of sheep I've ever seen; not even in Australia could a 'fleet' of that size be possible and we had to drive dangerously close to the outside edge of a mountain side, just to avoid them. It also provoked much wailing from Scottish Ted, who kept saying, 'There's a lot of doonness doon there, boss!'

We were also in a region where it seemed strawberries, cheese, cherries, bread and, of course, lamb were in huge abundance, and Ted happened to be very keen on strawberries. He's also keen on crates of lager and, on this occasion, was sitting in the middle of the aisle, banging on about something or other in his thick native brogue. He then decided he was full up with strawberries and lager, and did what jet planes sometimes do — offload. It's called projectile vomiting, and he's perfected it as an art form. As luck would have it, he performed the stunt over me, before going back to the crates to start all over again. The situation was unfortunate, to put it mildly. First, it happened just as we were approaching some town or other, where everybody seemed to know about our arrival, except us, and then it was down to me to act as spokesman for the visitors, to be their leader, I suppose. Well, I'd been sufferering from a bad cold, had not slept properly for hours, was unshaven and drunk. I now had Ted's contribution all over my smelly white shirt, moments before the convoy drew to a halt.

Outside, there were hordes of children and a multitude of wild-eyed horsemen on equally wild-eyed horses. While trying to focus, this guy came galloping over with a huge horn filled with about six pints of sweet red wine and, with cameras clicking and rolling, I was encouraged to sink the offering in one go, as a symbolic gesture of friendship. In this, I was encouraged by my ever faithful band, with sounds of 'Goo on, boss … goo on, boss' ringing in my ears. On completing the cultural nicety, I was then handed a bunch of mature roses, which I accepted by thorny stems, before my hands were tightly clasped together in a warm embrace of welcome. It was yet another arrival at which I regret the band were rolling around in the bus, making unintelligent noises, mostly in a single Scottish accent!

I feel so dirty
I feel so dirty
It's all worked out
You tell me I've been wrong
I've got no reason to live anymore
Nothing to do but curl up and die.

We were then escorted to the town, where on arrival at the hotel, I realised we had a problem, as all hell broke loose. The band poured off the bus, wearing shorts and t-shirts, and were, of course, drunk. The fact we carried bottles in our hands didn't help in an area where there were quite a lot of Muslim fundamentalists. The situation became even more confused, because of my association with *Jesus Christ* (the album, that is), and although the local organisers hadn't really heard of Deep Purple, they knew of course about Jesus, the great prophet, whom they held in very great respect. And so I was received by some as Jesus, with his faithful disciples, my interest in carpentry having also found its way into the translations, and therefore clinching it!

When they saw us take to the stage, it didn't seem to pose problems (as such), but I needed to keep alert as much as possible, to be prepared for huge leaps in thought and explanation sometimes!

It's one of the joys of being a rock musician, and being willing to travel, that you can learn so much — from the sublime to the ridiculous! In Russia, for example, if you are being directed to a particular place by car, you do not follow the lead vehicle, you lead it! That makes for quite a slow journey sometimes, and it's very irritating and confusing. Someone will open the door to a labyrinth, and usher you in first. So you are asking, 'This way?' with your head turning 180 degrees, and they say, 'No, that way,' and somehow you arrive at your destination feeling very flexible. As I say, this to me is what rock 'n' roll is about — taking my music and trying to find new audiences and fans, and I realise it's pointless adhering to your own home attitudes and values abroad. All you end up doing is upsetting people, so it's always best to be polite and try to respect others' traditions and points of view.

Of course, it's sometimes difficult. At one show, Graham and I watched as twelve Russian soldiers debated how to move my travelling wardrobe from the dressing room to the truck. It's not that big an item (well, I suppose it is quite big!), and is designed like a flight case, with grips and so forth. It's been round the world many times without causing hardship, but now it stood between these people, and there was much head scratching going on. It would regularly fall over until, finally, Graham and I decided my clothes had suffered enough, so we put out our cigarettes, went over, and popped it on the truck! Our feat brought no display of admiration — in fact, they seemed very unimpressed. I was later told that some military units are told that taking the initiative loses wars, so decisions need to be ratified on a group basis!

On the occasions that distances meant we had to fly, even then things were, well, let's say, very different. We found ourselves aboard this huge aircraft (it made a 747 appear quite small), and we seemed to be the only passengers aboard. I was still feeling quite unwell, with a bout of 'flu, which seemed determined to stay with me for the duration. So while I continued to shiver, the lads continued to make themselves as unwell as possible, with copious amounts of vodka and whatever else they had managed to find at the airport.

After a while, Tommy staggered up and suggested I take a walk with him to the far end of the plane, where there was an elevator, and it arrived just as we got there. A female flight attendant of considerable dimensions invited me into the lift with her and, as we travelled down to the hold, she kindly massaged my private parts, before we reached the bowels of the plane, where there was a party in progress. Almost the entire flight crew were there — perhaps they all were, since this was not busy airspace, and all of them were roaring drunk. They had an open-flame cooker burning, and were brewing coffee and knocking back alcohol as if there would be no tomorrow.

So, at 35,000 feet, they invited Tommy and me to join

them, Tommy coming rapidly to his senses when he fell against a loading door that hadn't been closed properly. In fact, it was held together by two pieces of rope! Still, if the crew didn't give a monkeys, we did, and the two of us returned upstairs, where I hoped to die!

There were more elegant moments, and many occasions when we were treated with great respect. At a Ministry of Culture do, I was asked to spend some time with students, where coffee was taken, before we eventually went to watch a tapestry being made by graduates. It was incredible to see as, in one area, three girls worked on a piece which depicted Russian soldiers attacking Georgians, with shovels as weapons. The project was based on an army unit returning from Afghanistan, where soldiers had come up against a nationalist movement. Their only weapons were shovels, not because they had lost their firearms, but because they had never been issued with them in the first place. The tapestry was sensational and memorable, because here in the West such brutality would have made headline news, and then been forgotten. But in these tapestries, the action would be a vital image for future generations to come.

The people we met in that part of the world were stunning hosts, doing so often what poor people do, which is to give much of their hard-earned money to provide hospitality to strangers and friends. Bron, her sister Julie and their mother, Sheila, came out to provide a period of sanity amidst the chaos, and my wife and I did what some people find strange. In Tbilisi, Georgia, we got married again. Our first was at home; we married again in Vermont; but in the USSR, the idea came from some journalists sent by the Tass news agency.

When we arrived in town, various things were put in place so the wedding could go ahead, There was no sign whatsoever as to who would be paying for it, or anything like that. In due course, this gentleman from the Georgian State

Orchestra came over and introduced himself. Everything had been taken care of, and what then followed can only be described as 'brilliant'. We were picked up by a horse-driven coach, and taken at break-neck speed through the town, where we were joined by riders in full regalia, and then escorted onwards. There was much evidence of vast quantities of wine, which weighed the horses down considerably, and also a huge amount of sword waving and yelling was going on, as we arrived at a building which resembled a medieval town hall in England.

We were now kitted out in national costume, and although Bron looked lovely, I looked very silly indeed! Strange as it may seem, my rock 'n' roll personality doesn't extend to every situation, and in front of my mates, I felt embarrassed. However, any feelings of inadequacy were my problem when all that was happening was a show of enormous goodwill and affection, for which words of thanks are inadequate.

Inside the civic building, there was the most beautiful music being performed, and a service was conducted in English and Georgian. We then signed a book and, with a temporarily sober crew and band, left to the sound of music, clicking cameras and applause from our hosts and assembled well-wishers. Back in the horse-drawn carriage, we were whisked back across the town with the now customary cavalcade, and arrived at the home of a traditional peasant family. Throughout the entire proceedings, a man named Kamal had acted as Bron's father in the 'giving away', and another from the community was my best man. None of my associates could be relied upon to respect the solemnity of the event in those roles!

These paternal figureheads continued in their responsibilities as the feast began, and then we were entertained by a number of dancers from the State Dance Company. I thought they were a bit good! The party had to be interrupted so we could do our show in Tbilisi but, as soon as it was over, we were brought back to continue with the celebrations. At that point, my brilliant band gave in to their way of dealing with happiness, and I'd like to think nobody present on that occasion can remember much about how it all ended.

Chapter 13

We came down to earth in July when we needed to promote *Naked Thunder* in Europe, and its release set off a huge tour. The show was based around 'Gut Reaction', 'Demon's Eye', 'Living for the City', 'Black Night', 'Puget Sound', 'Sweet Lolita', 'Nothing to Lose', 'Brazos', 'I Thought No', 'When a Blind Man Cries', 'Let It Roll', 'Knocking at Your Back Door', 'Speed King', 'No Good Luck', 'Smoke on the Water' and 'Lucille'. Sometimes we did 'New Orleans'.

The July 1990 period wasn't that busy and, in some ways, that was just as well, since the band needed time to recover. I basically did what was needed by the record company, which meant interviews, including the *Friday Rock Show*, and I generally made myself available for signings at outlets like Our Price in Newcastle, and then in Nottingham, and so forth. The management were basically setting things up for more work abroad, which gave us time to get over personality problems and clashes which had developed in the USSR.

Tommy's poor relationship with Al had continued throughout, and seemed to crop up over such issues as Tommy having been used to having his bags carried everywhere for him! Well, I guess that's how it's been for just about everybody on the tour — we'd all had our roadie to handle that sort of thing for us at some time or another, but Tommy would board the bus, having left his baggage in the hotel foyer. The Ian Gillan Band Tour just wasn't that kind of thing, and Al got more and more mad with Tommy, telling him to do his own dirty work. It all came to the boil at the airport when Tommy left his bags at the check-in area, and drifted off to the bar, as if to say to Al, 'You put them through!' So Al just went up to Tommy, gave him his tickets, and made it clear his bags were going nowhere, unless Tommy made them.

Now, on this occasion, I had two seats booked in the first-class section, and when that happened, I'd share the second on a rotation basis. Al had had enough by now, so he decided to give the spare seat to himself! We were in flight, chatting, and he was letting off steam about Tommy, when the musician himself came lurching down the aisle, totally out of his brains, to announce he'd not be working with Al any more. In fact, to be specific, he announced that Al would not be working with *him* any more, to which I said, 'Well, Tom, that's a real shame,' and then asked him what he proposed to do, which puzzled him.

After a pause, he asked what I was driving at, to which I said, 'Well, have you anything lined up ... something else to go to? Because if you're not going to be working with Al any more, I guess you have to find another gig.'

Tommy was stunned, and it needed me to tell him that Al was the finest tour manager I had ever worked with, and there was no way I was going to lose him. Tommy went berserk at this, and I had to put it to him straight. 'Tommy, I'm going to punch you if I hear another word about this. I'm getting so angry ... you are so out of control, that you are within seconds of being popped on the nose!'

Just to make the point, in case he still had any doubts, I added, 'If I even see you at the airport, I'm going to pop you on the nose; that's if I just set eyes on you, and you don't say a word!'

That was the last I saw of Tommy, until we picked up again in Brazil!

I saw her phone number written on the bathroom wall
She had a sweet reputation
She had done it all
She don't worry 'bout the acid rain
Because she's made no plans
For coming back again.

Some touring is hard, particularly the low-budget trips I like to do from time to time. But there's a limit as to how much football you can all play, how many jokes you can tell — even how much you can drink, I suppose! We did shows in São Paulo, Rio de Janeiro, Pôrto Alegre, Buenos Aires and Santiago, after which we came back to Ireland, and finished in Europe and the UK. The 1990 tour was a great and full trip, although the album stiffed and cost me money.

I have few regrets about that period. The record company didn't seem to quite share the 'rock 'n' roll' of what was going on. It never seemed to cross their minds that a perfectly good album might have failed, because it was never in the shops, nor was it promoted. So, now it was 'scapegoat time', and it seemed that most of the blame for the album's failure was laid at Steve Morris' doorstep. Whenever I mentioned Steve's name, it would either be ignored, passed off or dealt with in terms of, 'Oh, you're not going to work with him, are you?' The fact Steve's a great writer didn't seem to matter, and that left me telling people that I'll work with anybody who comes up with great ideas. It got to the stage where various flash young guitar players, who didn't know shit, would say, 'What's Ian doing with Steve around?' and then find it demeaning that Steve would play on the Liverpool cabaret circuit, to feed his wife and kids.

So it all became very difficult, and when it came to the next album, *Toolbox*, it was most strongly suggested that I work with new people — except Steve stayed on board! — as I played them at their own game.

The basic decision was that the best material would go on the album — a very obvious one if you think about it, but some things need spelling out sometimes. So I began with Bernie Tormé, Mel Galley and the massive Leslie West from the band, Mountain. Leslie came and stayed at the house with us, and everybody fell into the spirit of the album and the surrounding politics.

Eventually, the record company people came out to hear the demos, and the session began with, 'Now this is by Steve' and we'd run through some of that song, and then I'd say, 'And this has Leslie on it,' and they'd all say it was great, without being told that although Leslie was on it, Steve had written it, and was also playing! It became obvious that the people from the record company were very confused about what may or may not be a good song, finally to conclude that perhaps we should forget who wrote the material, and just select on merit!

Events would dictate that Steve would not play on the next Gillan tour, although he started with it as a musician, and worked on *Toolbox*.

For *Toolbox*, the pressure was really on!

'Come on Ian, we need a rock album ...'

'Yeah, right, I'm gonna scream from start to finish on every song!'

New blood was needed. The *Naked Thunder* tour had been one long drinking session, and my nearest and dearest were now laying it on the line.

'Enough is enough, Ian ... or it's going to be all over.'

I kept hearing that I had to stop drinking (fair enough); quit smoking (no problem); lose some weight (it'll just drop off), and that it was only when I got a grip that people in the business would take me seriously again. This was pretty much the chorus of comment from Phil Banfield, Al Dutton and B. In fact, Phil and Al said they'd quit unless I got my career under control again, and although B didn't go so far, it was plain something had to be done.

Now, believe it or not, I had no idea how much my image

was hurting me. I'd figured out that as long as I was writing and singing well, I'd just have to wait for the tide to turn, and yet here were my dear friends spelling out the reality. The thought of losing them was too much to bear, and so I decided to revive an old and much ignored promise. When Phil says 'jump', I jump! (Well, sometimes!)

Phil has a great attitude to management. He simply reckons he's been engaged to do a job honestly, and to the best of his ability, and that from time to time he'll do it so well, he'll be able to take some commission. Phil and I have never had a contract, and we've been together now for quite some time, during which we've both made our share of mistakes, but hopefully we've learned from them a bit.

At that time, Al was very much part of my inner circle, and although he is now working with other artists (his old buddy, Jeff Beck, and currently Judas Priest), we remain great mates. Whoever Al is with knows they have a person of refreshing openness; if there's something difficult to be said, you can rely on Al to say it. Tour managers are a special breed of no-nonsense types. One minute they'll be quietly putting their obnoxious charges to bed in a hotel that's had enough, and where the staff want to go home, and the next thing they'll be charming an airline out of $2,000 for excess baggage. The responsibilities are enormous, and many a hopeless situation has been rescued by the experience of people like Al and Colin Hart.

Toolbox was produced by Chris Tsangarides ('Tangled Hairdo', as he became known, and the 's' is silent). We went to Battery Studios in London, and the line-up was to change again for the project. Given the new impetus this time, Chris said that there was only one drummer we could possibly use to get what we were after, and so we drove out to Gatwick Airport to meet a flight from Oakland, California — the one and only Leonard Haze. Chris had briefed me a bit on Lenny's past with 'Y and T' (Yesterday and Today), when this funny-looking guy with a little pot-belly wheeled through customs.

I walked up, hand outstretched, and said, 'Leonard Haze ... I'm pleased to meet you! I understand you're known as The Mayor of Hell?'

He looked at me and wheezed, 'That's right ... and pretty soon I hope to become President!'

His words tailed away as he looked over my shoulder, and his eyes said, 'Hot dog!' So we went across to the stand, and Lenny ordered a couple with 'the works'.

I should mention that Chris was wearing some smart casual clothes, and as Lenny chomped his first bite, most of the works — mustard, chilli, ketchup, etc — exploded through his fingers on to Chris' new loafers.

We were staying at the Swiss Cottage hotel at the time, and Steve (Morris), Chris and I were frantically ploughing through our address books, in the search for a new bass player, at which moment Lenny woke up and said, 'I know just the guy!' So we bought him a pint of cider, and he delivered the goods — and I mean *the goods*! A couple of days later, we were back at the airport to meet one of the most imposing characters I'd ever come across — Brett Bloomfield (ex-Starship) from San Fransisco. I couldn't believe my eyes. The guy was about 9ft 4in, with a lean muscular frame, black, shiny hair down to his arse, and lips that made Mick Jagger's looked pursed!

His five-string guitars are made out of entire oak trees, and that man can play! So it was all in place when a storm cloud appeared. Not long before all this, I'd taken B to the John Radcliffe Hospital in Oxford, for tests on her heart. At the end of the day, we sat across the desk from her consultant, Brian Gribbin, and we both knew what was going to be said. He quietly explained that B needed an operation to replace a faulty valve in her heart, and that it should be carried out quite soon, as there was a real danger that she could fall in the garden, where she expended so much effort. A small tear trickled down her face as we rose and stumbled out to the car.

By the time we were home, she was making plans, and soon the coffee table was littered with medical books, as she learned everything she could about the heart. They looked interesting, lying alongside gardening stuff! Like everything B does, she approached this thing 'head on'; I've never known her to duck an issue, which is not to imply she's confrontational, but she does have great courage and strength. However, it was not the best moment to be making a new record!

There comes a time in your life when you go through a door, and that day for me was Wednesday, 24 April 1991, as I held my darling Bumble's hand — she was deathly white, the recovery ward was deathly quiet, and I went through that door. You can hardly see the scar now.

One of the questions I am very often asked is, 'What do you do when a tour ends, and you are back home?' I proudly reply, 'Exactly what my wife tells me!'

When I get back, and sometimes I've been away for months, I get exactly two days to reacquire a domestic attitude, by which I mean two days to get rid of strutting my stuff. Then it's, 'Here's a list of things which need doing round the house!'

Oh, and I'm only allowed to be a rock star on Fridays, and then, as I'm slipping outside the door for a pint at the local, there's an even chance I'll be thumbed back upstairs, because I'm not bleedin' colour co-ordinated! Now that's hard to take, but you'd be looking at a fool, if you thought I didn't love it!

So we finished *Toolbox*, which included 'Hang Me Out To Dry', 'Dirty Dog', 'Candy Horizon', 'Don't Hold Me Back', 'Pictures of Hell', 'Dancing Nylon Shirt' (Parts 1 and 2), 'Gassed Up', 'Everything I Need' and 'Toolbox' itself. And it was well liked, albeit with mixed reviews — 'Toolbox' is a reference to exactly what you think it is!

However, we felt let down by our label, East/West, who gave no real leverage to the project and its promotion — in fact, all the ideas seemed to flow from the artists' side, including the design, on which I started to work with Manjeet Khangura of Electric Echo. We got it right down to the condom freebies in the *Toolbox* packaging!

> *A hat shaped head*
> *A shoe shaped foot*
> *A kennel shaped dog*
> *A dancing nylon shirt.*
> *A man shaped woman*
> *Balloon shaped air*
> *Glass shaped beer*
> *A dancing nylon shirt.*

After *Naked Thunder*, it seemed that everybody was confused again. Chris Welch wrote in *Metal Hammer* something like, 'If *Toolbox* isn't a great success, then maybe rock 'n' roll is really dead.' Well, thanks Chris, but that's a lot of weight to carry! Rock 'n' roll will never die, because it's pro-active. It's also elusive to the pundits and the industry, and it always generates from 'underground'. It's very personal to musicians and fans alike, and you can't ever bag it. It's not fashion — it's an attitude.

So the album was out, and it was back on the road, this time with Steve Morris, the only musician surviving *Naked Thunder*. But now we had Lenny and Brett, plus tour manager Al Dutton, with Jim (Jim Bob) McLean as production manager and sound man. Graham (Squiffy) Underwood was there, too, and he and Lenny became attached at the hip!

At a time when the worldwide recession was really beginning to bite, and promoters were cancelling dates, the Gillan band was setting out on a tour, which would take us through 27 countries, and a few new places along the way:

July
Ukraine   Zaporozhye and Kiev

Latvia	Riga and Liepája
Russia	Moscow

With this line-up we then played intensively in the UK (October), moving through Europe in November — Germany, Austria, Switzerland, Poland, Czechoslovakia and Spain. 'Timing is of the essence' as Bill Reid used to say, and our tiny entourage travelled and played 'everywhere' — it was fantastic! Let it be beaten!

It's not just the shows that give life to a tour, it's the company you travel with, and the camaraderie that develops. It is this — the people you meet and the sights you see in far-away places — that makes rock 'n' roll what I believe in, what I search for.

On the banks of the River Dnieper, in Zaporozhye, Ukraine, and just a few klicks downriver from Kiev, we were invited to a barbecue. It so happens that the Cossacks of that territory seemed none too fond of the people of Kiev, so when it was my turn to make a toast, I became aware of mutterings, when I mentioned the name of the city, and the fact that we'd played there two nights before. Not wishing to offend my hosts, and now being well away from Kiev, I said (through the interpreter) that the water seemed much warmer here, than further upstream. The mood seemed to change as I explained to the Cossacks that this amazing phenomenon was probably caused by the fact that I'd pissed in the river, when I was swimming in the freezing waters of Kiev. There was much talking behind hands and, slowly, 'toothed smiles' turned to gales of unrestrained laughter, as my quickly contrived insult to their neighbours confirmed my status as a true friend! Much vodka was then consumed, the interpreter was given a break, and we continued in the international language of drunken, brotherly love.

The last thing I remember explaining was that my father came from Scotland, and I could not understand a single word he said to me until I was a man. And so we drank, laughed and talked around the fire, under the stars, deep into the night.

Meanwhile, rumblings of discontent began to be heard from the office back in London, as the tour drifted towards a new phase of shows, and the pressure to replace Steve (Morris) increased. The only personal criticism I could ever level at Steve was that his movement on stage made the pyramids look lively, but apart from that, he's a great guy, an impeccable musician and ongoing associate to this very day. It's just that the others felt the chemistry wasn't quite right, and he took the news like the big man he is.

It was replacement time, and after the show in Barcelona, (15 December 1991), Dean Howard — formerly with T'Pau — joined the band, having been introduced by Al Dutton.

Well, the first thing you notice about Dean if you look down is that his feet seem to be heading in almost opposite directions; sort of 'ten to two' on a clock face. Apart from that, I have to say that Dean was the perfect ingredient required to complete the recipe for this wonderful band.

From the first show in Istanbul, Turkey (30 January 1992), the magic was there. Even though he forgot every arrangement and key, his charisma and guitar playing gave me, Brett and Lenny the chance to deliver, and we most certainly did!

Brett was an awesome sight, wearing black tights and Doc Marten boots. He'd rampage around stage like a crazed rhino, while Dean would be every girl's dream in his tatty jeans, Docs and a silly grin on his face! Lenny and I would crack up all night, and things were picking up, as we played two great shows in Greece.

We then went to Australia for a schedule that took us through Sydney, Adelaide, Melbourne and Perth, then moving into Europe: Sweden, Denmark, Norway and Finland.

During all this, I got some good advice from a promoter, John Alphonso. Musing on the future in a hotel room, I asked John what he thought I should do with my career.

'Ian, it's up to you!' he said.

Simple words without embellishment, and I pondered on them for quite some time.

Still, I was with people I loved, and we travelled on, always breaking new territory, arriving in La Paz, Bolivia, on 30 April 1992.

Perched in a nest, high in the Andes, La Paz is the highest city in the world. After a long journey from London, via Miami and Bogota, we arrived just before dawn to scenes of great excitement. We were whisked away to a press conference at the airport, and the first question I was asked was, 'What do you think of Bolivia?' I was tired, and it was still the crack of dawn, so I replied, to my shame, 'It's very dark, isn't it!'

The point is that most people want to be thought of with affection, and I guess it's the same as me asking after a show, 'Did you enjoy it?' So I tend not to ask.

Music is a wonderful medium which can transcend all languages, cultures, religions, politics and general strife. Some people have made love and have conceived their children while accompanied by their favourite artists!

We arrived exhausted at a hotel, where tea was offered, made from coca leaves. It was explained to me that, in order to relieve aches and pains, the leaves from the coca tree are chewed by the Indians — it's been that way since time began, and it is as natural (and innocent) to Bolivians as tea is to Europeans. However, as the leaves are the source of the 'evil cocaine', this doesn't sit well with those who have the fingers of the world pointing at them.

In the climate of the football stadium at La Paz, I nearly passed out during the first song. The air is so thin at that altitude and strangers have a hard time doing anything physical. Lenny and I suffered that night, but it was worth it! As we flew out the next day, between towering mountain peaks, I waved farewell to this isolated little city, with its generous people and culture, so far removed from the exploitation of mankind.

The tour continued into Montevideo (Uruguay) and Brazil —

São Paulo, Belo Horizonte, Curitiba — and so on! Mexico followed, Chile, and then into Europe (Finland and Switzerland).

In South America, I met a bunch of British sailors after our show. They were waving the flag of their ship and, after a couple of beers backstage, CPO Taff Kemble and the lads invited us on board the next day, where they gave us a guided tour and a great time. So our confidence was sky high. Brett had taken to wearing a nifty little dress on stage, and Lenny looked like an over-ripe banana, in a tasty grow-suit that defies description! Dean was still cruising and grooving, and we'd written a few new songs, which were being brought into the shows. It's always good to let new songs grow into themselves, before going into a studio with them, but we were looking forward to going home and doing just that.

It was about this time that we were dropped by the record company, Teldec-East/West. We were almost expecting it, because record sales hadn't been brilliant, but here we were, two years after *Naked Thunder*, evolving into something a bit special.

It's a hard world, but we had total belief in ourselves — a 'let's do it' attitude. Although finances were tight, our management and associates were strongly behind us as we started recording in a shed near my home, with a small mobile studio. My cousin Paul 'Chad' Watkins, from projects at Kingsway Studios, came on board again, and we put down 'A Day Late 'n' a Dollar Short', 'Hard on You' and 'Sugar Plum', as well as 'High Ground' and 'Ticket to Your Heart'. We were all chuffed with the results, and sent the tape to Phil and Al who started punting them around. The reaction was not what we expected, and dejection set in. I wondered if my name was beginning to be a drawback to the band, and we talked about a change from something other than 'Gillan'. As we looked around the rehearsal-cum-recording shed we were using, at the litter of drumsticks, empty beer bottles and leads which didn't work, Lenny said, 'Jeez ... this place looks like a *repo depo*!' which is what a junk yard is, back where he comes from. So that dealt with the name of the band, as we set off on the ferry to the Hook of Holland, then driving in my Volvo and a Ford truck with all the gear, to try our luck at the studios of the famous Bolland Brothers. Bolland and Bolland from Holland — kinda rolls off the tongue, doesn't it?

Ferda and Rob have an impeccable background — 'Rock Me Amadeus' may jog your memory. These two guys are gentlemen, and I mean 'gentlemen'. They are professional, bright, but above all, have a sense of humour to add to their considerable business acumen. I had first met the Bollands when they kindly invited me to sing a couple of songs on a project called *Darwin*. It was based, not surprisingly, on the life of the 'great man', Charles, and the lyrics and music were, well, pure 'Bolland and Bolland'. Tim Rice would have approved!

A couple of hours after we arrived at the little hotel we'd arranged next to the studios, an El Al 747 flew into a block of flats in Amsterdam, and one of the engines landed quite near us.

Everything went quiet for a bit. My life was again in turmoil. You see, for six months or so, there had been gossip and moves afoot to reunite me in some way with Deep Purple. I've said nothing about their difficulties without me, and why should I? I knew what they were doing, but that was their business. However, it's fairly obvious to 'those who mattered' that what is often referred to as Deep Purple, is the Mark II line-up — Blackmore, Gillan, Glover, Lord and Paice. I've never been allowed to forget the time I said, 'I'd rather slit my throat, than sing with that band again', and it came up again with a reunion talk. When asked about other singers they'd had — David Coverdale, Glenn Hughes and Joe Lynn Turner, I simply turned the question back to whoever was asking and said, 'How would you feel if you found your lover with somebody else?'

When something gains momentum, it's hard to stop. When a flock of birds change flight, when dogs become a pack, when human minds compete collectively, single strengths move in alliance. Throughout my life, I have swum against the tide and, just once in a while, I realise it's necessary to take a deep breath, and 'go with the flow'.

In Amsterdam, it was unbearable, because I loved Repo Depo. I saw it as my future; my only future. We even had our logos organised. 'Man' (Manjeet Khangura) of Electric Echo (what a success that is today!) had come up with the whole 'promo' — the design, and even a band picture, which looked ultra cool. But, in reality, there was no record deal being offered, and I was 'on my uppers'.

Phil (Banfield) had come to the end of his tether, and I must have whinged one too many times. He sent me a fax saying, 'I quit!' Ashen faced, I walked into the kitchen of the Bolland studio, where Al was sitting quietly having a beer. I read the fax again, burst into tears, and looked at Al, who knew what was going on.

'I'll do it!' I said, and then rushed out, called Phil — still sobbing my heart out — and heard him doing the same at the other end of the line. I'd decided to go back to Deep Purple.

The journey home was uneasy. We all knew what was happening, and the usual banter was restrained. We had scraped together enough money for a couple of drinks, but stayed very sober. Everybody was tired, and politeness took away our fun. Dean drifted off from Harwich, and Brett and Lenny came back to my place for a day or so, during which time Lenny wrecked my car, before flying home to San Francisco.

I took a deep breath, and started work soon after with Roger Glover on the new Purple project, *The Battle Rages On*. (I saw Lenny quite recently — The House of Blues Tour, Los Angeles, in February 1998, and we also phoned Squiffy! That was great!)

Chapter 14

My return to the fold was not entirely joyful at first. Roger had come over to work with me, and we set up in a studio in the Thames Valley area — I believe it's where Jimmy Page used to live, and generally where the showbiz fraternity are in control. The Godfather in the area is Jon's friend, George Harrison, although he'd rather not be — the Godfather, that is!

Anyway, Roger and I were into the second day of delightful work, when I suddenly had this most horrendous awareness, the most disgusting feeling I've ever had in my life, as it suddenly dawned on me that I was not really being invited back into the band, I was being auditioned!

I took a deep breath, found some focus, and said to myself, 'My God, I'm being auditioned by the love of my life, Deep Purple, to see if I can hack it with my writing skills and vocals.' They'd actually sent Roger over for two days to the studio to check me out! I thought I was back in the band, but I wasn't!

I put the thought aside as best as possible, drank some wine with Roger, and quickly came to the realisation that Ritchie didn't want me back, but the record company, BMG, did.

Work already started with Joe Lynn Turner was obviously not acceptable, and everybody was now waiting to see what I did with the tapes. There was no feeling of certainty, no drive, just an 'anti' sort of feeling, and a guitar player who basically didn't want me around. I quickly picked up on the delicate situation that we were not on the same wavelength.

Been so many words, so much to say
Words are not enough to keep the guns at bay
Some live in fear some do not
Some gamble everything on who gets the final shot

The Battle Rages On was recorded at The Bearsville Studio in New York, and The Red Rooster Studio in Tutzing, Munich, while we also used the Greg Rike Studio in Orlando. Afterwards, Pat Regan and Roger mixed it at The Sound on Sound facility in New York. The record company was pleased with our work, which included 'Lick It Up', 'Anya', 'Talk About Love', 'Ramshackle Man', 'A Twist In the Tale', 'Nasty Piece of Work', 'Solitaire', 'One Man's Meat' and the one Ritchie didn't like (or, at least, preferred a different version of), 'Time to Kill'.

It's difficult these days to put music into a place in the charts. There was a time when this matter was dealt with by *NME*, *Melody Maker* and so forth, but now it seems different — so many different charts, for so many areas of music. There are the popular charts, the indie, heavy rock and so forth. So it's hard to know how something like *The Battle Rages On* really performed, in the way we could chart things in the past. However, I know it sold well, despite the problems.

With *The Battle Rages On* scheduled for release, plans were put in place (through Bruce's office) for the tour, beginning in Europe. With Colin Hart as the Tour Manager (Al Dutton came along with me), we travelled to Bregenz, Austria, on Saturday, 18 September 1993, where we rehearsed for three days. It was then on to Rome for another day of rehearsal, before we opened at Palaghiaccio on the 24th. A full programme was ahead:

September

25th	Palasport, Forli, Italy
26th	Palatrussardi, Milan, Italy
27th	Palasport, Turin, Italy
29th	Stadthalle, Villach, Austria

October

1st	Sporthalle, Schwerin, Germany
2nd	Ostseehalle, Kiel, Germany
3rd	Festhalle, Frankfurt, Germany
4th	Grugahalle, Essen, Germany
6th	Wesser-Ems-Halle, Oldenburg, Germany.

And so the tour continued: Berlin (7th), Hamburg (8th), Cologne (10th), Memmingen (11th), Nuremberg (13th), Munich (14th), Mannheim, Stüttgart, and on into France; Nancy 18th, Paris (19th); and into Switzerland for shows in Zürich and Lausanne (21st/22nd), Barcelona in Spain (and San Sebastian) on 23rd and 24th; finishing the month with shows in Austria, Czechoslovakia and Poland, where we played the Zabrze Sport Hall in Katowice on Sunday, 31st October.

The tour was going quite well, with virtual or complete sellouts wherever we went (including the bigger venues — around 13,000 at Stüttgart), and the material mixed the old with the new — 'Highway Star', 'Space Truckin'', 'Anyone's Daughter', 'Strange Kind of Woman', 'Speed King', 'Twist in the Tale', 'Child in Time', 'Smoke on the Water', 'Anya', 'The Battle Rages On', and so forth. Even 'Hush' was done a few times! Otherwise, there were the usual medlies the fans love, with 'Space Truckin'', 'Woman from Tokyo', 'Paint It Black' and 'Mandrake Root' thrown in; all in all, a lot of vintage Purple.

But there were also tensions — some obvious, such as Ritchie going on one occasion into a *Jesus Christ* riff in 'Black Night', and when I started to join in, he stopped in his tracks. For 'Lazy', I went to pick up on the guitarist's riff, at which point he stopped again!

I struggled to keep control sometimes, and didn't quite manage on every occasion! In Cologne I left the stage for a while (towards the end of 'Knocking at Your Back Door'), but there were many moments of high drama and musicianship from him (and the band for that matter), including the moment (at the same show), where he swapped his guitar and trashed the replacement, before throwing it into the audience. At the other extreme, his touch on songs like 'Anyone's Daughter' was sublime.

How can I rationalise this thing; this polarisation of Ritchie and me — with Jon, Ian and Roger in the middle? I suppose the best I can come up with is to say, 'Imagine a beautiful meal. A plate of food is in front of you, and it's fine, and that plate of food is Deep Purple — except for Ritchie and me. We're the knife and fork, on either side!'

Try as I may, I cannot claim to understand how he reasons things out, or how he arrives at his conclusions. I have certain ideas, but out of respect they must remain outside the public domain. It's one of those things to leave alone, at least until he and I are dead.

And so the shows continued to critical musical acclaim, with the problems kept pretty much to ourselves, as we went to Belgium to play Forest National in Brussels on 2 November and Rotterdam (Ahoy) on 3rd. It was into England, for Manchester (Apollo) on the 5th, the Brixton Academy (London) on 7th and 8th, and then to the 'big one' at the NEC in Birmingham on the 9th.

Ritchie had, by now, destroyed his visa, saying that he would not be going to Japan at the end of the month, but nobody could predict what would happen at Birmingham. Things were bad between us and, at Manchester, our roadies were trying to make sure we arrived on stage without taking the same route to it. Still, the show was fine, as was Brixton, particularly the second one, where Ritchie was great, and I met up with some old buddies afterwards, including Dean (Howard).

But in Birmingham, it was all to end. Stories vary about exactly what happened, depending on if you were on stage, in the audience, or in the wings. What had been arranged (and agreed by everybody) was that this show would be filmed. The director was Hugh Symonds, and it would be produced by Lana Topham. The atmosphere backstage was vile, and Ritchie was locked away in his room, signposted 'The Badger's Den'. He was party to the idea of the cameras, and so, not surprisingly, there were loads of guys wandering around — everywhere you turned, there seemed to be someone with a camera. Well, from my point of view, the days when an artist can demand to have the stage all to himself went out of the window years ago. All that precious behaviour stuff — I mean, there's always somebody under your feet, and you just have to learn to live with it. There's no point in letting something like that, something you'd wanted anyway, spoil your performance, but Ritchie did!

And so the lights went down, Ian Paice got things under way, Jon and Roger started up 'Highway Star' and I went on.

So I was at the mike, and realised something wasn't right. Jon was keeping things going, and I turned to see that Ritchie wasn't with us! I mean, when one-fifth of the band is not with you, it does sound a bit lame, particularly with the opening song! So it was decision time — either stop the show, or count in and get on with it, which is what I did. We reached the solo, and the guitarist appeared, played a few runs, and wandered off.

I'm told a beaker of water flew by me just after the congas, and we went into 'Black Night' with much the same — no guitar player.

Backstage, it seems Ritchie had taken exception to a cameraman, and thrown a bucket of water over him. He then found another bucket, and went for a second guy who was filming the whole thing. On chucking the water, the cameraman was not where Ritchie thought he was. Instead, it went all over my missus, as one thing led to another.

So I was on stage singing, and thinking, 'What's going on back there?' and finally put the mike down and went off, where I found B in tears. Having arrived at some kind of understanding of the situation, I said, 'I am now going to kill him — probably with a very slow bullet, called my right arm!'

B's reaction was, well, shall we say, brilliantly composed, as she said, 'Don't let it get to you. Just calm down and do a great show!' And she said it many times — 'Just do a great show!' In fact, she was warning me with such power; she was threatening me — bless her!

I was soon back on stage with the band, and the show continued, as the guitar player knocked the songs about, ending early, taking lumps out and generally leaving me stranded whenever possible. At the end, Ian Paice flew signed drum skins into the bemused audience, and shouted, 'We owe you a hell of a lot!'

I cannot begin to explain what Ritchie had in mind that night, whether he was aware of what was going on, or whether he was just hyper 'mind-fucked' and super tense, as he can be. Could the sight of some people with cameras really have upset him that much, or was it premeditated for his own inexplicable reason? I'm told (through *Darker than Blue*) that around midnight, the Badger's Den door opened, and he was seen being led out by a girl holding a lead, with a dog collar round his neck! He was dressed in his long black leather coat, and was wearing his roadie's witch mask which was sometimes used by the assistant on stage, plus a witch's hat! If that is true, it is also sad.

In many ways, I felt that until this moment, there were times, despite the tensions, when the five of us were as near as could be to the spirit of Deep Purple, and yet quite contrary to that, I remember writing down in my notebook that 'With Ritchie Blackmore, Deep Purple has no future.'

Such is the frustration and dilemma, and I always try to find answers. I look back and think of a young man who had been on the road with Screaming Lord Sutch, where he'd had to run off the edge of a ferry in a loin cloth; his fascination for the paranormal (not black magic, but communication with the spirits); when he wanted to borrow Roger's crucifix, and when it was refused, axed the door down to ask again! I think back to the man who loves football and animals — particularly his cats; to the man whose ultimate goal is (apparently) to live on a cobbled street, listening to medieval music. But, above all, to the musician who, like me, is totally in love with Deep Purple.

A video entitled *Come Hell or High Water* (without the incident) was made from the NEC show, and it has on it 'Highway Star', 'Black Night', 'Talk about Love', 'Twist of the Tale', 'Perfect Strangers', 'Beethoven', 'Knocking at Your Back Door', 'Anyone's Daughter', 'Child in Time', 'Anya', 'The Battle Rages On', 'Lazy', 'Space Truckin' ', 'Woman from Tokyo', 'Paint it Black' and 'Smoke on the Water'. BMG also brought out an album produced by Pat Regan, with recordings from Stüttgart (16 October) and the NEC.

Ritchie stayed with the band for the shows in Copenhagen, Denmark (12th); Stockholm, Sweden (13th); Oslo, Norway (14th/15th); he made Ishallen, Helsinki, Finland his last on the 17 November. It was all over.

Every so often, a project comes along which is different, and a (sometimes) welcome distraction from the cut and thrust of situations like Deep Purple. One such came about in June 1992, when Minos EMI and Phil Banfield arranged for me to go to Greece with B, to make a record with one of their major artists in the territory, Michalis Rakintziz. In fact, the idea first cropped up in February 1991, but other things prevented progress then. It's not the sort of project I normally do, but the artist has one platinum album to his name, and two gold and the label felt very enthusiastic about a collaboration.

So on 10 June 1992, B and I flew out, and were put up at The Hilton Hotel for the first night, and then moved to a suite at the Grand Chalet hotel. The next day we went to the Studio Sierra in Athens, and recorded an album with me singing on three tracks — 'Get Away', 'My Heart of Stone' and 'I Think I Know'. 'Get Away' was also released as a single.

Later on, I did three shows with Michalis at Thessaloniki, Patras and Athens, and the promoters gave it their 'all' in terms of advertising, TV and radio. It was really Michalis' gig, but I went on stage with him for 'Getaway', 'Smoke on the Water', 'When a Blind Man Cries', 'Black Night' and 'Woman from Tokyo'.

They had ping-pong balls made with our names on them, for throwing into the audience, and the whole experience was great. Michalis Rakintziz loves rock 'n' roll!

A particular highlight was when we did a video on an island somewhere. It was a hectic two or three days, with this particular producer. The man was so bossy, he must have thought he was Cecil B de Mille, the way he went around. He was even bossing Michalis, shouting, 'Stand there … stand there,' as we struggled in the wilting sun on this rooftop location. All the time it was 'You, you, you … Move over there. You … wait …You, stand still!'

There were moments when I thought, 'This is fucking ridiculous. I've had enough of this crap,' so after the first shot, I drifted off to find a moment of sanity, and wandered into a store, where my eyes fell on a replica Colt 38 … with bullets! And I thought, 'I'm going to kill that director with this,' and joyfully bought it, making sure the bullets were blanks, but also that it was noisy enough to bring him down to earth a bit.

I concealed the weapon in the black clothing we had to wear while we pranced around like prats on this rooftop, in touch with the gods and all that, until finally we came to this dramatic bit, a sort of tableau scene, where there was much posing going on.

Now, I realise what the guy was trying to do, but right now he was getting up my fucking nose, and although every so often I'd remind myself that they were giving us a great time,

and I was being well paid, he was still really pissing me off.

Watching this man shove my new mate around — a man who was a big star in his own country — well, it was too much! So I was ready to murder the director; execute him publicly on camera. OK, so I changed my mind, but he'd better not upset me like that again! It was a great few days!

Chapter 15

Ritchie leaving Deep Purple was critical, and we had to decide if we would carry on or not. There were major discussions, as we explored various ideas, until finally Mr Udo, our Japanese promoter of many years standing, suggested Joe Satriani. So Roger called him up to see if he was available and interested. As it happens, he'd just finished working in the studio, so our situation was talked through. We sent him a tape from the Stüttgart show — one where Ritchie stopped playing for a while, and one of the questions Joe asked was whether we wanted him to do the same! He told us he couldn't approach the project as anything permanent, looking at it more as helping us out, and so he arrived to join the Japanese leg on 29 November. As I said at the very beginning, Joe arrived, and was the perfect gentleman, the perfect professional and a consummate player. We had a couple of rehearsals booked, and he walked in and played faultlessly — first time.

We looked through the studio window, and there were Mr Udo, Colin Hart and the crew. After about four or five songs, everybody realised this was just a breeze — Joe was making it so easy for us and, turning round to catch our audience, they were all smiling and holding up cards, just like scoring in ice skating. And the figures were all 9.8s and higher!

So we got towards the end of the rehearsal, and it was 'Smoke on the Water' time. Somebody said, 'Oh, we don't have to do that, do we?' and Joe said, 'I'd kinda like to do it.'

'OK,' we said.

'Gee,' he said, 'I never thought I'd get to play "Smoke on the Water" with Deep Purple!'

After the usual pre-show preparations, we kicked off at Nagoya.

December

2nd	Rainbow Hall, Nagoya
3rd	Castle Hall, Osaka
5th	Yokohama Gym, Yokohama
6th/7th	Budokan, Tokyo
8th	Olympic Pool, Tokyo

For this tour, and without the presence of Ritchie, we played 'Highway Star', 'Ramshackle Man', 'Black Night', 'Maybe I'm a Leo', 'Twist of the Tale', 'Perfect Strangers', 'Pictures of Home' (Jon solo), 'Knocking at Your Back Door', 'Anyone's Daughter', 'Child in Time', 'Anya', 'The Battle Rages On', 'When a Blind Man Cries', 'Lazy' and 'Space Truckin'', with 'Hush', 'Speed King' and 'Smoke on the Water' for encores. Ideas to tour America with Black Sabbath in January 1994 had been abandoned after the Blackmore incident, and we picked up again in spring, still with Joe on board.

May

27th	Den Bosch, Holland
28th	Bielefeld-Seidenstickerhalle, Germany
29th	Kassel-Eissporthalle, Germany
31st	Flanders Expo, Gent, Belgium.

June

3rd	Waldbuehne, Berlin, Germany
4th	Rock Festival, Esbjerg, Denmark
5th	Eissporthalle, Halle, Germany
7th	Dortmund, Germany
8th	Sporthalle, Hamburg, Germany
10th	Rock Festival, Karlshamn, Sweden

And so the tour continued into Göteborg, Sweden (11th), Bielfield, Germany (13th), Kassel and Passau, also Germany (14th/15th), into Belgium, back to Germany, down to Italy (Lonigo, 21st and Genova, 22nd), up to Holland for a show at Den Bosch, across to Switzerland (St Gallen, 26th), into Spain for shows at Barcelona and Madrid (29th/30th), and finally wrapping up that programme in July:

July

1st	Burgos, Spain
2nd	Gijon, Spain
5th	Kaffenberg, Austria
6th	Bayreuth, Germany

The time had arrived when Joe needed to get back to his own projects. He had always been very open about his position, that it was a stopgap, and apart from his fantastic contribution as a band member, he played a crucial part in helping us to regain our confidence, and realise there was life after Ritchie. It was now time to sit down and look for someone permanent, and we all took a poll as to who wanted who.

Steve Morse was on everybody's list. Steve's a bit younger than the rest of us — born in Hamilton, Ohio in 1954, he cites his influences as Jeff Beck, Jimi Hendrix, Jimmy Page and Eric Clapton. He formed the Dixie Dregs in the Seventies with Andy West (bass) and Rod Morgenstein, and they made a number of albums, before breaking up in the mid-Eighties. He has worked, recorded and guested consistently, including with Kansas, and had, in fact, brought out a new album, *Structural Damage*, just before joining Deep Purple (with Dave La Rue, bass, and Van Romaine on drums).

Apart from being spoken of in the same breath as Joe Satriani, and voted overall best guitarist for several years running by *Guitar*, Steve is a great guy. When we explained our ambitions and the situation, there was just one question he put to us: 'Is there any dress code?' to which we said, 'Wear whatever you like!'

Outside the band, when he isn't constantly practising, he flies aeroplanes, and flew himself to a show on one occasion!

After three days of rehearsal, Steve's first tour with us was to Mexico City which we played on 23 November. We then went to Monterrey (also Mexico) for the 26th, and played Corpus Christi in Texas the following night. It was in Monterey that I noticed 'Rule 3' on the door of my hotel room. It said, 'It is strictly forbidden to bring into the hotel; (a) guns, (b) animals, (c) musicians.' Oh well ...!

From the very beginning, Steve entered into the spirit of the band, and we soon started to think about our next album for BMG; it became *Purpendicular*. However, I had another project which I'd been planning some time before, and which I'd been working on through to production and release in June 1994. That project was an album by the band with whom I first earned a performance fee — the Javelins.

It was Oslo, Norway (1992), and I was just unwinding after the Purple show, when somebody handed me a business card which said, 'Gordon Fairminer — Architect'. Well, needless to say, we met up, and I discovered that my old mate was now married to this beautiful girl, and they had two kids. We had a few beers, and started reminiscing, thinking it a bit sad that there were no recorded moments of a band that was great — I still think that to this day!

At that time, there were no such things as cassette recorders, only Grundigs or Phillips machines which were not good enough to record properly. So we toyed with the idea of getting together for a weekend, to find a hall somewhere, and just put a couple of tracks down, so we could each have a copy to take home.

Well, the idea developed from that, and we ended up at Parr Street Studio in Liverpool for a weekend! It took us several months to get everybody together at the same time, and then to decide what to record from the set list of 'yesteryear'. They were all covers, and reflected our influences at the time (they've not changed much), and I did a few backing tracks with Steve Morris — bare to the bone stuff, in the same original key and tempo.

Steve sent the tape down, I made copies and sent them to the rest of the guys; Tony Tacon (rhythm guitar), Gordon (of course), Keith Roach (drums) and Tony (Tubby) Whitfield of the sad bass guitar fall!

Career-wise, we were a printer, production manager, architect, cab driver and singer, but now, once again, for just a few days, we were the Javelins!

Because of the fact the lads had basically stopped playing all those years ago, when they picked up their instruments, they were able to capture the absolute essence of the time — it was exactly how we did it and, with Steve's help, we kept it that way — simple.

It was a great experience. They turned up on a Friday night, we set the gear up, and went to the pub for a few drinks. We got up in the morning, recorded, went for something to eat, and then down to the pub for a few more drinks. Got up on Sunday, and did the same again! There was some finishing off to do on Monday, and on Tuesday it was finished.

In the meantime, Simon Robinson had heard about it, and

had become interested in releasing it on his label, RPM Records. I handed the tape to him and, as usual, he did a great job, putting it in the shops, and it's been selling ever since!

In fact, I plan to do another one, hopefully sooner than 30-odd years away, and some work has already been done towards that end. However, I don't want to pass it on to the lads for any length of time — they might go off the boil. Heaven forbid they should turn up over-rehearsed. They never did!

'The record, called simply *The Javelins*, incorporates old R & B favourites, including 'Roll Over Beethoven', 'Poison Ivy', 'Blue Monday', 'Let's Dance', 'Too Much Monkey Business', 'Money' and a clutch of other great songs.

Back with Deep Purple, and with Steve Morse, we now knew for sure we'd found the right guitar player, and I was in a particular frame of mind for that next album, *Purpendicular*. There were a lot of things I wanted to write about, including experiences on the trip I did from Corpus Christi to Los Angeles with Al Dutton, and where I was able to have the freedom just to get in a car with my buddy and follow my nose. It's something I'd not done since I was a kid. The 'window' was too tight to go home, which I would have done had there been, say, a fortnight available, but in ten days, you somehow return, recover, and then you're packing your bags for another long haul. So we decided on the LA trip, where I wanted to spend some time with Pat Regan on my solo *Dreamcatcher* project, and working on thoughts for *Purpendicular*.

The ride was very spiritual, and we had some great times, including catching up with Mentor Williams, an old friend of B and a great songwriter. ('Gimme the beat, boy, to soothe my soul ...' remember that?) That meeting was pure coincidence, and in some hotel bar somewhere, we talked from about midday into the early hours.

Mentor likes his tequila and, after a few hours, we got the guitars out, and started giggling. As if, yeah, we can really write a song now! He told us about this place out on the Indian reservation, where communities live pretty much on their wits and the bread line. So he decided one day to take his horse, Neil, and go and hunt an elk, so he could feed them all. He packed, took his guns and dog, and disappeared into the forest, eventually to find what he was looking for. He shot the beast, and then tried to return with it on the back of his pack horse.

Unfortunately, it was too big, so, stuck out there, cursing, and realising the adventure's not going according to plan, he then figured out that that it was the rack which was jamming between the trees. Neil was also freaking out, because he had this lump of elk on his back.

Undeterred, Williams abandoned the carcass, and went back to get another horse, a round trip which took him three days. Returning, he found that the only way to get the thing back to the reservation was to cut it into five pieces, which seemed a strange calculation, but finally it all worked out, and he eventually reached the village.

It was now that he was reminded that the Indians use every part of an animal's carcass — the leather for clothes and moccasins, and so on. Each part has its value, and the meat was expected to keep many mouths fed for some days to come. However, instead of being grateful for his huge effort, they were furious that he'd butchered the animal as he'd done, and had spoiled much of the worth of the catch! The fact that he'd gone for days, and struggled to provide a lifeline for them, seemed to escape their grasp.

On another occasion, we were getting into the car just as the sun was starting to go down, and I said to Al, 'We're going west, aren't we?'

'Yep,' he said, nodding.

So we pondered the wisdom of two hours driving into the setting sun, and decided to find a beer and see how things panned out. We found some place where there was a pool table (of course), and were watched by some guys who wanted to take us strangers on. So we played doubles for a while, and got friendly over some more beers. Then two more arrived, and another couple, until we realised we were with about nine brothers, and they were all cowboys, coming in after a day in the saddle.

So we continued with them for a while longer, and then one of them asked if we were going to the Stage Bar that night. So I asked, 'Where's that?' and when told it was just at the end of town, and it was where everybody went, we agreed we'd go and check it out.

It turned out to be an inn, and we then settled on the thought that we'd not be needing the car until the next day. Once our bags had been offloaded, we went to the bar, which was empty, except for a four-piece band called the Hired Hands, who were setting up. Gradually the place began to fill up with cowboys and cowgirls, all dressed in immaculate boots, jeans and hats. It was an unbelievable sight, which I expected would turn into a bar room riot, of the kind you see in the John Wayne movies.

Believing we might die, we made sure our bar space was as near to the door as possible. But it didn't turn out as we'd thought. The band started playing, and everybody started dancing. It wasn't line dancing, but 'waltzing', like waves on the water or, more appropriately, the mass move of a herd of cattle, if you just watch their backs in motion. Only here at the Stage Bar, it was the most elegant herd of cowboys and girls; content, occasionally 'Yeehaaing', and immaculately behaved.

I bought a CD from the band, and recommend anyone who sets eyes on a Hired Hands album to get it! Their influences can be found on 'Country Mile' (*Dreamcatcher*), and, yes, many fans have picked up on recent life experiences and cultures in my music!

Under a desert sky it is closing in
Another day gone by
And I don't know where I've been
Said it before and it's true
All of my life I give to you

Our spiritual journey followed no particular order or route planning, and we took things as they came to us. It is little things in life, which make you smile; such as the arrival at another Indian reservation where the first (handwritten) sign you saw was 'Stop — Indians Ahead', and then another, 'Stop — Indian Jewelry', and then we reached the market where there were silks, artefacts, dreamcatchers and the like, and finally, as you leave, 'Stop — Nice Indians Behind!' We thought that much better than 'Au Revoir'!

At the ghost town of Calico, we found moments which would emerge on *Purpendicular*, and met Hard Rock Pete. Pete had a house built with a sloping floor, because he had one leg longer than the other. What he'd built was an experience of altered perspective, so when you walk into the room, you find a ladder leaning against a bookcase, and Hard Rock Pete climbs up it, and is leaning into the room. It was brilliant, as the two of us — each with our legs of equal length — tried to deal with magnetic poles and concepts of physics, in a building which tilted.

So there we were, leaning sideways, trying to be in harmony with the house and, after a while, the brain accepts it, and you feel upright! We even climbed up the ladder, and it was fine, leaning out into the room, and then leaning back. From up there, I could see across to a barrel of water, with a half section of guttering leading from the barrel *up* to the bucket, hanging at the other end. Pete took a ladle, poured water into the bottom of the bucket, and it flowed uphill! For the incredulous, the disbeliever, it's an amazing illusion!

So, finally, our glorious journey brought us to LA, where Pat had got together a great bunch of musicians, and we tried a few of the songs for *Dreamcatcher*. In fact, the effort didn't really work out the way we had hoped. It was nothing to do with the musicians, Pat, the studio — even me. It's just that the songs had a gentility born out of the time spent with Steve Morris in England, and rather like the wonderful story 'You Stole My Love for a Song', it just seemed that we were 'playing away'. We couldn't find the right spirit, and it came back home to be made.

To explain my reference to 'You Stole My Love for a Song', it was first written and recorded when I made *Naked Thunder*, and Simon Phillips played on it. It followed a version Steve had done for me with his drum machine. He'd programmed it to a particular groove he'd set up, and he then played to that feel. Now Simon has already been referred to with some reverence — he's an exquisite player, but on this occasion (for whatever reason), his live work simply didn't seem to give spirit to what we were looking for, which is why we didn't use his contribution, or the LA effort on the final production.

Dreamcatcher was released on a new label I had put together to look after some of my new projects and ideas (Caramba Music Limited), and apart from songs like 'Chandra's Coriander', 'Prima Donna', 'That's Why God Is Singin' The Blues', 'Gunga Din', 'Country Mile', 'You Stole My Love for a Song' and 'Any Way You Want Me (That's How I Will Be)', there's also a song for my wife — 'Sleepy Warm'. Then there are also three tracks written with Lenny Haze, Brett Bloomfield and Dean Howard from the Repo Depo project.

As with the LA/Simon Phillips experience, recording these songs on *Dreamcatcher* required a different feel to the work we did in Holland, but maybe we'll do a Repo Depo version one day. Why not?

For Deep Purple, we wanted *Purpendicular* to do what it seems to have done: bring a smile back on the faces of those who know and love the band, and realise that we are constantly searching to stay in the front line of our business. Terms like 'underground', even 'dangerous', were applied to us in the early days, and I never forget what I've said on more than one occasion — that I don't think it's right always to serve up the same old material and play safe, relying on past success. Perform it, yes, but offer new adventure, and I think that shows in our concerts. It certainly did when we toured the new album with Steve Morse.

In terms of presenting the project, we brought in Peter Bird to give the album a new look, and his contribution was very different. Peter basically took charge of the design and promotion, and brought to us his skills as a 'big ideas' man. He stands on top of hills to look down to make his plans, and has built his reputation working in exalted company, mostly with multi-national corporations. However, he, too, likes his rock 'n' roll, and took up the rather more modest creative and financial opportunity with great enthusiasm. The result was great — the album looked cool, and made a statement. However, I suspect he dipped his toe into the volcanic pool of the business, and found it vastly different to the oxygen-starved atmosphere of the boardroom, to which he is more accustomed! Still, he came out of the experience with his dignity intact, but others will have to decide about his sanity!

The songs on *Purpendicular* have been judged and analysed, and it was great to see it go straight to number one in the *Kerrang* charts in March 1996. The tracks on it are 'Vavoom: Ted the Mechanic', 'Loosen My Strings', 'Soon Forgotten', 'Sometimes I Feel Like Screaming', 'Cascades', 'I'm Not Your Lover', 'The Aviator', 'Rosa's Cantina', 'A Castle Full of Rascals', 'A Touch Away', 'Hey Cisco', 'Somebody Stole My Guitar' and 'The Purpendicular Waltz'.

Mother nature's been good to me
That's why I'm sitting in this cherry tree
But it's alright, it's alright
It's not so bad
I'm just a touch away

Although we'd gone through 1995 doing shows, they were basically confined to a brief spell in March and April, when we played South Korea, South Africa and India. Now it was back on the road with the new album, and a schedule of an intensity and fullness equal to anything I've done, if not greater. It was a tour which showed that Deep Purple's star is as bright as ever, and a sample of tour dates are listed here to show where we were taking the band, beginning in the UK.

February

15th	Pavilion, Plymouth
16th	Rivermead, Reading
17th	Guildhall, Portsmouth
19th	St David's, Cardiff
20th	Colston Hall, Bristol
29th	City Hall, Newcastle

March

1st	Capitol Theatre, Aberdeen
2nd	Barrowlands, Glasgow
4th	Apollo, Manchester
5th	Liverpool Empire
6th	City Hall, Sheffield
8th/9th	Brixton Academy

The rest of March saw us in Germany (including Ulm, Essen, Berlin and Düsseldorf); then to Rotterdam, Brussels, Paris and Grenoble; returning to Munich, Furth, Hanau and Hohenams.

April was a bit quiet — a day off on 'Fools' Day — then Wels (2nd), Vienna (3rd) and Budapest (4th), while on the 19th to 26th May we were in America, returning to Europe for the Esbjerg Rock Festival on 31 May (playing the night before at the Multihus Tobaksfabrikken, also in Esbjerg). In June we played:

June

2nd	The Arena, Posnan, Poland
3rd	Spodek, Katowice, Poland
4th	Hala Vitkovice, Ostrava, Czech Republic
6th	Palasport, Pordenone, Italy
7th	Palasport, Turin, Italy

And on to Milan, Bolzano and Bologna, then to Germany, Sweden, France, Finland and Russia, though not necessarily in that order! We went backwards and forwards, and July was the same!

OK, so to break this up, we played songs across the history of Deep Purple; in Europe, the set list we played from was 'Fireball', 'Maybe I'm a Leo', 'Vavoom: Ted the Mechanic', 'Pictures of Home', 'Black Night', 'Cascades', 'I'm Not Your Lover', 'Sometimes I Feel Like Screaming', 'Mary Long', 'The Purpendicular Waltz', 'No One Came' (my fear song — still unfounded!), 'Rosa's Cantina', 'Smoke on the Water', 'When a Blind Man Cries', 'Somebody Stole My Guitar', 'Speed King', 'Perfect Strangers', 'Hey Cisco' and 'Highway Star'. Other songs were used from time to time — 'Woman from Tokyo', 'Rat Bat Blues' and 'The Aviator'. On and on we went …

July

2nd	Fyrishov, Uppsala, Sweden
3rd	Slottsruinen, Oeland/Borgholm, Sweden
4th	Kungshamnsvallen/Smoegen/Kungshamn, Sweden
5th	Torget/Brottel, Halmstad, Sweden

We continued through Europe in September/October, then into Japan for the back end of that month. Then we were in familiar territory: Nagoya, Fukuoka, Osaka, Tokyo, Kawaguchi, Tochigi, Sendai, Sapporo and Yokohama. Then it was into Canada and America across the New Year, arriving in South America for spring 1997: Buenos Aires, Pôrto Alegre, Rio, São Paulo, Lima and La Paz.

We went into summer playing Germany, Baden-Baden and Lahr Airfield (5th/6th), and then on the 8th, the Mont La Salle Arena in Lebanon!

I have never been busier, and sometimes reflect back on that childhood moment with Grandad Watkins, when we put up the tent, and I dreamed of travel and adventure to exotic places.

So now it is 1998, and we are working on a new album, with our old friends at EMI. *Purpendicular* was the last with BMG, and I don't know quite what went on behind the scenes to bring about the change. As far as I'm concerned, BMG were lovely people, and there are various stories about the parting of ways. Some thought the NEC incident with Ritchie was the one that brought about the end – I will never know. Maybe it was that fateful day I met their top brass.

As I recall, three of them — one at least a 'squillionaire' — came to see a show, and it so happened that on the night in question, I was having trouble with the 'old rear gunner'. Unfortunately, there wasn't a private toilet/bathroom in the dressing room, which meant I needed to go into the arena area naked, but for a discreet towel. Across the corridor, there was a beautiful bathroom, and there I applied into my rear end what The Mayor of Hell calls 'Hoop Grease'.

Having finished I walked out into the corridor, with the towel now in my left hand, and 'Hoop Grease' on the second finger, as I saw Bruce Payne approaching with an army of BMG people dressed in Armani and Versace, and oozing wealth and success. In front of them stood their artist — long hair, towel held over my private parts. They came forward to greet me, arms outstretched in a warm 'Hello' attitude. I quickly withdrew my finger, to join the rest of the digits, but to no avail. All who met me that night were touched by the occasion!

We are recording in Florida again, but still journey out to play shows, while we complete the new album. The smile is there, the glint in the eye is back, as is the spirit and rock 'n' roll!

How, then, to end for now? Well, I'll go back to the beginning for that: 'Deep Purple, that enigmatic rock group I have always loved in torment. Jon Lord, the keyboard player, Roger Glover, the bassist, Ian Paice, the drummer, *and* Steve Morse, the guitar player, are essentially moderate people with good hearts and only the normal amount of wickedness.'

However, the see-saw itself is steady now, and as the singer of Deep Purple, I sit confidently at its fulcrum!

'I thank you.'

Discography

Ian Gillan Concise Discography
THE COMPLETE EPISODE SIX
GREAT BRITAIN : Sequel Records NEX CD 156 : 1991 CD
Ian Gillan made his first studio recordings with EPISODE SIX.
Compilation comprising all bands singles, plus six unreleased
tracks and the Neo Maya and Sheila Carter solo singles.

EPISODE SIX — RADIO ONE CLUB SESSIONS 68/69
GREAT BRITAIN : RPM Records RPM 178 : 1997 CD
22 track collection from live broadcasts made for Radio 1 Club,
includes many tracks not recorded by the band in the studio.
After leaving the band Ian Gillan sang on the following Deep
Purple albums recorded between 1969 and 1973.

DEEP PURPLE — CONCERTO FOR GROUP AND ORCHESTRA
Recorded September 24th 1969 at Royal Albert Hall, London.
GREAT BRITAIN : Harvest SHVL 767 : January 1970
Recommended CD version : GREAT BRITAIN : EMI CDP 7 94886
2 : 1990
CD includes two extra live tracks recorded the same evening :
WRING THAT NECK, CHILD IN TIME.

DEEP PURPLE IN ROCK
Speed King, Bloodsucker, Child In Time, Flight Of The Rat, Into
The Fire, Living Wreck, Hard Lovin' Man
Recorded between Aug 1969 & Feb 1970 at De Lane
Lea/Abbey Rd/IBC Studio's.
GREAT BRITAIN V1 : Harvest SHVL 777 : June 1970
Recommended CD version : UK : EMI 24383 401192 : 1995
Remastered with bonus tracks.

DEEP PURPLE GEMINI SUITE LIVE
Recorded Royal Festival Hall, Sept 1970.
UK : RPM Records RPM 114 : 1993 CD.

DEEP PURPLE FIREBALL
Fireball, No No No, Demon's Eye, (*Strange Kind Of Woman in
US and Japan), Anyone's Daughter, The Mule, Fools, No One
Came
Recorded between September 1970/May 1971, De Lane Lea &
Olympic studio's.
GREAT BRITAIN V1 : Harvest SHVL 793 : September 1971
Recommended CD version : UK : EMI CD DEEPP 1 : 1996
Remastered with bonus tracks.

DEEP PURPLE MACHINE HEAD
Highway Star, Maybe I'm A Leo, Picture's Of Home, Never
Before, Smoke On The Water, Lazy, Space Truckin'
Recorded Grand Hotel Montreaux Dec 1971/Rolling Stones
Mobile.
GREAT BRITAIN : Purple TPSA 7504 : May 1972 DS
Recommended CD version : UK : EMI 24385 95062 :
September 1997 2CD
Remastered plus unissued material and new remixes by Roger
Glover.

DEEP PURPLE MADE IN JAPAN
Highway Star, Child In Time, Smoke On The Water, The Mule
Strange Kind Of Woman, Space Truckin', Lazy
Recorded live in Japan, August 15,16,17th 1972.
GREAT BRITAIN : Purple TPSP 351 : Dec 1972 2LP
Recommended CD version : GREAT BRITAIN : EMI 24385 78642
: 1998 2CD
Remastered plus extra encore tracks.
Also recommended : GREAT BRITAIN : 7243 8 27726 2 0 : 1993
3CD
Special edition with all three shows from the Japanese tour for
collectors.

DEEP PURPLE WHO DO WE THINK WE ARE
Woman From Tokyo, Mary Long, Super Trouper, Smooth Dancer,
Rat Bat Blue, Place In Line, Our Lady
Recorded Rome July 72; Frankfurt Oct 72 on Rolling Stones
Mobile.
GREAT BRITAIN : Purple TPSA 7508 : March 1973
Recommended CD version : UK : EMI CDP7 48273.2 : 1987
(note : remastered CD version due late 1998)

DEEP PURPLE POWERHOUSE
Painted Horse, Hush, Wring That Neck, Child In Time, Black
Night, Cry Free
Recorded July 72, Rome. Royal Albert Hall Sept 24. 1969. Live
Aug 72, Japan. Live 1970 Studio out-take.
GREAT BRITAIN : Purple TPS 3510 : Nov 9th 1977
Compilation of Gillan era Deep Purple tracks, most of which are
being reallocated to the relevant CDs.

DEEP PURPLE IN CONCERT 1970–1972
Speed King, Wring That Neck, Highway Star, Strange Kind Of
Woman, Lazy, Never Before

Child In Time, Mandrake Root, Space Truckin', Lucille
Recorded BBC In Concert programme Feb 19.1970 (aired 22nd)
and BBC In Concert programme Mar 6.1972
GREAT BRITAIN : Harvest SHDW 412 : December 1980
Recommended CD version : GREAT BRITAIN : EMI CDEM 1434 :
1992 2CD
CD includes two tracks - Maybe I'm A Leo and Smoke On The
Water - which didn't fit on the vinyl.

DEEP PURPLE SCANDINAVIAN NIGHTS
Wring That Neck, Speed King, Into The Fire, Paint It Black,
Mandrake Root, Child In Time, Black Night
Recorded Stockholm Konserthus, Nov 12th 1970
GREAT BRITAIN : Connoisseur DP VSOP LP 125 : Oct 17. 1988
2LP
Recommended CD version : GREAT BRITAIN : Connoisseur DP
VSOP CD 125 : October 1988 2CD

Ian Gillan Sessions/Productions 1969/73.

JESUS CHRIST SUPERSTAR
GREAT BRITAIN : MCA MKPS 2011/2 : October 1970 2LP
Gillan sang the part of Jesus & was chosen over Robert Plant
when producers heard the rough mix of Child In Time.

CHER KAZOO
GREAT BRITAIN : RPM 104 : 1992 CD
Assembled from home produced sessions begun in 1972 but
never released.

JERUSALEM - JERUSALEM
GREAT BRITAIN : Deram SDL 6 : May 1972 (produced by Ian
Gillan)

SAMMY
GOO GER WOOGIE/Big Lovin' Woman Philips 6006 227 : UK :
1972 (produced by Ian Gillan)
PUSSY
FELINE WOMAN/Ska Child Deram DM 368 : UK : 1972
(produced by Ian Gillan)

IAN GILLAN BAND DISCOGRAPHY 73-84

IAN GILLAN BAND CHILD IN TIME
Lay Me Down, You Make Me Feel So Good, Shame, My Baby
Loves Me, Down The Road, Child In Time, Let It Slide
Recorded Musicland, Munich Dec 1975–Jan 1976. Produced by
Glover.
GREAT BRITAIN : Polydor/Oyster Delux 24901 36 : 1976
CD : UK : Virgin CDVM 2606 : 1989 remastered with extra
tracks

IAN GILLAN BAND CLEAR AIR TURBULENCE
Clear Air Turbulence, Five Moons, Money Lender, Over The Hill,
Goodhand Lisa, Angel Manchenio
Recorded Kingsway Studio's, London, Dec 1976.
GREAT BRITAIN : Island ILPS 9500 : April 1977
CD : UK : Virgin CDVM 4 : 1989 remastered

IAN GILLAN BAND SCARABUS
Scarabus, Twin Exhausted, Poor Boy Hero, Mercury High, Pre-
Release, Slags To Bitches, Apathy, Mad Elaine, Country Lights,
Fools Mate
Recorded Kingsway Studio's, London, July/August 1977.
GREAT BRITAIN : Island ILPS 9511 : Oct 7. 1977
CD : UK : Virgin CDVM 3 : 1989 remastered with extra track

IAN GILLAN BAND LIVE AT THE BUDO-KAN VOL 1 & 2
Clear Air Turbulence, Smoke On The Water, Money Lender,

Scarabus, Twin Exhausted, Over The Hill, Child In Time, Smoke
On The Water, Mercury High, Woman From Tokyo
Recorded Tokyo Budo-Kan Hall, September 22nd. 1977.
GREAT BRITAIN : Virgin VGD 3507 : August 1983
Originally issued as two single albums in Japan in 1977, not
issued in Europe until 1983.
CD : UK : Virgin CDVM 3507 : 1989
Nine tracks from the original Japanese set. The tenth track (My
Baby Loves Me) was added to the CD of Scarabus (see above)

GILLAN GILLAN
Second Sight (inst), Secret Of The Dance, I'm Your Man, Dead
Of Night, Fighting Man, Message In A Bottle, Not Weird
Enough, Bringing Joanna Back, Abbey Of Thelema, Back In The
Game
Recorded Kingsway Studios July/August 1978.
JAPAN : East World Sound EWS 81120 : 1978
CD : UK : RPM Records RPM 113 : 1993 Original album plus
bonus tracks.

GILLAN MR. UNIVERSE
Second Sight, Secret Of The Dance, She Tears Me Down, Roller,
Mr. Universe, Vengeance, Puget Sound, Dead Of Night,
Message In A Bottle, Fighting Man
Recorded Kingsway Studio's June/July 1979.
GREAT BRITAIN : Acrobat ACRO 3 : Oct 12. 1979
CD : UK : Virgin CDVM 2589 : 1989 remastered with extra
singles tracks.

GILLAN GLORY ROAD
Unchain Your Brain, Are You Sure?, Time And Again, No Easy
Way, Sleeping On The Job, On The Rocks, If You Believe Me,
Running White Face City Boy, Nervous
Rec. Kingsway April/May 1980.UK

GREAT BRITAIN : Virgin V2171 : October 1980
CD : UK : Virgin CDVM 2171 : 1989 remastered with extra
tracks from Gillan Fans (see below).

GILLAN FOR GILLAN FANS ONLY
Higher & Higher, Your Mother Was Right, Abbey Of Thelema,
Trying To Get To You
GREAT BRITAIN : Virgin VDJ 32 : October 1980
Free with Glory Road, an album of band out-takes, including
the above numbers featuring Ian Gillan.

GILLAN FUTURE SHOCK
Future Shock, Nightride Out Of Phoenix, (The Ballad Of) The
Lucitania Express, No Laughing In Heaven, Sacre Bleu, Bite The
Bullet, If I Sing Softly, Don't You Want The Truth, For Your
Dreams, New Orleans
Rec. Kingsway Studio's. January 1981.
GREAT BRITAIN : Virgin VH 2196 : April 1981
CD : UK : Virgin CDVM 2196 : 1989 remastered with extra
tracks

GILLAN DOUBLE TROUBLE
I'll Rip Your Spine Out, Restless, Men Of War, Sunbeam,
Nightmare, Hadely Bop Bop, Life Goes On, Born To Kill, LIVE -
No Laughing In Heaven, No Easy Way, Trouble, M.A.D., If You
Believe Me*, New Orleans
Rec. Kingsway Aug 81; Reading Aug 29.81; *Mar 4. 81
GREAT BRITAIN : Virgin VDG 3506 : October 1981
CD : UK : Virgin CDVM 3506 : 1989 remastered with extra
tracks.

GILLAN MAGIC
What's The Matter, Bluesy Blue Sea, Caught In A Trap, Long
Gone, Driving Me Wild, Demon Driver, Living A Lie, You're So

Right, Living For The City, Demon Driver (Reprise)
Rec. Kingsway July/August 1982.Charts : UK .
GREAT BRITAIN : Virgin V 2238 : September 1982
CD : UK : Virgin CDVM 2238 : 1989 remastered with extra
tracks.
Following this album Ian Gillan had a year out with Black
Sabbath (see below).

GILLAN WHAT I DID ON MY VACATION
CD : UK : Virgin. DIXDCD 39 : 1986 General Gillan Band collection

GILLAN THE VERY BEST OF GILLAN
UK : Music Club MCCD 032 : 1991 CD
Standard compilation of Gillan Band tracks.

GILLAN - ROCK PROFILE
UK : Connoisseur VSOP CD 214 : 1995 CD
Compilation tracking Gillan's career from early days up to his
Naked Thunder CD.

GILLAN - LIVE AT READING 1980
UK : Raw Fruit FRSCD 002 : 1990 CD
Six tracks recorded at Reading Aug 1980 by BBC for
transmission on Friday Rock Show.

GILLAN — BBC TAPES Vol 1 — DEAD OF NIGHT
UK : RPM Records RPM 185 : 1998 CD
11 tracks from BBC In Concert Sept 1979 and Reading 79 BBC
broadcast.

GILLAN — BBC TAPES Vol 2 — UNCHAIN YOUR BRAIN
UK : RPM Records RPM 186 : 1998 CD
12 tracks from BBC In Concert Sept 1980.

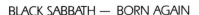

BLACK SABBATH — BORN AGAIN
Trashed, Stonehenge, Disturbing The Priest, The Dark, Zero The
Hero, Digital Bitch, Born Again, Hot Line, Keep It Warm
Rec. Manor Studio's Oxfordshire May/June 1983
GREAT BRITAIN : Vertigo VERL 8 : September 1983
CD : UK : Castle ESMCD 334
After the Black Sabbath sojourn, Ian was able to participate in a
long-awaited Deep Purple reunion.

DEEP PURPLE — PERFECT STRANGERS
Knockin' At Your Back Door, Under The Gun, Nobody's Home,
Mean Streak, Perfect Strangers, A Gypsy's Kiss, Wasted Sunsets,
Hungry Daze, Not Responsible *
Recorded Vermont USA July 10th - August 26th 1984. Charts :
UK 5/US...
GREAT BRITAIN : Polydor POLH 16 LP : Oct 29th 1984 LP
GREAT BRITAIN : Polydor 823 777-2 CD : Oct 29th 1984 CD
CD contains bonus track taped at same sessions*.

KNOCKING AT YOUR BACK DOOR — THE BEST OF DEEP PUR-
PLE IN THE 80's
UK/EUROPE : Polydor POL 899 511438-2 : 1992 CD
Compilation includes non album track SON OF ALERIK.

DEEP PURPLE — THE HOUSE OF BLUE LIGHT
Bad Attitude, The Unwritten Law, Call Of The Wild, Mad Dog,
Black & White, Hard Lovin' Woman, Spanish Archer,
Strangeways, Mitzi Dupree, Dead Or Alive
Mk 2. Recorded Vermont USA May/June 1986. Charts : UK /US .
GREAT BRITAIN : Polydor POLH 32 : Jan 12th 1987 LP
GREAT BRITAIN : Polydor 831318.2 : Jan 12th 1987 CD
CD has longer versions of some tracks.

DEEP PURPLE — NOBODY'S PERFECT
Highway Star, Strange Kind Of Woman, Perfect Strangers, Child
In Time, Lazy, Space Truckin', Hard Lovin' Woman, Bad Attitude,
Knocking At Your Back Door, Black Night, Woman From Tokyo,
Smoke On The Water , Hush
Recorded Irvine Meadows USA May 23; Phoenix USA May 30;
Oslo Aug 22; Italy Sept 6. Hush Feb 26, UK
GREAT BRITAIN : Polydor PODV 10 835 897.1 : July 5th 1988 LP
LP lacks Dead Or Alive.
GREAT BRITAIN : Polydor 835 897. CD
CD lacks Space Truckin', Dead Or Alive & Bad Attitude - you
need the single. After Ian Gillan had recorded the live album
NOBODY'S PERFECT, during Dec 88/Jan 89 he was ousted from
the band.

HUSH/DEAD OR ALIVE (Milan Sept 4)–BAD ATTITUDE
UK : Polydor PZCD 4 887 636.2 : June 1988 5" CD

SOLO / SPIN-OFF PROJECTS

GILLAN/GLOVER : ACCIDENTALLY ON PURPOSE
Clouds And Rain, Evil Eye, She Took My Breath Away,
Dislocated, Via Miami, I Can't Dance To That, Can't Believe You
Wanna Leave, Lonely Avenue, Telephone Box, I Thought No (+
Chet, Purple People Eater, Cayman Island on CD).
Recorded Oct 86 Monserrat/Sept 87 New York.
GREAT BRITAIN : VIRGIN CDV 2498 CD : Feb 1988.

SOUTH AFRICA/ JOHN
UK : Virgin VST 1088 12" : 1988
Specially recorded song written by Bernie Marsden and sung by
Gillan. Tracks later added to the CD edition of the MAGIC album
in 1989. See above.

Chris Tetley Presents THE GARTH ROCKETT & THE
MOONSHINERS Story
I'll Rip Your Spine Out, No Laughing In Heaven. Interview with
Ian Gillan.
GREAT BRITAIN : Rock Hard ROHACD 3 CD : 1990
Two live tracks from Manchester Ritz 1989 (the full show was
issued as a video).

ROCK AID ARMENIA
SMOKE ON THE WATER (various inc Ian Gillan) / PARANOID
(Black Sabbath 1970 version)
Life Aid Records Arment 001 : 1989 CD
Charity release with vocals mostly by Ian Gillan.

IAN GILLAN — NAKED THUNDER
Gut Reaction, Talking To You, No Good Luck, Nothing But The
Best, Living On Borrowed Time, Sweet Lolita, Nothing To Lose,
Moonshine, Long And Lonely Ride, -Love Gun, No More Cane
On The Brazos
EUROPE : Teldec 9031 71899 CD : August 16th 1990

NOTHING BUT THE BEST/HOLE IN MY VEST
GERMANY : Teldec 9031 72040 : 1990 (non LP b-side)
NO GOOD LUCK/ROCK N ROLL GIRLS
GREAT BRITAIN : Teldec YZ513 9031 72377 : Aug 1990 (non LP
b-side)

PRETTY MAIDS
IN SANTA'S CLAWS/A MERRY JINGLE
HOLLAND : CBS 656499 : November 1990 7"
IAN GILLAN guests on the b-side taped during Scandinavian
tour in Sept 1990.

THE BOLLAND PROJECT
Holland : Dino Music 90 70 117 : 1991 CD
Ian Gillan did two spoken tracks and one vocal
on this concept CD.

IAN GILLAN — TOOLBOX
Hang Me Out To Dry, Toolbox, Dirty Dog, Candy Horizon,
Don't Hold Me Back, Pictures Of Hell, Dancing Nylon Shirt
(pt 1), Bed Of Nails, Gassed Up, Everything I Need,
Dancing Nylon Shirt (pt 2)
Europe : East West Records 9031 75641-2 : October 1991

THE BEST OF IAN GILLAN
GERMANY : East West 4509 91304-2 : 1992 CD
Compilation of NAKED THUNDER and TOOLBOX
album tracks.

GILLAN/RAKINTZIS — ETZEI M'APEEEI
GREECE : Minos 7243 4 78766 : 1992 CD/LP
Ian sings vocals on three tracks — GETAWAY, MY HEART OF
STONE and I THINK I KNOW - on this set by Greek MOR
artist Rakintzis.
After this brief spell away from Deep Purple, Ian was asked back
for the band's twenty fifth anniversary tour.

DEEP PURPLE — THE BATTLE RAGES ON
The Battle Rages On, Lick It Up, Anya, Talk About Love, Time To
Kill, Ramshackle Man, A Twist In The Tale, Nasty Piece Of Work,
Solitaire, One Man's Meat
UK : BMG / RCA 74321 15420-2 : July 26. 1993 CD
UK : BMG / RCA 74321 15420 : July 26. 1993 LP

DEEP PURPLE — COME HELL OR HIGH WATER
Highway Star, Black Night, Twist In The Tale,
Perfect Strangers, Anyone's Daughter, Child In Time, Anya,
(Lazy*, Space Truckin*, Woman From Tokyo*)
Speed King, Smoke On The Water
UK/Europe BMG 74321 23416 2 : November 1994 CD
Single CD edited from shows in Munich, Stuttgart and
others in 1993. Tracks marked * only on Japanese edition but
are edits. Ritchie Blackmore left the band during the 1993 tour
and was eventually replaced on a full-time basis by guitarist
Steve Morse.

DEEP PURPLE — PURPENDICULAR
Vavoom : Ted The Mechanic, Loosen My Strings, Soon
Forgotten, Sometimes I Feel Like Screaming, Cascades : I'm Not
Your Lover, The Aviator, Rosa's Cantina, A Castle Full Of Rascals,
A Touch Away, Hey Cisco, Somebody Stole My Guitar, The
Purpendicular Waltz (Don't Hold Your Breath*)
UK / EUROPE : BMG 7 4321 33802-2 : Feb 1996
America : BMG Prominent 1001-2 : April 16th, reissued Sept
10th 1996
Carried bonus track *Don't Hold Your Breath.

DEEP PURPLE — LIVE AT THE OLYMPIA '96
CD 1 : Fireball, Maybe I'm A Leo, Ted The Mechanic,
Pictures Of Home, Black Night, Cascades : I'm Not Your Lover,
Sometimes I Feel Like Screaming, Woman From Tokyo,
No One Came, Purpendicular Waltz
CD 2 : Rosa's Cantina, Smoke On The Water,
When A Blind Man Cries, Speed King, Perfect Strangers,
Hey Cisco, Highway Star
UK : EMI June 1997 2CD
Recorded at Paris Olympia, June 17 1996, featuring Steve
Morse line-up.

IAN GILLAN — DREAMCATCHER
UK : Ark 21 : November 1997 CD : 7243 8 21246 2 : Chandra's
Coriander, Prima Donna, All In My Mind, That's Why God is
Singin' The Blues,, Gunga Din, Hard On You, Sleepy Warm,
County Mile, You Sold My Love For A Song, A Day Late 'N' A
Dollar Short, Sugar Plum, Anyway You Want Me (That's How I
Will Be).
Recorded at Ocean Road Studio, Warrington and Parr Street
Studios, Liverpool, with Steve Morris.

DEEP PURPLE — ABANDON '98
New album released May 1998 : Any Fule Kno That, Almost
Human, Don't Make Me Happy, Seventh Heaven, Watching The
Sky, Fingers To The Bone, Jack Ruby, She Was, Whatsername,
'69, Evil Louise, Bludsucker.

Note : this discography concentrates on UK releases, plus any
rare non-UK tracks.
Discography assembled by Simon Robinson / Deep Purple
Appreciation Society, April 1998. Fuller entries for most of these
records, including vinyl and foreign editions, can be found in
the society's discography, and on the Deep Purple Archive
discographies being added to our web site -
www.rpmrecords.co.uk/purple